Praise for Loren Coleman and his landmark book
Mysterious America

"There are a lot of strange 'things' happening in these United States
(and other American countries), and a goodly number of them are
described in Loren Coleman's *Mysterious America* . . . out-of-place
animals, 'phantom' cats, mystery kangaroos, mad gassers, and even
The Jersey Devil himself. In short, it's a potpourri, with something
for almost any lover of the strange and the unusual."
—*Cryptozoology*

"Coleman has done more than sit in a library reading room, he has
collected information in the field. . . . I recommend it to everyone
who is interested in the strange, bizarre, and unusual."
—*Fate* magazine

"An entertaining and open-minded book. . . . A useful reference
tool as well as a record of the unexplained."
—*Library Journal*

"The lists are worth the price alone."
—*Critique*

"Objective, painstaking, exhaustive."
—*London Times*

BIGF

OOT!

The True
Story of Apes
in America

Loren Coleman

PARAVIEW POCKET BOOKS
New York London Toronto Sydney

To
John Green

The author gratefully acknowledges Barbara Smith for permission to
use the lyrics that appear on page 207.

An *Original* Publication of PARAVIEW POCKET BOOKS

PARAVIEW
191 Seventh Avenue, New York, NY 10011

POCKET BOOKS, a division of Simon & Schuster, Inc.
1230 Avenue of the Americas, New York, NY 10020

ISBN-13: 978-0-7434-6975-3
ISBN-10:   0-7434-6975-5

First Paraview Pocket Books trade paperback printing April 2003

20   19   18   17   16   15   14   13   12   11

POCKET and colophon are registered trademarks of
Simon & Schuster, Inc.

For information regarding special discounts for bulk purchases,
please contact Simon & Schuster Special Sales at 1-800-456-6798
or business@simonandschuster.com

Printed in the U.S.A.

Acknowledgments

This book is the result of decades of work, and my thanks for the assistance that hundreds of people have provided in making this volume a reality.

First off, a deep appreciation to Caleb and Malcolm, my two honor-roll, baseball-player, artistic sons, for coming along with me on the quest.

The book is dedicated to John Green, who, from the beginning, served as a model of morality and open exchange in a field that oftentimes gets caught up in personalities during the pursuit of these elusive new apes.

Foremost thanks go to Patrick Huyghe, for the years of friendship, editorship, and his suggestion to write this book. Another tip of my bush hat goes to Mark A. Hall, for years of intellectual stimulation and research exchanges. For numerous bits of information regarding primatology and hominology, I thank the following *Homo sapiens,* who with friendship and grace, shared moments and insights with me: Grover Krantz, Diane Horton, Dmitri Bayanov, Bernard Heuvelmans, Jeff Meldrum, Gordon Strasenburgh, Carroll Riley, George Agogino, Carleton Coon, Matt Bille, Karl Shuker, and Phil Sirois.

Very specific acknowledgments are to be given for permissions to use materials in this book. Special thanks to Chris Kraska for his photograph of a Colorado road sign, to Zack Clothier and Craig Wooleater for photographs, to Janet Bord for the FPL images noted throughout, to Jim McClarin, Richard Noll, Roger St. Hilaire, Brian Wyatt, John Green, Kyle Mizokami, *Fate, Fortean Times, The Anomalist,* and Ivan T. Sanderson for permission to quote from their interviews and written material, to songwriter Jaime Mendoza-Nava of Highmeadow Music

V

Company to quote lyrics from *The Legend of Boggy Creek*, and Steve Newmark of Hen's Tooth Video for use of *The Legend of Boggy Creek* image.

A variety of materials, reports, casts, ideas, and suggestions flowed from a wide selection of Bigfooters who shared much with me. The top folks on my list, with apologies to all those not mentioned, are Alexis Rockman, Allen Greenfield, Amy Hayes, Andrew D. Gable, Archie Buckley, Berthold Schwarz, Bill Grimstad, Bill Rebsamen, Bjorn Kurten, Blake Mathys, Bob Betts, Bob Hieronimus, Bob Jones, Bob Tarte, Bob Titmus, Bobbie Short, Brad Steiger, Brent O'Donnell, Brian Wyatt, Burt Warmeister, Carol Michels, Chad Arment, Chester Moore, Chris Kraska, Chris Woodyard, Constance Cameron, Cosma Shalizi, Craig Heinselman, Craig Woolheater, Curt Krumpe, Curt Sutherly, Curtis Fuller, Dan Porter, Daniel Cohen, Daniel Perez, Darren Naish, David Barkasy, David Bittner, David Downs, David Fideler, David Grabias, David P. Mikkelson, David Walsh, David Webb, Dennis Pilichis, Des Miller, Don Keating, Don Worley, Donald Shannon, Dorlores Phelps, Doug Tarrant, Dwight Whalen, Eric Altman, F. Henner Fahrenbach, Gary Mangicopra, Gene Duplantier, George Earley, George Eberhart, George Haas, George Wagner, Gilbert Miller, Gordon Rutter, Graham Conway, Gregg Hale, Grover S. Krantz, Hank Davis, Harry Trumbore, Henry Bauer, Henry Franzoni, Ira Walters, Jacob Davidson, Janet Bord, Jay Garon, Jeff Glickman, Jeff Meldrum, Jerome Clark, Jim Auburn, Jim Boyd, Jim Lyding, Jim McClarin, Joan Jeffers, Joe Beelart, Joel Hurd, John A. Keel, John Kirk, Jon Downes, Karl Shuker, Kenn Thomas, Len Aiken, Libbet Cone, Linda Godfrey, Lisa Stone, Lou Farish, Louise A. Lowry, Marcello Truzzi, Mark Dion, Mary Margaret, Matt Drudge, Matt Moneymaker, Matthew Johnson, Michael Bershad, Michael Goss, Michael Newton, Michel Raynal, Mike Oxbig, Monte Ballard, Pat Bontempo, Paul Bartholomew, Paul Herman, Paul Johnson, Paul Willis, Pauline Strawn, Peter Byrne, Peter Hassall, Peter Jordan, Peter Rodman, Phil Sirois, Philip Levine, Phyllis Galde, Rachel Carthy, Ramona Hibner, Ray Boeche, Ray Crowe, Ray Nelke, René Dahinden, Rich La Monica, Richard Brown, Richard Crowe, Richard Hendricks, Richard Leshuk, Richard Noll, Richard Smith, Rick Fisher, Rob Riggs, Robert Downing, Robert Goerman, Robert Mason, Robert

Neeley, Robert Rickard, Robert Stansberry, Roberta Payne, Rod Dyke, Roger St. Hilaire, Ron Dobbins, Ron Schaffner, Ron Westrum, S. Miles Lewis, Sara Garrett, Scott Lornis, Scott McNabb, Sean Foley, Stacy McArdle, Stan Gordon, Stephen Foster, Steve Collins, Steve Hicks, Sunny Franson, T. Peter Park, Terry W. Colvin, Thomas Archer, Tim Church, Tod Deery, Todd Lester, Todd Neiss, Todd Roll, Tom Adams, Tom Miller, Tom Page, Tom Slick, Ron Winebrenner, Toni Campbell, Tracy Boyle, Troy Taylor, Warren Thompson, Wayne Laporte, William Corliss, William Gibbons, William Zeiser, Zack Clothier, and last, but by no means least, my old mentor, long-gone-but-not-forgotten friend Ivan T. Sanderson.

Additionally blessings go to my mom, sister, and brothers, for their encouragement. I send out gratitude to my late dad, whom I miss being able to talk with, about *Wild Kingdom,* Bigfoot, and baseball. Thanks, Desmond, for letting me know you played that Bigfoot game as a kid. And finally to Leslie, for the female companionship that nourished this ape in many ways, thank you.

With appreciation,
Loren Coleman
Portland, Maine
October 20, 2002

viii

ENTS

INTROD

My body is soaked from trogging miles through heavy underbrush, literally drenched from my own sweat and the heavy mist in the forest. The object of my quest seems just ahead, around the next bend, right after that ridge. I'm after Bigfoot, and I push on. I've sunk waist deep in the swamps of southern Illinois, frozen overnight in a tent in the Trinity-Shasta area of California, looked at the stars from the Sasquatch Provincial Park in British Columbia, interviewed witnesses from Maine to West Virginia, Florida to California.

Bigfoot hunting has been my passion for over forty years. I'm convinced these creatures are out there to be discovered. A dream? I grew up with dreams. I am the son of heroes, the son of a city firefighter and a mother who speaks proudly of her Cherokee legacy, the grandson of a retired farmer who worked a field of dreams as the head groundskeeper for a minor league baseball team. I wanted to become a naturalist, in the original meaning of the word, and trek around the world seeking all sorts of animals. Instead, I did one better; I became a cryptozoologist, one who searches for new animals, yet to be discovered.

1

When I was young, growing up in Decatur, Illinois, I found myself outdoors all the time, camping, hiking, and, yes, at baseball games. My brothers and I, as kids, explored the "hollers and hills," the local name for the wild parts near the edges of town and beyond. In the 1950s, those were the safe feral places farther out, past the trailers and the cemeteries, the swampy, rugged, unexplored, and forgotten lands unused by farmers and as yet undiscovered by developers. Animals used them as natural greenways to travel from place to place, unnoticed.

I explored these and gathered snakes, turtles, toads, and other animals for my summertime zoo. I would keep, observe, and then let the animals go. In preparing to be a naturalist, I wanted to handle the things I read about in the books by Roy Chapman Andrews and Raymond Ditmars. I had visions of being a zoologist, but never could I have imagined what awaited me.

I now look back on one March evening in 1960 as a critical juncture that changed my life. I was watching the broadcast on the local Decatur TV station of a science fiction movie, a Japanese picture entitled *Half-Human: The Story of the Abominable Snowman* (Ishiro Honda, 1957), about the search for the Abominable Snowmen in the mountains of Asia. It was fascinating, for even though I knew it was fiction, there appeared to be an underlying truth to this tale of an expedition in pursuit of an unknown species of hairy, upright creature. One does not pick their entry point into mysteries, I suppose; for me this just happened to be the one.

I went to school the next week and asked my teachers about this elusive, mysterious creature called the Abominable Snowman. They were discouraging and lacked interest. They told me that I was wasting my time on a "myth." But their words did little to put out the fire in my belly. I was one very curious young man. I began looking for everything I could read on the Abominable Snowman. I discovered a large literature on the Yeti and soon found out, through the writings of Ivan T. Sanderson in magazines in 1959 to 1961, and in a book published in

1961, about North America's version of the Abominable Snowman, the Bigfoot of the Pacific Northwest and the Sasquatch of Canada.

I started writing to people all around the world who were investigating and searching for these creatures. Soon, I was corresponding with more than four hundred people, including the likes of Ivan Sanderson, John Green, Peter Byrne, Bernard Heuvelmans, and others. Then I decided to do some research, to look for old newspaper reports about Bigfoot, to interview witnesses, and to go out in the field myself and seek out these creatures.

In his book *Abominable Snowmen: Legend Come to Life,* Ivan T. Sanderson mentioned some cases from the U.S. Midwest and South he liked to call Little Red Men of the Woods. This is where I would start, and before I knew it, I was interviewing witnesses and tracking the beasts in Illinois, Indiana, Missouri, and Kentucky.

My interest in Bigfoot led to some specific life decisions. For example, I picked my college and its location — Southern Illinois University in Carbondale — because folklorist John W. Allen had written of authentic sightings of these animals by a minister and farmers from the area's bottomlands. I studied anthropology, minored in zoology, to have some scientific background to pursue these Bigfoot.

Sometimes my classes would suffer because I was hitchhiking deeper into southern Illinois to look into more cases, or to farther-away places such as Mississippi, to interview more witnesses. While I was in Carbondale from 1965 to 1969, I explored the swamplands of the area, ran down reports of strange, hairy creatures thereabouts, and spent endless hours in the microfilm sections of the libraries at SIU, as well as getting materials from Indiana University on local cases. I explored places that would later become familiar in Midwestern Bigfoot lore — Murphysboro, Chittyville, and other places in Little Egypt, as that part of Illinois is called.

I sent reams of material — raw reports, transcripts of eighteenth-century articles, and modern news clippings — to my correspondents.

Eventually, I became Ivan Sanderson's and John Green's "man in the East." Sanderson was so excited by what I was finding outside of the Pacific Northwest that he wrote in 1967, "Yes ... Please ... any reports you have ... Little Red Men of the ... or Giant Hairys of the suburbs. The whole bit is getting hotter and hairier by the month." John Green and John Keel, among others, mentioned me in their books, as the source of many accounts I had forwarded their way.

Finally, in 1968, Lou Farish, a correspondent in Arkansas, suggested that I begin writing articles on my own. A year later, I began writing about Bigfoot in the Midwest. Soon Ivan Sanderson introduced me to Mark A. Hall, and John Keel introduced me to Jerry Clark. The old generation was mentoring the new.

In 1974, I constructed a cross-country trek, from Illinois to California, via a southwestern route, stopping at various locales that had histories of Bigfoot reports, from the Ozarks to the Sierras. I lived in California for parts of two years, working closely with George Haas and Jim McClarin, and meeting and discussing Bigfoot with many others, including René Dahinden, Archie Buckley, and John Green. When I decided to move back East for my long-delayed entry into graduate school, I once again used my journey as a way to see parts of the Bigfoot story, on-site, staying not in motels or RVs but in a sleeping bag, under the stars or, on rainy nights, in a tent. From the mid-1970s, from my base in New England, I continued to crisscross the country seeking Bigfoot and Bigfoot reports.

I have written much, consulted on documentaries about Bigfoot, and done more than that boy in Illinois could ever have dreamed. By the turn of the twenty-first century, I had been on treks, hikes, expeditions, and explorations in forty-eight states. I have canoed the backwaters of the Everglades, Okefenokee Swamp, Hockomock Lake, Honey Island Swamp, Caddo Lake, and dozens of other Bigfoot locations throughout the land. I have explored the most likely habitats of these creatures. I have climbed peaks from

Yosemite to Fort Mountain, from the Trinities to Mt. Blue, looking for signs of Bigfoot. I have interviewed hundreds of Bigfoot witnesses. Four decades later, I'm convinced that ordinary people are having extraordinary but real encounters with these creatures, these hairy giants. This is what I now know about them.

Coast to Coast The classic Bigfoot is a real animal living in the montane forests of the Pacific Rim, specifically the United States of America's and Canada's Pacific Northwest wilderness areas up through southern Alaska. There probably exists a much rarer Eastern subspecies or regional race of primates with distinctive behavioral and physical characteristics. The American Bigfoot, also known historically as Sasquatch in western Canada, has affinities to giant, hairy, apelike hominoids reported from the western mountains of Central and South America, as well as the forested areas of China, Tibet, and Indochina, although this volume will focus only on the North American variety.

It has been estimated that the population of Bigfoot in the Pacific Northwest is between two thousand and four thousand individuals, with the greatest concentrations around Bluff Creek, California, and with other random spots such as the Skookum Meadows region of Washington State getting routine visitations. I tend to think the number may be smaller, only 1500 Bigfoot.

Witnesses have reported seeing Bigfoot in groups, including females and juveniles, demonstrating that breeding groups do exist. Detailed descriptions of the young of the Bigfoot are rare, but we do find some records of encounters at the edge of forested areas abutting new human habitats.

In general, the upright Bigfoot ranges in height from six to nine feet at maturity, with the conditions of available light, temporal length of the encounter, and the hair covering of the animals causing an often exaggerated estimate of greater stature. Their hair-covered, stocky bodies have enormous barrel torsos, with well-developed buttocks in both genders, penises seen on males, and large breasts clearly visible on older females. The breasts are often reported to be hair-covered except for the nipple area. Their heads are relatively small and peaked with no visible neck or forehead, with a heavy brow-ridge that sports a continuous up-curled fringe of hair. Both genders exhibit a sagittal crest, the peaked ridge found in fossil hominoids and modern great apes, which runs from the front to the back of the top of the skull where the muscles of the jaws are attached. Their jaws project forward markedly. Canine teeth that are noticeable enough to be called fangs are only rarely reported in males. The skin seen on the faces of the young is generally light-colored, while that of older individuals tends to be dark. Their eyes are small, round, and dark.

The hair of Bigfoot is reported to be relatively short and shaggy with no difference in length between body and head hair. In the young, the hair is usually dark, moves into shades of red and brown with age, and finally, at extreme maturity, evidences some silver, as in male mountain gorillas ("silverbacks"). Among the eastern North American subgroup of Bigfoot, piebald, or "two-tone," coloring has been reported.

Evidence of these animals, as their name implies, is often in the form of large tracks found in mud, sand, and snow. The Bigfoot foot has an hourglass outline and measures 4 to 9 inches in width by 11¾ to 20 inches in length. Unlike in the human foot, halfway down the Bigfoot foot is a "split-ball" or double-ball arrangement that is unique for these primates. Each foot has five toes, all aligned together, with some individual variation in number of toes either showing in the prints left behind or actually existing. Four-toed prints are rare but not unknown.

Bigfoot do not wear clothes of any kind and never display weapons or tools. They seem to nest in caves or beds made in the open and in trees. They appear to be vegetarian, though they have been seen to take small rodents and fish on occasion. Bigfoot are highly vocal, making high-pitched whistles, animal-like screams, howls, and such sounds as *eeek-eeek-eeek* and *sooka-sooka-sooka*.

Bigfoot are nocturnal, with sightings also at dawn and dusk. They are retiring, alert, and clever, generally avoiding humans, though firsthand encounters and native folklore plus a few modern reports indicate they have been known to kidnap humans. Bigfoot are intelligent. They appear to have a heightened sense of smell and avoid metal objects such as guns, cameras, and human dwellings in general. The Eastern variety has routine negative interactions with dogs, and an intriguing curiosity about such domestic animals as horses and cows. Sightings are scarcer than generally acknowledged, and close encounters in which good details are reported are extremely rare.

Undiscovered in North America?

Could a bunch of large, hairy, near-human ape-men, or hirsute giants, be living unfound in America? A parallel story, from just fifty years ago, suggests that this is a very real possibility.

The largest land animal in Canada, the wood bison, had been disappearing from all over North America for centuries when the last animals were officially declared extinct in 1940. Then in 1957, a wonderful discovery occurred. During a regular air patrol, federal wildlife officers flying over a remote part of the Wood Buffalo National Park, Alberta, spotted a small, isolated herd of two hundred wood bison. They had gone completely unnoticed for decades—and had kept physically and genetically separate from their cousins the plains bison, so familiar to Americans as the buffalo. The wood bison were found about one hundred miles from a new road being built from Alberta to the arctic circle and within fifty miles of a mission station that had existed for a hundred years. Inspection of these animals showed that they were indeed the last remaining pure wood bison *(Bison athabascae),* an enormous Ice Age species not known to exist in a pure strain anywhere else in the world.

The rediscovery of a hidden group of wood bison in a remote valley in Canada is as remarkable as the discovery of the coelacanth, the mountain gorilla, and the giant panda. I don't believe those who insist that North America has no new secrets. One day Bigfoot will be officially recognized as a living creature.

I hope to see that day soon. In the meantime, the sightings continue, the number of Bigfoot seekers keeps growing, and the search is still afoot.

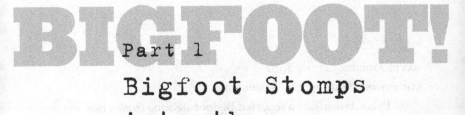

BIGFOOT!

Part 1
Bigfoot Stomps into the Twenty-First Century

1   The Summer of Sasquatch

DATE: Monday, June 10, 2002
LOCATION: Near Sappho, Washington

Police investigate a reported Bigfoot sighting from a man living on Burnt Mountain Road, about thirty miles northeast of Forks. The man, whose name was not released, said he spotted the hairy, humanlike creature near his house.

"We were unable to locate, identify, or capture the Sasquatch," Forks police chief Mike Powell told the Associated Press. An animal control officer checked the area but found no signs of the creature.

Local authorities noted this was not the first recent report in the area. They mentioned that the sighting happened in the same general area where, in June 2000, Gene Sampson found two sets of large footprints in the woods behind his home on the Hoh Indian reservation.

Clallam County undersheriff Joe Martin said he heard of Sasquatch sightings on the North Olympic Peninsula about once every five to ten years. "Out West, that's not an uncommon thing," he said.

10

DATE: January 16, 2002

LOCATION: Near Multnomah Falls, Oregon

An Idaho family has a run-in with a Bigfoot that almost turns into a roadkill. Linda Boydson claims she and her son came within inches of running over an unusually slender Bigfoot. Rounding a corner on the freeway at night, Boydson saw a "very, very skinny, nine-foot-tall, hairy man" standing in the slow lane. She remarked that the thing was bony, as if it needed to eat, but was otherwise muscular like a well-toned athlete. She nearly hit the creature.

There is nothing remarkable about these Bigfoot reports from 2002. Bigfoot sightings happen all the time in North America, especially in the Pacific Northwest. While the media may cite two or three reports per month during spring, summer, and fall, people are probably seeing Bigfoot and finding footprints at the rate of about ten unpublicized encounters a week. More than 550 reports a year. Year after year. Accounts of Bigfoot in America go back as far as this land is mentioned in history, and in legends and folklore long before that.

What's remarkable about these reports is that, despite the overwhelming evidence for the existence of Bigfoot, the media and most scientists largely act as if the creature is a joke, a mass delusion. The truth is that at least one unknown species of primate exists in America. It's a big story and it's not getting the attention it deserves.

But it almost did in 2000. So many sightings were reported by the media in the summer of that year, with so much positive press attention, that it's now referred to as the Summer of Sasquatch. The sightings actually began popping up in the papers in the spring.

On March 28, 2000, at about five-fifteen in the morning, James Hughes was delivering the little local newspaper, the *Black River Shopper,* along County Highway H, near Granton, Wisconsin, when he noticed a figure standing in the roadside ditch and carrying what appeared to be a goat. At first he took it to be a large man, but then he saw it was about eight feet tall and had an apelike face.

"He was all covered with hair, a real dark gray color, with some spots that looked a honey color. It was walking on two legs, and it was mighty, mighty big," Hughes said. In its left hand it held what Hughes at first took to be a goat but later thought might have been a small sheep. But he was certain it was a dead animal. When the Bigfoot-like beast turned to look at him, Hughes said he floored the gas pedal and sped away, scared.

"I didn't call it in [to the Sheriff's Department] until the next day, because people would think I'm crazy. And I don't drink, I don't use dope, and I was wide-awake," Hughes said.

Hughes finally did file a report with the Clark County Sheriff's Department, and a deputy was dispatched to the scene but could not find any large footprints or other evidence. The Sheriff's Department said Hughes gave a detailed description, but without tracks or other evidence suggesting a creature was in the area, the officers had to finally call off their searches.

In April 2000, two fly fishermen discovered a series of huge, humanlike footprints, seven miles apart along the banks of Colorado's Eagle River. Bill Heicher, a wildlife biologist at the Colorado Division of Wildlife, evaluated the evidence and drew two conclusions. He told Theo Stein of the *Denver Post* that the tracks were not faked and were not made by a bear. Heicher observed, "It's no animal that we know of."

Reports of footprint finds and sightings then appeared throughout the Pacific Northwest. On May 7, 2000, campers found a set of Bigfoot tracks in the wilderness along the Sandy River, near Troutdale, Oregon. On May 18 at Grants Pass, Oregon, a motorcyclist told of having seen a Bigfoot beside Highway 101. On June 3 a family found large footprints on their property in Orting, Pierce County, Washington. Two days later, near Orting again, an elderly woman saw a hairy giant pass by her car.

Meanwhile, back East, on Friday, June 9, 2000, at approximately 7 A.M., a woman was driving to work on Route 30 between Jeannette and Greensburg, Pennsylvania, when she spotted a Bigfoot. She had slowed down to look at a car for sale when she turned to her right and spotted a creature six to seven feet tall standing on the back road, she told investigators Eric Altman and Stan Gordon. The creature was covered with black hair and appeared neckless. When the manlike creature crossed the stretch of road, she lost sight of it as it took three long strides into a nearby wooded area.

On June 16 giant bare footprints were found along the Mountain Loop Highway in Darrington, Snohomish County, Washington. On June 21 hikers climbing the 5,324-foot-high Mount Pilchuck, Washington, found huge footprints. And on June 24 large Sasquatch footprints were discovered in Washington State's Olympic National Park, along the Sol Duc River.

Three days later Gene Sampson found giant footprints behind his home on the Hoh Indian Reservation, near Port Angeles, Washington. Hearing strange *bam, bam* noises, Sampson searched and discovered two different and distinctive sets of footprints, which he measured at fourteen inches and seventeen and a half inches in length, and seven and eight inches in width. Cliff Crook, a local Bigfooter, made casts of the prints. To the late Grover Krantz, a Bigfoot researcher and retired Washington State University anthropology professor, who examined them within days, the footprints on the Hoh reservation indicated the presence of one male and one female Sasquatch. Soon after Sampson's encounter, a forestry manager for the Suquamish First Nation saw a Bigfoot in the forest on the Kitsap Peninsula in Washington State.

Then on July 1, the true media storm began when a psychologist reported seeing a Bigfoot while hiking with his family near the Oregon Caves National Monument, Selma, Oregon.

Grants Pass psychologist Matthew Johnson was squatting in the woods, near one of the monument's backwoods trails, hiding behind a tree, taking a bathroom break, and keeping his family in sight. Then he heard grunting and smelled something strong and unpleasant.

"I turned my head quickly, and I saw this very tall, dark, hairy animal walk from behind one tree and over to another tree," he told me.

The creature was watching his wife and children too, Johnson said. Terrified, he ran back to his family and hustled them away from the area. "I didn't immediately tell them what I saw," Johnson would repeat many times later to me and others. "I didn't want to freak my kids out. I didn't want to freak my wife out." When the family stopped along the trail for a water break, Johnson just had to tell his wife. "I said, 'You're not going to believe this, but I saw Bigfoot.' She said, 'I believe you.' "

Johnson would later tell reporters such as Tim LaBarge of the *Statesman Journal,* "It was nothing else but a Sasquatch. I swear to God. I lived a lot of years in Alaska. I've been chased by a grizzly bear. This was no bear."

Media attention to Dr. Johnson's sighting was the big event of the summer, if one was to judge by how much newspaper, radio, and television coverage the sighting received. Johnson was interviewed widely, appeared on several morning and news programs, and was videotaped by filmmakers from around the world. His sighting was taken seriously, although some within the Bigfoot study ranks were upset that the press would treat a Ph.D. so nobly when the media ignores reports from truck drivers, farmers, and hunters every week.

The incident did catch the attention of some Bigfoot researchers in northern California, who spent parts of the summer retracing the Johnson family's steps along the monument's Big Tree Trail. Soon after the July 1 incident, investigator Scott Herriott and Bigfoot Field Researchers Organization's John Freitas, accompanied by Park Ranger John Roth, followed the family's path along the monument's pathways. Johnson said they found a large "impression in the ground." He termed it a partial footprint.

On July 3, near Concrete, Skagit County, Washington, hikers found giant footprints near Highway 20. Then in August 2000, two hikers forced by stormy weather to camp in the high wilderness north of Crested Butte, Colorado, emerged with quite a tale, reported the *Denver Post*. They told of having been shadowed for two nights by at least one Bigfoot that came close to their tent and camp.

The media kept covering the Bigfoot story as the summer ended. Chris Wright, who lives on the Mountain Loop Highway near Granite Falls, Washington, just wanted his midnight cigarette that Sunday night, September 24, 2000, according to Everett, Washington's the *Herald*. But he got more than he bargained for—a close encounter with a Sasquatch.

"I was not a firm believer in Bigfoot," Wright, twenty-nine, a broadcast communications tower manager, told local authorities. "But after last night, I'm rethinking that."

Wright stepped out on the back porch of his residence near Iron Mountain rock quarry, lit his cigarette, and walked off the porch and into the yard. That activated the motion detectors, and on came his security lights.

"At that point, I heard a loud, high-pitched yell," he recalled. "I turned and looked to my right and that's when I saw him. I was looking right at the son of a gun."

The beast was only seventy-five feet away from the tree line. The Bigfoot stood upright, about seven feet tall, was dark in color, and appeared to be covered with hair. "When the lights came on, he ran into the woods," Wright said. "It sounded like a human running through the woods." Being a hunter, Wright knew it wasn't a bear: "Bears don't run like that."

Running back into his home, Wright went after his rifle.

"I have guns in a gun case, and I was going for them when I decided to wake up my roommate and tell him what I saw," Wright noted. "At first, he sort of laughed at me. But then he could see how shaken I was, and he began to believe me."

Herald reporter Leslie Moriarty interviewed Wright and learned that he had seen a television show on Bigfoot sightings a few weeks before the sighting. On that documentary, a recording of a Bigfoot yell was played.

"What I heard sounded just like that," he told Moriarty. "That's why I know this was Bigfoot."

The next morning, Wright looked for footprints but found none.

Granite Falls police received no calls about Bigfoot sightings that Sunday night. "I haven't ever gotten any in the five years I've been here," officer Rich Michaelsen said.

"I thought all those guys who said they saw Bigfoot were loony," Wright said soon after his sighting. "But I know what I saw. . . . It had to be Bigfoot. Nothing else is that big or that tall."

Meanwhile, the most dramatic event of the year was occurring just due south, also in Washington State, not far from Mt. St. Helens and Ape Canyon, where a group of Bigfoot hunters had set a trap for Bigfoot. Their effort would produce one of the most concrete pieces of Bigfoot evidence to date—the Skookum cast.

2 Strange Cast of Skookum

The Native American Chinook word *Skookum,* according to linguists, is another name for Sasquatch or Bigfoot, and settlers in the West employed it to name geographical sites. Over two hundred Skookum place names are found in Oregon, Washington State, British Columbia, Idaho, and Alaska. During September 2000, Richard Noll, Matt Moneymaker, and eleven other individuals on an expedition looking for evidence of Bigfoot made a remarkable find, as chance would have it, near Skookum Meadow in the Gifford Pinchot National Forest in southern Washington State. In a mud trap they created, they obtained a half-body print—literally a butt print—of a Sasquatch. If authentic, noted Benjamin Radford, editor of the *Skeptic Inquirer,* the cast would be "arguably the most significant find in the past two decades."

A Powerful Name More than three thousand years ago, the Chinook First Nation, Native American traders extraordinaire, dwelt at the mouth of the

Columbia River, Washington. Their trade routes reached east as far as the central Great Plains, as far north as Sitka, Alaska, and as far south as the Monterey Peninsula and Taos, New Mexico. According to the records of the Hudson's Bay Company, about 90 percent of all furs shipped to Europe and Asia passed through the Chinooks first. While the Indians today are practically extinct, their name survives in the trade language they created and used, known as Chinook jargon. It is composed of two-fifths Chinook, two-fifths other Native American tongues, and the remainder English and Canadian French. One of the first to record the language was the great Pacific Northwest anthropologist Franz Boas, in reports for the Smithsonian Institution, beginning in 1894. Authentic snippets of it can even be heard in the Clark Gable movie *Across the Wide Missouri*.

Of the one hundred or so Chinook words that remain today, perhaps none is more intriguing than *Skookum*. When Chinook was in its purest form, before 1790, the word *Skookum* appears to have simply meant "powerful," according to Chinook historian Joel Freeman. A southwest Washington stream, Skookumchuck, for example, translates as "power water," denoting a swift stream.

Others see a more direct link between Skookum and Sasquatch. In 1867, U.S. geodetic surveyor F. W. Brown of Tacoma would write in his journal of the humanlike monsters that left tracks and were seen by the natives near Mount Rainier and Boisfort Peak. The Indians called the monster Skookum Quash, or in English, "strong terror." Bigfoot researcher and First Nation worker Henry Franzoni's interest in Skookum goes back to his first experience with Bigfoot in 1993. At a place called Skookum Lake, Oregon, Franzoni and his companion encountered what he would later call the "Bigfoot phenomenon." After his encounter, Franzoni began collecting Native tales and started noticing the links between Skookum and other names and the sightings of the creatures. Not coincidentally, Franzoni discovered that *Skookum* was another name for Sasquatch or Bigfoot. He has identified 214

Skookum place names all found in Oregon, Washington State, British Columbia, Idaho, and Alaska. It's a common name in the Pacific Northwest, as common as reports of the classic Bigfoot or Sasquatch.

In the book *Oregon Place Names,* written in 1928, author Lewis A. MacArthur explained, "The Indians, particularly of the Coast Range region, were fearful of a number of lakes and localities that were supposed to be inhabited by skookums, or evil wood-spirits. Some of the lakes are still called Skookum lakes, others are called Devils lakes. Many Indians avoided these places and considered them haunted."

In 1998, Franzoni outlined his thoughts about *Skookum.* "The modern Chinook jargon meaning," he stated in an e-mail to me, "is 'big, strong, and swift' whilst the original Chinook village meaning is 'Evil God of the Woods.' Places have to be examined as to when they were named, and often a correlating old story has to be located to really suggest that a particular skookum place is worthy of our Bigfoot interest. A number of skookum places fit the bill just fine after being investigated though. Places like Mt. Duckabush in the Olympic Range was once named 'Mt. Arleta' by Lt. Patrick O'Neill, who led the second group ever across the Olympic Mountains in 1890. O'Neill mentioned in his diary that the native guides he had with him called it skookum and believed their gods lived on it. His native guides abandoned him and his group when a panther shrieked at their camp continuously one night. Oddly enough, most native peoples of the Olympic Peninsula did not venture into the interior, because they thought their gods lived there. There are some interesting parallels between some stories of the Himalayan Shangri-la and native legends of a hidden valley in the Olympics, guarded by Skookums. . . . The Chinook jargon does have many different interpretations for the word *skookum* depending on which expert is consulted. I used MacArthur's 1924 definition, but for me the Bigfoot connection was strong once I went to a skookum place and figure that I stood ten feet from a smelly Bigfoot on my very first day of looking."

Franzoni's experience is remarkably similar to that of others. Paul Kane (1810–79), who was a well-known painter of Native Americans, mentioned in his journal entry of March 26, 1847, of hearing that Skookums at Mt. St. Helens, in what is now Washington State, had eaten a man. At Skookum Lake, Clackamas County, Oregon, Bigfoot was encountered in 1991, 1993, and 1995. As the twenty-first century was breaking, Kyle Mizokami, a former Bigfooter, who was on a casual hike at Skookum Creek, Washington, found two fourteen-inch-long Bigfoot tracks. The biggest prize, of course, was to take place at another Skookum place.

Imprint of the Century

When reports of twisted trees and hair alerted investigators to new activity in the spring of 2000, the Bigfoot Field Researchers Organization (BFRO) decided the Skookum Meadows area was a good location to search for Bigfoot. Frustrated by past searching there, they decided in September 2000 to get a group of specialists together to look anew and use a variety of techniques. Those there included tracker Richard Noll, psychiatrist and pheromone expert Greg Bambenek, zoologist LeRoy Fish, wilderness guide Jim Henick, local Gifford Pinchot Park guide Jeff Lemley, assistant Erin Lee, bait expert Thomas Powell, animal tracker Derek Randles, communications professional Alan Terry, and BFRO founder, director, and expedition leader Matt Moneymaker. Joe Beelart was the off-site equipment supplier, and a film crew from the British television series *Animal X* was along to see what they could find.

As the group established base camp on September 16, 2000, they were well prepared. They had infrared cameras, night-vision goggles, sound equipment, and a sexual attractant. Since no Sasquatch pheromone has ever been gathered, Bambenek (nicknamed Dr. Juice) created a mixture of human and gorilla scent. They placed samples of this special fragrance on trees near their camp, in hopes that a Bigfoot would come for a visit. They also set out fruit in and around a "mud trap" they constructed, in the hope of getting some Bigfoot tracks.

They also broadcast a sound recording of what was supposedly a Bigfoot call from California, recorded in 1999. Soon they heard "answers" to these screams. Rick Noll told reporter Mark Hume of the *National Post* that the responses "sounded sort of like a high-pitch scream by a woman, trailing off to a gurgle."

On September 22, Noll, Randles, and Fish checked on the fruit "traps" and noted the fruit was gone from two locations. Whatever took the fruit from those places did not leave behind any footprints. When they came to what they called the Skookum Meadows "mud site," however, the three noticed that half of the six locally grown apples were gone. They also noted the presence of older tracks of coyote, bear, deer, and elk.

Then, suddenly, Noll was startled to see another large impression at the edge of the muddy patch. Fish and Randles came over to view what Noll had found, and they all quickly agreed that it seemed to show an animal, indeed the animal they were pursuing.

Others from camp rushed to the site, and photographs and other recordings and measurements of the area were made. Noll was transporting some casting material, Hydrocal B-11, in his truck and thus had a larger amount than normal. A casting of this half-body print was taken by Noll, Fish, and Randles. Meanwhile, Lemley, Terry, and Bambenek helped in the making of the cast—holding a sun shade, retrieving water, lifting the cast out of the ground, and removing food debris and hair from the cast site. Moneymaker coordinated the whole effort.

It took 325 pounds of casting material to capture the imprint, while the crew from *Animal X* videotaped the event. The BFRO folks were stunned to realize that they had a good plaster copy of a Sasquatch's butt, ankles, testicles, hip, thigh, left arm, and apparent hair on the body. They believe the impression was made as the creature sat down and reached over to pick up the bait. The imprint of hairy buttocks in the mud is the strongest hint yet that Bigfoot is roaming the American Pacific Northwest, according to the Bigfoot Field Researchers Organization, which sponsored the expedition.

Other evidence was gathered, such as portions of the apple the creature had chewed, to see if any Sasquatch salvia could be found.

Details of the events at Skookum Meadows were widely reported in daily newspapers, by Channel 5 in Seattle, and in the *New Scientist*. The media had a field day with the Skookum cast discovery, with several wire service stories playing with the obvious "butt" imprint humor in their headlines and articles. Nevertheless, a serious piece of the puzzle had been found, and the investigation kicked into full gear after the BFRO members returned from the rain forest.

Skookum Cast Analyses

One individual, Cliff Crook, a sometimes thorn in the side of the Bigfoot community and the former director of Bigfoot Central, quickly came forward and convinced some in the media to print his theory that the cast collected was nothing more than impressions from the chest or belly of a kneeling elk. Crook called the Skookum cast either the "Spoofem" or "Wapiti" cast. "Wapiti," Crook e-mailed to Bigfooters across the country, "is the name given to the elk by the Shawnee Indian Tribe and means 'white rump.'"

Crook didn't convince many of his theory. In response, BFRO's Richard Noll pointed to the fact that besides the hair of coyote and elk, unknown primate hairs and a Bigfoot footprint was found in the Skookum cast area. "The imprint," Noll wrote to Bigfoot researchers, "is consistent with an animal that can use its forelimbs as leverage separate from the hind limbs in raising its body from a sitting position. There are no elk prints behind the heel marks, nor in the main body of the cast impression, as would be expected if it were a four-legged animal. It apparently could use one of its limbs to support its weight and thrust it out of the mud to leave this imprint."

Meanwhile, Grover Krantz and others not on the expedition began to examine the Skookum cast. I got a chance to examine the cast of the leg imprint when Rick Noll showed it to me at a Bigfoot conference in 2001. And anthropologist Jeff Meldrum of Idaho State University also examined the cast. In an article published in *New Scientist,* Meldrum noted that the imprint seems to have been made by a large, hair-covered hominoid more than 2.5 meters tall. Meldrum found markings that look like human dermal patterns (such as those found on human feet) on the heel print. "All we're trying to say at this stage is that there's evidence that justifies objective consideration," Meldrum wrote.

In rebuttals to the *Skeptical Inquirer*'s attacks on the Skookum cast, Sasquatch chronicler John Green stated, "Some of the holes in the mud, not readily identifiable in that form, turned out in the cast to be beautiful prints of huge, humanlike heels, complete with hair patterns on the Achilles tendon—good enough to cause the author of a text on primate anatomy to reverse a long-held opinion as to the existence of the Sasquatch. And those poor fools who have found the cast completely convincing include several people with relevant doctorates and careers, one of them considered by many to be the greatest field zoologist of our time. Primatologists at the Smithsonian Institution, on the other hand, have said they will not look at the cast even if someone drives clear across the country to show it to them. Who are the scientists and who are the believers?"

In June of 2002, the Discovery Channel gathered three noted anthropologists in an Edmonds, Washington, hotel to tape them examining anew and commenting on the Skookum cast. Financing for Sasquatch searches is wanting, but cable television subtly supports the efforts of interested parties in at least attempting to gather information and in scrutinizing the evidence. University of Washington professor emeritus Daris Swindler, American Museum of Natural History anatomist Esteban Sarmiento, and Idaho State University anatomy professor Jeffrey Meldrum were gathered together to investigate the cast of the imprint for the filming of a documentary on the science behind the search for the Sasquatch. The presence of Sarmiento, a functional anatomist who has concentrated on African gorilla populations and the study of hominid skeletons, constituted the first sign of interest in Bigfoot by the New York–based American Museum of Natural History.

David Fisher, a reporter for the *Seattle Post-Intelligencer,* was allowed to observe the anthropologists' examinations. According to Fisher, one impression "lined with hair marks," said Sarmiento, "could have been made by a huge hindquarters." Meldrum pointed out for the camera that "a deep knob-shaped hole with a fluted groove running into it could have been made by the back of a huge heel jammed into the mud. Fine lines, reminiscent of the fingerprint patterns on human heels, are faintly visible."

Meldrum feels all the evidence points to an eight-foot-tall Bigfoot's having left the overall impressions at Skookum Meadows.

During 2002, zoologist LeRoy Fish and anthropologist Grover Krantz, both strong Skookum cast supporters, died. The Discovery Channel documentary, entitled *Sasquatch: Legend Meets Science,* was shown in January 2003. The program highlighted the scientific analysis of various pieces of purported Bigfoot evidence, including the Skookum cast.

As exciting a find as the Skookum cast is, the decisive quest still remains — for the animal that made the hairy-buttocks impression.

"Obviously, to me," remarked Sarmiento of the American Museum of Natural History, "the ultimate evidence that this thing exists is if somebody found one and brought it back."

"Bringing one back" to prove they exist has not always been the goal of people knowledgeable about Bigfoot. For the first people on the continent, the Bigfoot were simply cohabitants, the giant hairy neighbors in the woods.

BIGFOOT!
Part 2
A Look Back

3　Native Traditions

Our knowledge of Bigfoot in America begins with Indian tales, folk-lore, and legend, which demonstrate a prehistoric knowledge of unknown hairy, erect primates on the continent.

The stories are familiar. Almost two centuries ago, native Indonesians passed along elaborate stories of their "wild men of the woods," which today we know as orangutans, and native Africans told of their local "monster ape" (the *ngagi* and *ngila*) that allegedly kidnapped and killed natives, which is recognized by zoology today as the mountain gorilla. So too we have lessons to learn from the First Nations of North America about apes still in our midst. Their fantastic tales have an underlying reality that appears to point, oftentimes, to actual animals.

In a survey of native traditions of Bigfoot that Mark A. Hall and I first published in 1970, we wrote: "A vast folklore and a belief in a race of very primitive people with revolting habits is found from northern California up into the Arctic lands themselves. This tradition covers not only the whole stretch of the Pacific coast, but much of the rugged territory to the east, even into Greenland. Generally, these subhominids are described as very tall, fully haired, and retiring. Sometimes they are described as carnivorous."

When Europeans colonized from the East to the West, their initial encounters were with the rare, eastern Bigfoot, which the natives they met spoke about. The first Americans acknowledged these hairy races, and their tales come down to us in the records that ethnographers, folklorists, and anthropologists have preserved in overlooked essays on hairy-giant legends and myths. Examining these closely, a pattern begins to emerge of Bigfoot revealed.

Eastern Traditions

In eastern North America, a specific subvariety of manlike hairy hominoid allegedly exists. It exhibits aggressive behavior, hair covering the face in a masklike fashion, occasional piebald coloring, an infrequent protruding stomach, and distinctive curved, five-toed sprayed footprints. (A few hominologists have labeled these unknown primates Taller or Marked Hominids, and others have written of them as Eastern Bigfoot. What may be in evidence is actually an Eastern geographic race, perhaps a subspecies, of the more classic Bigfoot, but more of that later.) They are inhabitants of the northern forests of the East. The local Native American, Native Canadian, and Inuit accounts discuss the ancient traditions of these hairy, humanlike beings with words special for each linguistic and tribal group. Nevertheless, a casual practice has begun to develop in the East in calling these hominids *Windigo* in association with a commonly used Native regional name from long ago. The Algonquian linguistic groups of the East and upper Midwest of the United States and lower Canada have used the terms *Windigo, Wendigo, Weetigo, Wetiko, Wittiko,* and other variant names for these reported giants of the bush covered in hair.

The antiquity of this subject matter is marked by places in geography and language. The Wetiko Hills, the Misabi Range, and numerous Windigo and Wendigo Lakes take their names from giants known to American Indians. *A Dictionary of Canadianisms on Historical Principles* mentions eighteenth-century versions of Bigfoot called the *Weetigo*. The *Weetigo* were feared cannibals known to the Cree living in the vicinity of Hudson Bay. The Ojibwa knew the *Wendigo*. A nineteenth-century account relates, "The *Muskegoes,* who inhabit the low and cheerless swamps on the borders of Hudson's Bay, are themselves reproached by the other tribes as cannibals, [and] are said to live in constant fear of the *Windegoag.*"

There was a free exchange of information on these manlike, hairy primates among many First Nations in eastern North America. In the eastern provinces of New Brunswick and Nova Scotia down into Maine, the Micmac tell of the *Gugwes*. "These cannibals have big hands, and faces like bears," noted folklorist Elsie Clews Parsons in her 1925 paper in the *Journal of American Folklore.* "If one saw a man coming, he would lie down and beat his chest, producing a sound like a partridge." While the behavior attributed to this creature is puzzling, the theme of the one-tone whistle (i.e., the call of the gray partridge, *Perdix perdix,* of southeastern Canada) appears elsewhere as part of the unknown primate's behavior in America.

The cannibalism attributed to the *Windigo* is specific to these Eastern hairy hominids. Anthropologist Grover Krantz, who seemed not to have studied these traditions closely, is to be excused for falling into the usual misunderstandings of these traditions of the *Windigo* when he too quickly sensed they have all been based on stories of cannibal Indians. The Natives clearly thought of these hairy cannibal giants as non-Indians.

The Micmac know the cannibal giant by the names *Gugwe* or *Koakwe* and *Djenu* or *Chenoo*. However, Wilson D. Wallis and Ruth Sawtell Wallis in *The Micmac Indians of Eastern Canada* note that "*Gugwes* is a grotesque creature; in 1911–1912 he was commonly compared to a baboon; in 1950 he was described as a giant."

In the state of Maine, the Penobscot tell of the *Kiwakwe,* a cannibal giant (Speck 1935b: 81). "The giants, or *Strendu,* the averred enemies of the Wyandot," relates C. M. Barbeau in recording beliefs of the Huron and Wyandot in the area of Lake Huron, "were dreaded on account of their extraordinary size and powers. Some describe them as being half-a-tree tall and large in proportion. Their bodies were covered all over with flinty scales, which made them almost invulnerable." The *Strendu* too are said to be cannibals.

In upper New York State similar beings were known as Stone Giants. "The Iroquoian Stone Giants," notes Hartley Burr Alexander in *Mythology of All Races,* "as well as their congeners [a member of the same kind, class, or group] among the Algonquians (e.g., the *Chenoo* of the Abnaki and Micmac), belong to a widespread group of mythic beings of which the Eskimo *Tornit* are examples. They are . . . huge in stature, unacquainted with the bow, and employing stones for weapons. In awesome combats they fight one another, uprooting the tallest trees for weapons and rending the earth in fury. . . . Commonly they are depicted as cannibals; and it may well be that this far-remembered mythic people is a reminiscence, coloured by time, of backward tribes, unacquainted with the bow, and long since destroyed by the Indians of historic times. Of course, if there be such an historical element in these myths, it is coloured and overlaid by wholly mythic conceptions of stone-armoured Titans and demiurges."

More of these peculiar "primitive" tribes are identified, as noted, by these First Nations as the *Windigo* of Algonquian origin. Knowledge of the *Windigo* is extensive and well documented in eastern and central Canada. The Tête-de-Boule of Quebec use different names for the same being: *Witiko, Kokotshc, Atshen.* The *Chenoo* of the Micmac seems to be similar to the *Witiko* of the Cree, for John Cooper in his article on the *Witiko* in *Primitive Man* observes, "Both have the same characteristics. . . . The very name *Chenoo* seems to be identical with the Montagnais and Tête-de-Boule (Cree) name, *Atcen,* for the *Witiko.*" According to anthropologist Frank Speck, among the Naskapi "the nearest analogy in name and character with *Atcen* among neighboring peoples is the *Chenoo (Tcenu)* of Micmac legend."

The traits of the *Witiko,* recorded by the Reverend Joseph Guinard, in his article "*Witiko* Among the Tête-de-Boule," in *Primitive Man,* recall traditions elsewhere: "The *witiko* wore no clothes. Summer and winter he went naked and never suffered cold. His skin was black like that of a negro. He used to rub himself, like the animals, against fir, spruce, and other resinous trees. When he was thus covered with gum or resin, he would go and roll in the sand, so that one would have thought that, after many operations of this kind, he was made of stone."

A similar habit, observes John Cooper in "The Cree *Witiko* Psychosis," in *Primitive Man,* "is ascribed to the Passamaquoddy *Chenoo,* who used to rub themselves all over with fir balsam and then roll themselves on the ground so that everything adhered to the body. This habit is highly suggestive of the Iroquoian Stone Coats, the blood-thirsty cannibal giants, who used to cover their bodies carefully with pitch and then roll and wallow in sand and down sand banks."

Windigo are without lips, and "the voice of the *witikos,*" notes the Reverend Joseph Guinard in his 1930 *Primitive Man* essay, "was strident and frightful, and more reverberating than thunder. The sound of his voice was a long-drawn-out one, accompanied with fearful howls." He is a huge individual, notes Guinard, "who goes naked in the bush and eats Indians. Many people claim to have heard him prowling in the woods." Also in Quebec, the Grand Lake Victoria Band knows tales of the *Misabe,* a giant with long hair, according to D. S. Davidson in 1928 articles in the *American Journal of Folklore.*

Canadian commentators on the unknown began remarking on the place of the *Windigo* in the context of other creatures almost a half century ago, bringing it forth in time. Explorer-author Pierre Berton commented on the *Windigo,* as did Canadian folklore researcher R. S. Lambert (1955). Lambert wrote that the *Windigo* or

Wendigo was "a Canadian entity, half phantom, half beast, who lives in the forests and preys on human beings, particularly children. The belief in this horror dates back to the earliest Indian legends and it is said that the *wendigo* will eat the flesh of its victims."

The Little Windigo

The Natives of the North Woods gave many names to the *Windigo*, but they were all the *Windigo*, nevertheless. Sometimes they also apparently noted differences among the *Windigo*, including perhaps the existence of juveniles or children of the clan of the *Windigo*. An example comes from the Ojibwa of northern Minnesota and is provided by Sister Bernard Coleman, who wrote about the *Memegwicio*, or men of the wilderness, "Some called them a 'kind of monkey' ... and were described as being about the size of children ten or eleven years of age ... faces covered with hair."

The Timagami Ojibwa know the *Memegwesi* as "a species of the creature which lives in high remote ledges. They are small and have hair growing all over their bodies," according to Frank A. Speck in "Myths and Folklore of the Timiskaming Algonquin and Timagami Ojibwa," *Anthropological Series*. The Cree around James Bay are familiar with the *Memegwecio*, according to Regina Flannery in *Man in Northeastern North America*, "the diminutive being who looks like a human except that he is covered with hair and has a very flat nose."

Other tales of little people are found among the Cherokee, Iroquois, and other Eastern First Nations, which closely match these traditions. These all may be efforts to characterize immature offspring and the juveniles of the *Windigo*.

Western Traditions

Creatures that are manlike and hairy and said to be part of the real world, not the spirit one, were familiar to the first inhabitants of this land. In the West the creature was known by a variety of names, from *Oh-Mah* to *Skookum*. A few chroniclers and researchers have also liked the Native-sounding nature of *Sasquatch,* the name that J. W. Burns, Indian-agent teacher of the Chehalis Indian Reserve, coined from Native British Columbian words, including *sokqueatl* and *soss-q'tal,* for the hairy giants.

Wayne Suttles, a Portland State University anthropologist who edited *The Scientist Looks at the Sasquatch I* and *II* with Grover Krantz, had this to say about the origins of *Sasquatch* in the second volume of the series: "The word *Sasquatch* is an anglicization of the word *sésqec,* which occurs in the mainland dialects of the Halkomelem language. This language, a member of the Salish language family, is spoken in southwestern British Columbia in the Lower Fraser Valley from Yale to the mouth of the Fraser and on southeastern Vancouver Island from Nanoose bay to Malahat."

Many contemporary authors have noted the widespread nature of Native traditions of Bigfoot-like creatures in the Pacific Northwest. Indeed, in his review of the folklore of Bigfoot, Ivan T. Sanderson felt the term *Oh-Mah,* used in the Klamath area, among the Hoopa, was preferable to *Bigfoot,* in addition to the Canadian *Sasquatch.* The Hoopa or Huppa called the large, hairy beings in their legends *Oh-mah-ah,* which was later shortened to *Oh-mah* or *Omah* by Bigfoot researchers like Sanderson.

A similar western-Washington legend is the Nisqually tribe's *Tsiatko,* who are described as gigantic and hairy, with eighteen-inch-long feet. In the interior of British Columbia, the Kaska Indians told stories of men with coarse, thick hair, according to ethnographer James Teit writing in 1917, in the *Journal of American Folklore.* Among the Kaska, another anthropologist, John Honigmann, found that memories of the *Big Man* or *Tenatco* were mentioned by his informants in the first half of the 1900s. These *Tenatco* dug a hole in the ground as a place to sleep and kidnapped adults and children. Tales of bearlike men are mentioned by another Athabascan group, the Sinkoyne, according to folklorist E. W. Gifford, writing in a 1937

article in the *Journal of American Folklore*. The Anderson and Seton Lake Indians related to W. C. Elliot, another folklorist writing in the *Journal of American Folklore*, in 1931, of giants in British Columbia. The Lillooet people knew of beings they call the *Hailo' Laux*, who were said to be tall, hairy, and strong, noted the above-mentioned ethnographer Teit. Diamond Jenness writing in the *Journal of American Folklore*, in 1934, recounted that the Carrier First Nation told of a monster that left enormous footprints in the snow, had a face like a human being, was covered in long hair, and was exceedingly tall.

Agent J. W. Burns discovered in 1938 just how real Bigfoot was to the Indians, during the May 23 celebration of a festival known as Indian Sasquatch Days, held at Harrison Hot Springs, British Columbia. "Having obtained special permission from the Department of Indian Affairs at Ottawa," Burns writes in the *Wide World Magazine* (1940), "I took several hundred of my charges to the event. Unfortunately, in his opening speech over the radio, a very prominent official of the British Columbia Government made a bad slip, thus offending all the Indians present who understood English. After a few preliminary remarks, this personage went on: 'Of course, the Sasquatch are merely legendary Indian monsters. No white man has ever seen one and they do not exist today in fact. . . .'

"Thereupon," continues Burns, "his voice was drowned by a great rustling of buckskin garments and the tinkling of ornamental bells as, in response to an indignant gesture from old Chief Flying Eagle, more than two thousand Red men rose to their feet in angry protest. Chief Flying Eagle then stalked across to the open space where the speaker stood, surrounded by important dignitaries and others. Absolutely ignoring the entire groups, Chief Flying Eagle turned to the microphone and thundered in excellent English: 'The white speaker is wrong! To all who now hear I say: Some white men have seen Sasquatch. Many Indians have seen them and spoken to them. Sasquatch are still all around here. I have spoken!' "

The well-known California anthropologist Alfred Kroeber reached an interesting conclusion in his classic volume, *Handbook of the Indians of California,* published by the Bureau of American Ethnology in 1925. After his decades of studying the folklore of the Karok and Yurok Indians, he concluded that the impression clearly existed "of the idea [of] an ancient prehuman but parallel race."

Should we be surprised that the early Europeans would find more than just the Indians inhabiting these distant shores?

4   Wildmen, Gorillas, and Ape Canyon

The first reports of hairy, upright creatures by European visitors to the New World come from the eastern fringes of North America and are very old. In A.D. 986 Leif Eriksson wrote of encountering monsters that were ugly, hairy, and swarthy with great black eyes. In 1603, during Samuel de Champlain's first voyage to eastern Canada, the local natives informed the explorer of the *Gougou,* a giant hairy beast that lived in the northern forests and was much feared by the Micmac.

More and more, newspapers picked up the thread. A *London Times* article of 1784 records the capture of hair-covered hominids by local natives, near Lake of the Woods, in south-central Canada. In the *Boston Gazette* of July 1793, a dispatch appeared from Charleston, South Carolina, May 17, 1793, concerning a creature seen in North Carolina. The account centers on Bald Mountain, where the local residents call it *Yahoo,* while the Indians give it the name *Chickly Cudly.* [Investigator Scott McNabb notes the term *Chickly Cudly* could be an English variant on a Cherokee name, *ke-cleah (Chick Lay)*, which means "hair" in Cherokee, and/or *kud-leah (Cooed Lay)*, which means either "man" or "thing." The term *kud-leah* in Cherokee can also mean a "man bear" or a "bear thing," and thus *Chickly Cudly* = *ke-cleah kud-leah* = hairy man/thing.]

For much of the nineteenth century, the native words for these creatures were substituted almost universally by the word *wildman*.

Newspapers' Wildmen

An old North American newspaper account appeared in the *Exeter Watchman* of New York on September 22, 1818. The item told of a sighting of a "Wild Man of the Woods" near Ellisburgh, New York, on August 30, 1818. The hairy creature was said to bend forward when running and left footprints showing a narrow heel with spreading toes. Such accounts were followed by reports of hairy, child-sized creatures seen in Indiana and Pennsylvania, in the 1830s. Then, beginning in 1834, in Arkansas, a giant "wildman" was seen by many people in the Ozarks. Even the journal *Scientific American* for March 1846 mentioned this "monstrous wild man" with twenty-two-inch-long footprints as being seen in the swamps near the Missouri-Arkansas state line. The *Memphis Enquirer* of May 9, 1851, reported on the Arkansas sightings of the previous March, noting, "This singular creature has long been known traditionally in St. Francis, Greene, and Poinsett counties, Arkansas, sportsmen and hunters having described him so long as seventeen years since." The wildman was said to be of gigantic stature, hairy, and with shoulder-length hair on its head. Footprints found measured fourteen inches long.

From the thumb of Michigan, Mark A. Hall chronicles in his 1999 book, *Living Fossils,* that hair-covered, formidable, manlike beings were seen in the 1860s, near Lake Saint Claire and Lake Huron. The group reportedly included adult males and females, as well as three or four small or young ones. One male had a bristly

beard, while another had a bald head and white beard. They had enormous stomachs, long arms, and were strongly muscled. (Similar hairy hominids in this specific area of Michigan were reportedly sighted in 1910, 1969, 1981, and 1983, according to Hall's research, and were chronicled by others into the twenty-first century. Furthermore, the aggressive encounters with the Sister Lakes and Monroe, Michigan, "monsters" of 1964–65 closely mirror the earlier descriptions of these "wildmen.")

Various researchers—from Mark A. Hall and myself in 1970, through John Green in 1978, and Gary S. Mangiacopra and Dwight Smith in 2002—have found reports of "wild men" in nineteenth-century newspapers. Mangiacopra and Smith, for example, discovered old records of a "wild boy"—covered with hair—seen near East Davenport and Gilbert, Iowa, in 1869; of a giant, hairy "wildman" seen in Lancaster, Berks, and Chester Counties, Pennsylvania, in 1874; and of a hairy "wildman" seen near Lagrange, Indiana, beginning in 1895, and again two years later.

The Winsted Wildman was the rage of 1895 Connecticut. The reports began with a sighting on "a sultry August day" that year, say newspaper clippings from the time. A local town official, Selectman Riley Smith, was the first to spy the "wildman." Others soon saw the creature too, but Smith's encounter was said to be the most credible. According to Frank Wentworth's 1929 book, *The Winsted Wildman and Other Tales,* Smith went up to pick berries near the Colebrook town line on Lowsaw Road in an area known then as Indian Meadow. "While [Smith] was stooped over picking berries, his bulldog [Ned], which is noted for its pluck, ran with a whine to him and stationed itself between his legs," accounts from the August 21, 1895, *Winsted Herald* report. "A second afterward a large man, stark naked and covered with hair all over his body, ran out of a clump of bushes and, with fearful yells and cries, made for the woods at lightening [*sic*] speed where he soon disappeared. Selectman Smith is a powerful, wiry man and has a reputation for having lots of sand, and his bulldog is also noted for his pluck, but Riley admits that he was badly scared and his dog was fairly paralyzed with fear."

Local posses of searchers and newspaper reporters from New York and Boston were never able to track down the Winsted Wildman.

Near the Traverspine River, Labrador, come the 1913 accounts of the apelike creature said to stand upright and yet also go about on all fours. This Traverspine white-maned primate reflects the piebald conditions so common in the reports of these unknown primates, and others, such as Old Yellow Top, the name given to distinctively light-color-maned hominids seen in 1903, 1926, and 1970, in Cobalt, Ontario. Also, this Traverspine River creature was seen more as an ape than a "wild man."

Gorillas in Our Midst

By the end of the nineteenth century, references to the "wildman" became references to the "gorilla." This was directly related to the media attention about gorillas whipped up by Du Chaillu's sensational travels in Africa and his book *Exploration and Adventures in Equatorial Africa: With accounts of the manners & customs of the people & the chase of the gorilla, crocodile, leopard, elephant, hippopotamus . . .*, which was published in 1861. "After [Du Chaillu's] trip, which lasted from 1856 to 1859," wrote Vernon Reynolds in his *The Apes*, "Du Chaillu returned to the United States, where he received widespread acclaim." In 1863, another famous gorilla/travel book was published, written by American explorer Winwood Reade, after he spent five months in gorilla country. As a result, many nineteenth-century articles about "strange creatures"—whether real or imagined—labeled them "gorillas."

The record of "gorillas" in America begins in 1869 with two news accounts uncovered by Mark A. Hall. The first concerns reports from Gallipolis, Ohio, on the Ohio River. The account appeared on

January 23, 1869, in an article headlined "A Gorilla in Ohio." It told of a hairy creature haunting the woods near the town that had jumped on a man riding in a carriage. The man's daughter, who was also in the carriage, threw a stone at the animal as it struggled with her father. The rock hit the animal's ear and the "gorilla" departed.

The second incident occurred on the western fringes of the bottomlands along the Osage River of Missouri and Kansas. During the summer of 1869, in the Arcadia Valley, Crawford County, Kansas, people started seeing a "wild man or a gorilla, or a 'what is it?'" Called Old Sheff by the locals, it was seen by more than sixty people. "It cannot be caught and nobody is willing to shoot it," reported the *Osage City Journal Free Press* of August 6, 1869. The debate of the day was whether it was of the "human family or not." The writer of the piece noted that it "probably will be found to be a gorilla or large orangutan that has escaped from some menagerie in the settlements east of here." The item, signed "M. S. Trimble," was reprinted in Missouri and Minnesota newspapers. The creature allegedly had a stooping gait, long arms, and immense hands. It walked on its hind legs but sometimes went on all fours. The gorilla escapee theory, upon closer examination, hardly holds any water.

Researchers Mangiacopra and Smith found one of the most intriguing early "gorilla" reports in old archives of the Williamsport *Sun-Gazette* (February 1871), which reprinted a long article from the Californian *Antioch Ledger* of October 1870. The statement republished in the Eastern newspaper details sightings of "California Gorillas" during two decades. Beginning with the encounters of gold hunters coming to the minefields in 1849 and 1850, up through 1870, miners had observed two "gorillas," indeed mates, in the mountains about twenty miles south of Antioch, California. The tracks discovered were "a man's" but "of immense size." The creature was described as stocky, a little over five feet tall, with a head smaller than would be expected for the body seen. It gave forth a "shrill whistle."

The Pennsylvania naturalist and folklorist Henry W. Shoemaker once wrote a short essay called "The Gorilla," about the sightings of such an animal in Pennsylvania late in 1920 and early in 1921. Thanks to research by Chad Arment, we hear again of the oft-repeated, but hardly credible, escaped-animal explanation in Shoemaker's writings. Shoemaker pondered, "The papers have told us how a gigantic man-ape escaped from a carnival train near Williamsport, and seeking the South, fled over the mountains to Snyder County, where it attacked a small boy, breaking his arm, held up automobiles, rifled smokehouses and the like, and then appeared in Snyder Township, Blair County, still further South, his nocturnal ramblings in that region proving an effective curfew for the young folks of a half-dozen rural communities. This story sounds thrillingly interesting, but as gorillas live on fruit, and do not eat flesh, the animal in question would have starved or frozen to death at the outset of his career in the Alleghenies, and there the unknown quantity of the real story begins. The newspapers have only printed the most popular versions of the gorilla mystery, only a fraction of the romance and folklore that sprang up mushroom-like around the presence of such an alien monster in our highlands. Already enough has been whispered about to fill a good sized volume, most of it absolutely untrue, yet some of the tales, if they have not hit the real facts, have come dangerously close to it."

Wild Wild West There were several exceptional nineteenth-century news reports on what would more than a half century later be known as Bigfoot. One appeared in the *Bishop Creek Times* of 1882, which referred to sightings of a large, hairy beast roaming the hills of Round Valley, California. We also have the "wild man" of Mt. Diablo, reported in the San Joaquin, California, *Republican* on September 19, 1870. And we have the hairy-gorilla reports from the Antioch, California, *Ledger* of October 18, 1870.

But one news article took on an almost legendary status. The story of Jacko—that of a small, apelike, young Sasquatch said to have been captured alive in the 1800s—is a piece of folklore that refuses to die, despite a superb investigative article published in 1975, coauthored by John Green and Sabina W. Sanderson.

The investigation into the Jacko story did not begin until decades later. During the 1950s, a news reporter named Brian McKelvie became interested in the then-current stories of the Sasquatch being carried by his local British Columbian papers. McKelvie searched for older reports. What he found was the *Daily British Colonist* July 4, 1884, article about Jacko. The account detailed the sighting of a smallish, hairy creature ("something of the gorilla type") supposedly seen and captured near Yale, British Columbia, on June 30, 1884, and housed in a local jail.

McKelvie shared the Jacko account with researchers John Green and René Dahinden. McKelvie told them this was the only record of the event due to a fire that had destroyed other area newspapers of the time.

In 1958 John Green found and interviewed a man (August Castle) who remembered the Jacko talk of the time, but he said his parents did not take him to the jail to see the beast. Other senior citizens remembered the talk of the creature, but no one could produce any truly good evidence for or eyewitness accounts (other than the *British Colonist* story) of Jacko.

The story's appearance in Ivan T. Sanderson's 1961 *Abominable Snowmen: Legend Come to Life* propelled the Jacko incident into history. Other authors, including John Green, René Dahinden/Don Hunter, Grover Krantz, and John Napier, would follow. The story was repeated again and again.

John Green continued digging into the story and finally discovered that microfilms of British Columbia newspapers from the 1880s existed at the University of British Columbia. Green then found two important articles that threw light on the whole affair.

The New Westminster, British Columbia, *Mainland Guardian* of July 9, 1884, mentioned the story and noted, "The 'What Is It' is the subject of conversation in town. How the story originated, and by whom, is hard for one to conjecture. Absurdity is written on the face of it. The fact of the matter is, that no such animal was caught, and how the *Colonist* was duped in such a manner, and by such a story, is strange."

On July 11, 1884, the *British Columbian* carried the news that some two hundred people had gone to the jail to view Jacko. But the "only wild man visible" was a man, who was humorously called the "governor of the goal [jail], who completely exhausted his patience" fielding the repeated inquiries from the crowd about the nonexistent creature.

As Green has pointed out, the *Colonist* never disputed its critics. Green (with Sanderson's widow) wrote of the Jacko story as a piece of probable journalistic fiction in the article "Alas, Poor Jacko," in *Pursuit,* published in 1975.

Unfortunately, a whole new generation of hominologists, Sasquatch searchers, and Bigfoot researchers are growing up thinking that the Jacko story is an ironclad cornerstone of the field, a foundation piece of history proving that Sasquatch are real. But in reality Jacko seems to be a local rumor brought to the level of a news story that eventually evolved into a modern fable.

The Roaring Twenties With the turn of the century came a renaming of such creatures—and the world's attention turned to Tibet. Before Bigfoot and Sasquatch, there was the *Abominable Snowman,* a phrase coined, accidentally, by a *Calcutta Statesman* newspaper columnist, Henry Newman, in 1921.

It happened when Newman wrote about the 1921 sighting by Lieutenant Colonel (later Sir) C. K. Howard-Bury and his party, who saw *dark* forms moving about on a twenty-thousand-foot-high snow-

field above their location, the Lhapka-La pass on the Tibetan side of the Himalayan mountains, and viewed them through binoculars. This is the first credible Western sighting of what to Westerners had been mostly a shadowy tale of strange, hairy, upright creatures in Tibet, Bhutan, Sikkim, Mustang, and Nepal. Howard-Bury would later find footprints "three times those of normal humans" at the site where the dark forms were moving about.

The Sherpas insisted that the prints were those of the *metoh-kangmi,* as Howard-Bury rendered it. *Kang-mi* loosely means "snow creature." But the *metoh* part should have been written as *met-teh,* which translates as "man-sized wild creature."

Newman's mistake was caused in part by Howard-Bury's mis-transliteration of the Sherpa word. Howard-Bury did not understand that the Sherpas recognized several types of creatures; on this occasion they had used a generic, not a specific, term. The error was compounded when Newman changed Howard-Bury's *metoh-kangmi* to *metch kangmi,* which he explained as a Tibetan word meaning "abominable snowman."

In any case, this proved to be a pivotal event in cryptozoological history. As Ivan T. Sanderson wrote, "The result was like the explosion of an atomic bomb." In his monumental book on the subject, *Abominable Snowmen: Legend Come to Life,* published in 1961, Sanderson pondered, "Thus, the 'birth' of the Abominable Snowman per se may be precisely dated as of 1920." The melodramatic name *Abominable Snowman* spurred gigantic press interest. Newspaper coverage multiplied as more and more expeditions sought to climb Mount Everest.

Meanwhile, Ivan Sanderson noted that "the turn of the year 1920 to 1921" was also worth noting in British Columbia. "I have often wondered," he wrote, "what would have happened if the Squamish word for these creatures in their country, instead, had happened to have been mistranslated as something equally fetching.

I suppose we would then, in time, have witnessed a *New York Journal American* Expedition to Harrison Lakes, and Admiral Byrd flying skin-trophies to Chicago from the hamlets of the Alaskan panhandle. It is nothing more than a quirk of history and a series of harmless mistakes that has put Nepal instead of Vancouver Island on the map in this respect."

Sadly, the events unfolding in the Pacific Northwest would go unnoticed by the new science of anthropology.

Paradigm Shifts The intellectual climate within anthropology, however, would indirectly influence the search for Bigfoot. At the time, the school led by anthropologist Franz Boas, often called Historical Particularism, was coming to a climactic end. Boas and his students were mostly "antitheory," feeling the need to gather ethnographic data before constructing any grand theory. Research focused on cultural rules and particulars, and one of the major areas of interest to Boas, where he and his students did research, was the Pacific Northwest. Boas had institutionalized and created the four-subfield organization of anthropology (sociocultural, linguistic, archaeological, biological/physical) that still exists today and continues to influence how we "look" for Bigfoot evidence.

Meanwhile, the school dominated by Bronislaw Malinowski, termed Functionalism, came into being as the 1920s began. It noted that all humans have three basic types of needs—biological (e.g., food, shelter), instrumental (e.g., education, law), and integrative (e.g., religion). Functionalists searched for cultural universals, thus the similarity in hairy-giant reports from culture to culture were emphasized, as opposed to differentiated. Meanwhile, Psychological Anthropology came on the horizon, with Ruth Benedict and Margaret Mead, also in the 1920s. Studying each culture independently, the importance of societal enculturation was studied. While

 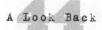

Bigfoot might be a biological entity, Psychological Anthropology was more interested in why it was significant to a culture, as opposed to any parallel biological existence that might be taking place.

Alfred Kroeber, who has been called the "first prominent Boasian student" by anthropologists Stephen O. Murray and Regna Darnell in their 2000 article in *Journal of Youth and Adolescence,* on paradigm shifts within anthropology during the 1920s, studied in California during the 1910s and 1920s. His far-reaching influence led anthropologists to treat Sasquatch reports as mere "folklore." The Boasian influence can clearly be seen in how Ruth Benedict, another of his favorite students during the 1920s, and later Mead's mentor, wrote a dissertation on beliefs in guardian spirits among aboriginal North American First Nations. Boasians were interested in mapping and showing how cultures had diffused traits, folklore, and stories. But Mead would break with that view, instead taking on a psychoanalytic analysis of cultural artifacts from tattooing to tales. The battle between the old and new Boasian anthropologists in the 1920s left little room for any insights by *physical* (now termed *biological*) anthropologists who might have had an interest in Sasquatch reports coming across their desks.

Nevertheless, big, hairy, upright creatures were being seen in the woods. In the East, a *Windigo*-like creature was sighted in July 1923, in a blueberry patch near Cobalt, Ontario. Near Alton, Illinois, a manlike beast covered in brown hair and having an apelike face was seen in June 1925. Creatures like Bigfoot were reported from Oklahoma, near Goodwater and Mountain Fork River, in 1926.

As with the majority of accounts from the 1920s in the East, most of those from the West have come down to us as remembrances or recent stories published in newspapers some fifty to eighty years after the events. For example, the report that twenty-eight people saw a Bigfoot near Yankton, Oregon, in 1926, surfaced in 1968. Even the now famous Albert Ostman case of the camper kidnapped and kept prisoner at Toba Inlet, British Columbia, in 1924 (which we shall be examining in chapter 13), is one man's story, which first came to the attention of Sasquatch researchers in the 1950s.

The one great landmark case from the 1920s that is supported with several contemporary news accounts is that of the incident at Ape Canyon. Taking place in July 1924, near the Muddy, a branch of the Lewis River, eight miles from Spirit Lake, near Mt. St. Helens, Washington State, it has Bigfoot attacking the cabin of prospectors.

Ape Canyon The wonder of Ape Canyon is that we have detailed news articles from the time, and much since then, to substantiate the events of that summer. The Portland *Oregonian,* for July 12, 1924, notes these encounters were not the first. The article begins by calling these "the fabled 'mountain devils' or mountain gorillas of Mount St. Helens" and mentions that "Smith and his companions had seen tracks of the animals several times in the last six years, and Indians have told of the 'mountain devils' for sixty years."

In the news article, the "devils" are described as "huge animals, which were about seven feet tall, weighed about four hundred pounds, and walked erect." Tracks "thirteen to fourteen inches long" were found where the animals were seen.

The Ape Canyon incident is often told in the Bigfoot literature. It has become a classic. The familiar version has carefully been bowdlerized by writers who have cited it as further evidence that an unknown flesh-and-blood hominoid exists in the wilderness of the Pacific Northwest. Fred Beck's 1967 version, on the other hand, suggests something rather different. The following is based upon Beck's own account from an obscure, out-of-print booklet, *I Fought the Ape-man of Mt. St. Helens,* which Beck and his son R. A. Beck wrote and published privately. Some people feel that his son's additions to the story outweigh Fred Beck's true sense of the events. Do they?

Beginning in 1918, Fred Beck and his partners—Marion Smith,

 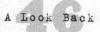

his son Roy Smith, Gabe Lafever, and John Peterson—began prospecting for gold in the Mt. St. Helens and Lewis River area of southwestern Washington. Before they built a cabin, they lived in a tent below a small mountain called Pumy Butte. Nearby a creek flowed, and along it there was a moist sandbar about an acre in size where the prospectors would wash their dishes and get drinking water.

Early one morning in about 1922, one of them came running to the camp and urged his fellows to follow him back to the creek, where he showed them two huge, somewhat humanlike tracks sunk four inches deep in the center of the sandbar. No other tracks were nearby. Because the nearest spot it could possibly have jumped to was 160 feet away, the men reasoned the creature had a huge stride, or "something dropped from the sky and went back up."

As time passed, the miners came upon similar tracks, which they could not identify. The largest of them was nineteen inches long. (In the original 1924 articles, however, as noted above, the miners had mentioned much smaller prints.) After they had built their cabin, Beck and the four other miners working their gold claim—the Vander White, named after their "spirit guide"—would hear a strange "thudding, hollow thumping noise" in broad daylight. They could not find the cause, though they suspected one of their number might be playing tricks on them. That proved not to be the case, since even when the group was gathered together the sound continued all around them. They thought it sounded as if "there's a hollow drum in the earth somewhere and something is hitting it."

These were not the last strange sounds they would hear. Early in July 1924, a shrill whistling, apparently emanating from atop a ridge, pierced the evening quiet. An answering whistle came from another ridge. These sounds, along with a booming "thumping" as if something were pounding its chest, continued every evening for a week.

Now thoroughly unnerved, the men had taken to carrying their rifles with them when they went to the spring about a hundred yards from the cabin. Beck and a man identified only in his booklet as

"Hank" to avoid embarrassment to his family (but who was noted in 1920s press accounts as Marion Smith) were drawing water from the spring when suddenly Hank yelled and raised his gun. Beck looked up and saw, on the other side of a little canyon, a seven-foot apelike creature standing next to a pine tree. The creature, a hundred yards away from the two men, dodged behind the tree. When it poked its head around the tree, Hank fired three quick shots, spraying bark but apparently not hitting the creature, which momentarily disappeared from sight. It reappeared two hundred yards down the canyon, and this time Beck got off three shots before it was gone.

Hurriedly, Beck and Hank returned to the cabin and spoke with the other two men there (the third was elsewhere at the time). They agreed to abandon the cabin—but not until daybreak. It would be too risky, they felt, to try to make it to the car in the darkness. The four got their belongings together, then settled down for a good night's sleep, which, as it turned out, they did not get.

At midnight they awakened suddenly to a tremendous thud against the cabin wall. Some of the chinking knocked loose from between the logs fell across Hank's chest. This disoriented Hank, and Beck helped to get it off him. Then, as they heard what sounded like many feet tramping and running outside, they grabbed their guns, prepared for the worst. Hank peered through the open space left by the dislodged chinking (the cabin had no windows) and spotted three "apes" together. From the sound of things, there were many more.

The creatures pelted the cabin with rocks. Though terribly frightened (the other two miners were huddling in the corner in shock), Beck said they should fire on the creatures only if they physically attacked the cabin. This would show that the miners were only defending themselves.

Shortly afterward the "apes" began attacking the cabin. Some of them jumped on the roof, evidently in an effort to batter it down. In response, Beck and Hank fired through the roof. They were also

forced to brace the door with a long pole taken from the bunk bed, since the creatures were furiously attempting to smash it open. Beck and Hank riddled the door with bullets.

The attacks continued all night, punctuated by brief quiet interludes. At one point a creature reached through the chinking space and grabbed an ax by the handle. Beck lunged forward, snatched the blade, and turned the ax upright so that the ape couldn't get it out. As he was doing so, a bullet from Hank's rifle narrowly missed its hand. The creature withdrew its arm and retreated.

Finally, just before daybreak, the attack ended. The embattled miners waited for daylight, then cautiously stepped outside, guns in hand. A few minutes later Beck spotted one of the creatures about eighty yards away, standing near the edge of the canyon. Taking careful aim, he shot three times and watched as it toppled over the cliff and fell down into the gorge four hundred feet below.

As quickly as possible, the miners departed, heading for Spirit Lake, Washington, and leaving $200 in supplies and equipment behind. They never returned to claim it.

At Spirit Lake, Hank told a forest ranger about the experience. Once back home in Kelso, the story leaked to the newspapers and caused a sensation. Reporters found giant tracks at the scene, but no other trace of the creatures. The canyon where the episode had allegedly occurred became known as Ape Canyon and still bears that name today.

In his booklet Beck reveals that all his life, from early childhood on, he had numerous psychic experiences, many of them involving supernatural "people." He says that they found the mine they were working in 1924 through guidance from two "spiritual beings," one a buckskin-clad Indian, the other a woman after whom they would name their mine (Vander White).

Of the "apemen," Beck writes, "they are not entirely of this world. . . . I was, for one, always conscious that we were dealing with supernatural beings and I know the other members of the party felt the same." Beck believes the creatures now known as Sasquatch or Bigfoot come from "another dimension" and are a link between human and animal consciousness. They are composed of a substance that ranges between the physical and the psychical, sometimes one more than the other, depending upon the degree of "materialization." Because of their peculiar nature none will ever be captured, nor will their bodies ever be found.

Fred Beck, as seen through the writing of his son, viewed the whole mining experience as spiritual, the thumping as poltergeist activity, and the Bigfoot as spirits. "Our time spent in Mt. St. Helens was a series of psychic experiences," he wrote. The booklet he wrote with his son is filled with Fred's thoughts on spirits, the spirit world, and flying saucers. Yes, UFOs. (I will return to this topic in chapter 12.) Beck tells of being a psychic, a "chairvoyant" [sic], and how he held spiritual meetings and "saw visions." Many have ignored—or forgotten—this other material. In general people have taken what they want from Fred Beck's sighting and left behind that the man had a devout Adventist spiritualist worldview.

Was Beck's 1967 book merely the fantasy of an old man? Or was it due to the overly contemporary 1960s influences of his son, who wrote large sections of the book?

It's worthy of noting, however, that Fred Beck never mentioned the paranormal when Bigfooters interviewed him about his experiences in the early 1960s. The paranormal elements appear to be merely reflections of Beck's temperament when he or his son would retell or write down the story that resulted in their 1967 book. The news articles from the 1920s seem to be closer to the actual details of the event.

Let me be clear. While I sense Beck and his associates had actual experiences with real Bigfoot, this event has been screened through his and others' worldviews and retold with such heavy editing as to be confusing today. But to truly understand the mix of culture and creature, we must not be afraid to look at the whole story, to get at the true essence of Sasquatch the animal, and to reconstruct the biological reality behind the human context.

Similarly, Mark A. Hall pointed out to me recently that when Fred Beck told his story in the 1960s, the tracks were said to be nineteen inches long and the creature's height was said to be eight feet or more. However, the Bigfoot was shorter and the tracks smaller in Beck's 1924 account. Hall believes that Beck in his later years gave a version of the story that was altered to meet the larger, modern expectations for Bigfoot, as opposed to the more modest, realistic figures given in the 1924 reports. The news articles of the 1920s also mention four stubby toes, as opposed to the five toes mentioned in modern Sasquatch reports.

What we have here is a series of stories issuing from the Kelso area from about 1918 to 1924. The Native Americans, according to newspaper articles in 1924, called these reported creatures *Seeahtiks, Siatcoes,* and *Selahtiks.* In July of that year the sheriff sent out people. Search parties were formed, but only tracks were found. In Green's retelling of the encounter he mentions that an article of the time "makes it clear that many parties of ape hunters were running all over the area."

Marian Place, a newspaper reporter and writer of Bigfoot books in the 1960s and 1970s, credits most of what she knows of these events from the news articles she used for her books. In her 1974 book, *On the Track of Bigfoot,* she devotes a whole chapter, "Giant Hairy Apes on Mount St. Helens," to this episode. She explores the notion that this area has been a focus of human interest in "spirits," "mountain devils," and Bigfoot for well over a hundred years. Place makes the point that the Beck group's "mine was only a ridge or two away from Spirit Lake, so named by the Indians who believed it was the abode of evil spirits they called *Siatcoes* or *Selahtiks.*"

Ape Canyon Today Ape Canyon and Ape Cave live on as active tourist locations to mark these events. But travelers beware: today rangers are saying incorrectly that Ape Cave was named in honor of a local youth group called the St. Helens Apes, who hiked and explored on Mount St. Helens. Of course, ask yourself, why were they called the St. Helens Apes? Needless to say, it is because of the 1924 flap. The eventual naming of both the cave and the canyon come from these events.

Underlying the modern rangers' canned program on Ape Cave and Ape Canyon is the tale of a cover-up that occurred soon after the miners' cabin was attacked. In 1924, news reports had rangers claiming that boys from a YMCA camp had thrown rocks on the Smith-Beck cabin and caused the Ape Canyon incident. But the YMCA camp was at Spirit Lake, some miles from the site of the incident.

The Ape Canyon incident of 1924 remains a classic, but what exactly happened, unfortunately, is slowly being lost in mountain fog.

5 Fruit Crate Label Art and Ruby Creek

Curiously, there are no contemporary accounts of Bigfoot in California from 1900 through 1957. As Bigfoot researcher John Green recently observed, "Checking my files, there are several dozen reports from California before 1958, but all are recollections of one sort or another. Not a single one is from a newspaper story in the 1900s. That is indeed odd."

Though news accounts of Bigfoot for this era are not available, some stunning cultural evidence for the existence of Bigfoot in California in this period does exist. I recently found a fruit crate label that appears to have a direct bearing on Bigfoot in early-twentieth-century California.

"Fruit crate labels," so called even if the items being packaged were vegetables, were in common use from the 1920s through 1950s. These labels were originally designed to get the attention of distributors and wholesalers. The labels were glued to the ends of wooden crates of produce so as to distinguish one grower's product from another's. The label art reflected local items of interest and were made to be highly visible in the fruit and vegetable auction sales. The most desired brands were those that could be recognized from a distance and were distinctive, often by taking advantage of a local pun. When new technologies and cardboard replaced these labels, the old labels became prized as art and have been highly sought after items among collectors of printed ephemera.

In October of 2000 I stumbled upon a fruit crate label called the California Giant while scanning items for sale on eBay. The vendor from whom I purchased it, Dwayne Rogers of Chico, California, informed me this specific label would simply be called Giant, or California Giant, among fruit-crate-label collectors.

The label shows a large, hairy, humanlike form not unlike what we have grown to know from the descriptions of Bigfoot. The California crate label references either the Giant brand lettuce or carrots from the Salinas area. From a label collector's point of view, Rogers told me, the fact the California Giant is actually carrying a crate of lettuce with the same label is unique in crate label art.

Since I knew that such labels essentially disappeared in the 1950s, I decided to track down, if possible, the age of this particular art. I thought it curious that a hairy giant would be on a California crate, and that no one in cryptozoology had ever mentioned this before. Rogers thought it dated back to the 1930s, perhaps from the 1940s, but certainly before 1950. Rogers also remarked that a black-and-white image of this label is dated to the 1930s in Gordon McClelland's 1983 book, *Fruit Box Labels*.

Rogers suggested I talk to agrilitholigist Thomas P. "Pat" Jacobsen, dean of fruit crate art and author of *Pat Jacobsen's Millennium Guide to Fruit Crate Labels!!*

Jacobsen did some digging for me and sent me these findings: "I have gone into my collection, and found a few samples of the label 'California Giant' or 'Giant.' There are two different versions of the artwork that I know of; one says 'carrots,' the other says 'lettuce.' One of the labels I have says 'lettuce' on it and was made by the L. A. Miller Label Co., in business from 1925 to 1934 when they ostensibly merged with H. S. Crocker Co. Then, in December of 1936, I have a dated file copy from Schmidt Lithograph Company, the largest in the West, whose basement I acquired. On the bottom of the label in green letters is their name. This is the only printing of 'carrots' that I know of. Another copy is dated August 1941 and still [has] the green Schmidt name. In 1950, it is produced again with a black Schmidt name and 'Produce of the USA' added in the bottom border. So I am sure [this California Giant label] was used between 1934 and 1950 . . . probably more like the Depression era (1932, 33, but it may be older)."

California Giant = Bigfoot

The image on the California Giant brand lettuce fruit label definitely shows a large, hairy, hominid form. The figure looks strong, well muscled, with brown, short hair all over the body but on the face. The neck is unusually solid-looking and well defined. It is a rather typical image of a Bigfoot.

The label itself serves as a scale for how large this "Giant" is. The label is nine inches long, and the artistic mirror image of the label itself is three-quarter inches in length. The image of the repeating California Giant label on the label tells us how big this creature is. Basically, the label shows items that are on a 1:12 scale. Therefore, we find that the hairy giant depicted is about ten feet tall and has a foot that is approximately twenty to twenty-four inches long.

These dimensions are comparable to Roger Patterson's "Giant Hairy Ape" (a creature he discussed in his 1966 book), which had humanlike footprints measuring twenty-two inches long and was taller by several feet than the regular Bigfoot reported at the time. John Green also noted some reports from the 1950s and 1960s that told of hairy men with giant, almost two-foot-long foot tracks.

I am convinced the label speaks to knowledge of reports and traditions of hairy giants in northern California in the 1920s and 1930s, when the label was first created. In the absence of news articles on Bigfoot sightings in California from these early years, I find this surprising bit of evidence from a fruit crate label worth pondering.

But can this label truly be regarded as cultural evidence for the existence of hairy-giant motifs in early-twentieth-century California? Or is this no more than yet another example of folklore immortalized through art? What do we know about the connection to realism in other fruit crate art?

Reality-Based Labels?

Fruit crate labels embellished boxes of Louisiana sweet potatoes, French plums, Washington State apples, and California oranges with vivid artwork of cats, butterflies, beautiful women, cowboys, lions, peacocks, baseball players, and many other reality-based images from nature and history. The labels I have examined rarely show mythical or fanciful creatures, though Santa Claus, knights, and romantic historic figures are sometimes illustrated.

However, one image, familiar to most of us, parallels the California Giant, which we must not ignore. This would be the Jolly Green Giant. If the Jolly Green Giant is mythical, as we must assume, is there perhaps nothing to the California Giant? But let's look for a moment at the tradition underlying the Green Giant, as it was originally known.

In 1903, Green Giant was founded in Le Sueur, Minnesota, as the Minnesota Valley Canning Company. In 1925, a pale, giant, boy-like figure with a leafy bit of clothing was introduced to market the company's new line of giant, sweet, early green peas. The name *Green Giant* for this marketing image soon followed, with the giant figure's skin then turning green. Eventually the Green Giant came to symbolize not only the peas, but the company as well. In 1950, Min-

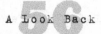

nesota Valley Canning Company disappeared completely behind the trademark it had created and became officially the Green Giant Company. Today, the *Jolly Green Giant* is the name of the giant figure, having evolved from the youthful figure of 1925.

In our search for the origins of the California Giant in the tales of the California Bigfoot, should we be disturbed that Jolly Green Giants are not running around Minnesota? Perhaps. Perhaps not. First and foremost, the tradition of the Green Giant appears to have a direct link, in terms of artistic imagery, with the folklore and widespread art of the European Green Man.

Green Giants to Bigfoot

From ancient times, the archetypal figure shown as the Green Giant is commonly referred to as the Green Man, or leafy man, and has been discussed throughout European texts, especially in England, and as well as in France, where it is called *Le Feuillou,* and in Germany, where it is known as *Blattqesicht.* Authors have written extensively on the pagan and Celtic traditions of these Green Men, and books and Web sites about them are abundant.

Scholars, furthermore, see a direct link between the European traditions of the Green Man and the old tales and encounters with real Wild Men. "The wildman (who may be the same as the 'green man')," Myra Shackley notes in her book *Still Living? Yeti, Sasquatch and the Neanderthal Enigma,* "also takes on the role of the spirit of the woods, a kind of pagan nature god. . . . Over two hundred European families have wildmen as heraldic emblems, and many more as supporters. Any nude figure in heraldry is called a 'savage', 'wildman,' or 'woodman,' and the terms are interchangeable. There is little variation in the way they are portrayed, leafy decorations and a club being the rule. . . . Wildmen (or green men) also appear carved in wood and as architectural adornments in the Middle Ages. . . . Green men are frequently shown as a face with foliage emerging from the mouth, and fifty or more of these are known from England alone. The green man is also found carved in stone, as a gargoyle. . . . In the Elizabethan period wildmen, or green men, were often employed to clear the way for processions, wielding sticks."

Clearly the Green Man comes from the tradition and evolution of the art form of the burly wildmen, the woodsmen, and thus the man of the woods and greenery. Shackley notes, "Wildmen are important figures in medieval paintings and illuminated manuscripts. They may be called 'wodewoses' or 'woodhouses,' and are frequently shown covered with long hair or fur. An additional class of picture shows actors in plays, masques, and dramas who are depicted in wildman costumes. . . . The name *wodewose* is derived from the Anglo-Saxon *Wudewasa* and thence from *Wudu* (late Old English for 'wood'; *Wudewasa* seems to mean 'man-of-the-wood.' "

The "wildmen" are an active topic in hominology, and some researchers feel the Wildmen and Green Men are a remembrance of Neandertal. As Shackley, Ivan T. Sanderson, and others have noted, we must view the interrelationship between the hairy wildfolk lurking in the remote woodlands of the Middle Ages and the European wildmen, regardless of whether they were called wodewose or green men.

So the graphic transmutation of the survival of late Neandertals in Europe to Wild Men and Green Men, with an artistic connection to the Green Giant and the Jolly Green Giant, is worth serious consideration. There appears to be a link between that label on a can of peas in your kitchen and the possible existence of relict hairy hominids, even if uncomfortably so.

Just as the encounters of European wildmen survive in medieval carvings and other graphic representations, so too is the early-twentieth-century California Bigfoot evident in an artistic form. Depression-era painters appear to have captured the giant, hairy hominid on at least one fruit crate label. The containers for lettuce, carrots, and, yes, green peas may have much to teach us in Big-foot studies, beyond our wildest imaginations.

Ruby Creek Incident Although Bigfoot would not break into public consciousness until 1958, the modern history of this creature is widely thought to have begun with a 1941 encounter labeled by John Green as the Ruby Creek Incident because it happened a half mile east of that little settlement in British Columbia. Although only the Chapman family was involved in this encounter, others in the Ruby Creek area also saw the footprints.

Ivan Sanderson wrote up the Chapmans' story soon after he interviewed them and then published his account in *True* magazine in 1960. I will let Sanderson retell the story in his own words, directly from his firsthand interview, in order to do full justice to the Chapmans' account:

"The modern history of the Sasquatch really dates from September, 1941, when one of these creatures paid a visit—in broad daylight—to an Indian family named Chapman. While the Amerindian stories have usually been dismissed as legend, or laughed off because Indians are not supposed to be reliable, too much physical evidence to be ignored accompanied this experience. The Chapman family consisted of George and Jeannie Chapman and children numbering, at my visit, four. Mr. Chapman worked on the railroad, and was living at that time in a small place called Ruby Creek, thirty miles up the Fraser River from Agassiz, British Columbia, in Canada's great western province.

"It was about three in the afternoon of a sunny, cloudless day when Jeannie Chapman's eldest son, then aged nine, came running to the house saying that there was a cow coming down out of the woods at the foot of the nearby mountain. The other kids, a boy aged seven and a little girl of five, were still playing in a field behind the house bordering on the rail track. Mrs. Chapman went out to look, since the boy seemed oddly disturbed, and they saw what at first she thought was a very big bear moving about among the bushes bordering the field beyond the railway tracks. She called the two children, who came running immediately. Then the creature moved onto the tracks and she saw to her horror that it was a gigantic man covered with hair, not fur. The hair seemed to be about four inches long all over, and of a pale yellow-brown color. To pin down this color Mrs. Chapman pointed out to me a sheet of lightly varnished plywood in the room where we were sitting. This was of a brown-ochre color. This creature advanced directly toward the house and Mrs. Chapman had, as she put it, 'much too much time to look at it' because she stood her ground outside while the eldest boy—on her instructions—got a blanket from the house and rounded up the other children. The kids were in a near panic, she told us, and it took two or three minutes to get the blanket, during which time the creature had reached the near corner of the field only about one hundred feet away from her. Mrs. Chapman then spread the blanket and, holding it aloft so that the kids could not see the creature or it them, she backed off at the double to the old field and down onto the river beach out of sight, and then ran with the kids downstream to the village.

"I asked her a leading question about the blanket. Had her purpose in using it been to prevent her kids seeing the creature, in accord with an alleged Amerindian belief that to do so brings bad luck and often death? Her reply was both prompt and surprising. She said that, although she had heard white men tell of that belief, she had not heard it from her parents or any other of her people, whose advice regarding the so-called Sasquatch had been simply not to go further than certain points up certain valleys, to run if she saw one, but not to struggle if one caught her as it might squeeze her to death by mistake. 'No,' she said, 'I used the blanket because I thought it was after one of the kids and so might go into the house

to look for them instead of following me.' This seems to have been sound logic as the creature did go into the house and also rummaged through an old outhouse pretty thoroughly, hauling from it a fifty-five-gallon barrel of salt fish, breaking this open, and scattering its contents about outside. (The irony of it is that all those three children *did* die within three years; the two boys by drowning, and the little girl on a sickbed. And just after I interviewed the Chapmans they also were drowned in the Fraser River when a rowboat capsized.) Mrs. Chapman told me that the creature was about seven and a half feet tall. She could estimate its height by the various fence and line posts standing about the field. It had a rather small head and a very short, thick neck; in fact really no neck at all, a point that was emphasized by William Roe and by all others who claim to have seen one of these creatures. Its body was entirely human in shape except that it was immensely thick through its chest and its arms were exceptionally long. She did not see the feet, which were in the grass. Its shoulders were very wide and it had no breasts, from which Mrs. Chapman assumed it was a male, though she also did not see any male genitalia due to the long hair covering its groin. She was most definite on one point: the naked parts of its face and its hands were much darker than its hair, and appeared to be almost black.

"George Chapman returned home from his work on the railroad that day shortly before six in the evening and by a route that bypassed the village so that he saw no one to tell him what had happened. When he reached his house he immediately saw the woodshed door battered in, and spotted enormous humanoid footprints all over the place. Greatly alarmed—for he, like all of his people, had heard since childhood about the 'big wild men of the mountains,' though he did not hear the word *Sasquatch* till after this incident— he called for his family and then dashed through the house. Then he spotted the foot-tracks of his wife and kids going off toward the river. He followed these until he picked them up on the sand beside the river and saw them going off downstream without any giant ones following.

"Somewhat relieved, he was retracing his steps when he stumbled across the giant's foot-tracks on the riverbank farther upstream. These had come down out of the potato patch, which lay between the house and the river, had milled about by the river, and then gone back through the old field toward the foot of the mountains where they disappeared in the heavy growth.

"Returning to the house relieved to know that the tracks of all four of his family had gone off downstream to the village, George Chapman went to examine the woodshed. In our interview, after eighteen years, he still expressed voluble astonishment that any living thing, even a seven-foot-six-inch man with a barrel chest, could lift a fifty-five-gallon tub of fish and break it open without using a tool. He confirmed the creature's height after finding a number of long brown hairs stuck in the slabwood lintel of the doorway, above the level of his head.

"George Chapman then went off to the village to look for his family, and found them in a state of calm collapse. He gathered them up and invited his father-in-law and two others to return with him, for protection of his family when he was away at work. The foot-tracks returned every night for a week and on two occasions the dogs that the Chapmans had taken with them set up the most awful racket at exactly two o'clock in the morning. The Sasquatch did not, however, molest them or, apparently, touch either the house or the woodshed. But the whole business was too unnerving and the family finally moved out. They never went back. After a long chat about this and other matters, Mrs. Chapman suddenly told us something very significant just as we were leaving. She said: 'It made an awful funny noise.' I asked her if she could imitate this noise for me but it was her husband who did so, saying that he had heard it at night twice during the week after the first incident. He then proceeded to utter exactly

the same strange, gurgling whistle that the men in California, who said they had heard a Bigfoot call, had given us. This is a sound I cannot reproduce in print, but I can assure you that it is unlike anything I have ever heard given by man or beast anywhere in the world. To me, this information is of the greatest significance. That an Amerindian couple in British Columbia should give out with exactly the same strange sound in connection with a Sasquatch that two highly educated white men did, over six hundred miles south in connection with California's Bigfoot, is incredible. If this is all hoax or a publicity stunt, or mass-hallucination, as some people have claimed, how does it happen that this noise—which defies description— always sounds the same no matter who has tried to reproduce it for me? These were probably the last words on the Sasquatch that the Chapmans uttered and I absolutely refuse to listen to anybody who might say they were lying. Admittedly, honest men are such a rarity as possibly to be nonexistent, but I have met a few who could qualify and I put the Chapmans near the head of the list."

Before 1958, Sasquatch was merely a regional monster, a hairy forest tribe of the Indians. The California fruit-crate hirsute beast was little known outside of the lettuce- and orange-growing regions. Stories of "wildmen" and "gorillas" had faded from news reporters' memories. Over in the Himalayas, the Abominable Snowmen were getting some notice, but it had little bearing on America. Something big was about to happen, though. And that something was Bigfoot!

6   "Bigfoot" Discovered

Today, when people talk about stories of monsters in the woods, wildmen in the forests, giants on the tundra, hairy bipeds in the suburbs, and apes in the swamps, whether in Maryland or Maine, California or Kansas, the word used in the popular media and in the public mind is *Bigfoot. Bigfoot,* of course, is the post-1958 name for those unknown hairy hominids found in the Pacific Northwest of the USA with large, humanlike footprints and an upright stance.

The Times   The year 1958 is special. Change is in the air and exploration is at a new cutting edge. The first atomic submarine, the *Nautilus,* built in 1954, travels under the north pole. Outer space begins to occupy world interest with *Sputnik 2* being launched by the Soviet Union on November 3, 1957, and *Explorer I* by the Americans on January 31, 1958. The United States establishes NASA (the National Aeronautics and Space Administration) to advance the space race. Nikita Khrushchev becomes premier of the USSR. Fidel Castro is leading a band of guerrillas in the mountains of Cuba. Washington is in an uproar when President Eisenhower's assistant Sherman Adams (who was called the Abominable No-Man) resigns because he has accepted a vicuña coat from Boston industrialist Bernard Goldfine. In the midst of the Cold War, the world would soon see the advent of JFK's New Frontier and Castro's new Cuba. The sleepy Eisenhower years were coming to an end.

In 1958, television is in its heyday, although the year's scandal regarding the rigging of the game show *Twenty-One* shakes up the politics of the networks. *The Garry Moore Show,* television's first celebrated daytime news and variety program, ends its successful eight-year run in June, having introduced America to its frequent guest Moore's "animal man," early cryptozoologist Ivan T. Sanderson. *Lolita* is a best-seller, despite its embarrassingly (for the time) off-color subject of a love affair between an older man and a young girl. Boris Pasternak wins the Nobel Prize for literature, but the author is unable to travel from behind the Iron Curtain to receive the award.

Drive-in theaters are all the rage. Invented in 1933, and growing to 820 screens by 1948, the drive-in peaks ten years later at 4,063. Perhaps reflecting this, the movies are lighthearted, with *Gigi* winning the Academy Award for Best Picture. Science fiction films are popular, with bizarre beasts having dominated the cinemas since 1954's *Them!* Nineteen fifty-eight sees Steve McQueen being pursued by *The Blob.* Vincent Price tackles *The Fly.* Ed Wood makes his *Plan 9 From Outer Space.* Of special interest to us is the particular truth that three movies, all released in the United States in 1957, are making the drive-in and movie-theater circuit in 1958. They are *Half-Human* and *The Abominable Snowman of the Himalayas,* both about hairy, apelike creatures, Yetis. The third one stars Michael Landon and is *I Was a Teenage Werewolf.* Hairy monsters are called Abominable Snowmen and Werewolves as 1958 begins, and not yet Bigfoot.

"Bigfoot" The direct labeling *Bigfoot* did not occur until a man named Jerry Crew appeared at a northern-California newspaper office with the plaster cast of a large humanoid footprint. That's when *Humboldt Times*' "RFD" columnist and editor Andrew Genzoli coined the word *Bigfoot* and published it on October 5, 1958. He was always proud that he had discovered the well-kept secret of the Hoopa Indians regarding Bigfoot. Genzoli died in 1975.

The coinage of *Bigfoot* was a significant cultural event. To deny this would be to ignore how intrinsic *Bigfoot* has become in North Americans' day-to-day living, from a special type of pizza, to snow skis, to characters in films, as well as scores of other commercial examples. Before 1958, there was scant recognition of the widespread Native American folklore about unknown anthropoids, shaggy forest giants, and cannibals. Most media attention regarding Pacific Northwest hairy-biped reports was limited to a few minor stories on the Canadian *Sasquatch*, a little-heard-of term in the United States before the advent of the post-1958 articles on Bigfoot. Today, most grade-school children in Canada and the United States of America can talk with authority about and draw a picture of Bigfoot.

But why did the catalyst have to happen in a place called "Bluff" Creek?

Bluff Creek If you look in any good book on Bigfoot, you will find the modern era of Bigfoot stories begins with a retelling of the famous 1958 Gerald "Jerry" Crew affair. Some chroniclers such as John Green have correctly pointed out it had as much to do with the wife of another member of the work crew, Jess Bemis, and her letter to Genzoli. But most of the Bigfoot book treatments have rehashed each other for so many years that names are dropped, dates are telescoped, and events are overlapped. This blurring of facts has happened so often that the creative treatment of the event bears little resemblance to what actually transpired.

Few people have read or recall that more than just Jerry Crew was immersed in those events. To rediscover the other actors (e.g., Wilbur and Ray Wallace) who were involved sheds a much deeper understanding of these historic 1958 events. Typically, the author of each new Bigfoot book takes the Crew story as gospel and then quickly moves on to other reports of more recent interest.

For example, John Napier, the late anthropologist and director of the Primate Program at the Smithsonian Institution, gave only a short but typical examination of the case in his definitive 1972 work, *Bigfoot: The Yeti and Sasquatch in Myth and Reality*. Napier writes, "One day in October of 1958, Jerry Crew, the catskinner, came upon some tracks in the mud. They were very big tracks deeply impressed in the soil and had the look of human footprints. They measured all of 16 in. long and 7 in. wide and they were all over the place. They went up hill and down dale and continued into situations that seemed to defy the ingenuity of a hoaxer with a footprint machine. Mr. Crew and his team had observed tracks like these for several weeks, but on this occasion Jerry Crew made a plaster cast of one of the prints. His photograph holding the cast, which stretches from his collar to his belt, was widely publicized and immediately elicited stories of previous footprint discoveries and earlier Sasquatch encounters. The Crew footprints were seen in the Bluff Creek Valley." Napier appears to be promoting Jerry Crew to the status of team leader, thus completely distracting readers (and Bigfoot investigators) from the need to look more closely at Crew's real bosses, Wilbur and Ray Wallace.

This series of incidents marked the beginning of all Bigfoot investigations in the United States. Yet some books ignore it altogether. In such old books as Colin and Janet Bord's *The Bigfoot Casebook*, the encounters are never even mentioned, not in the text of the book nor in their extensive chronological listings of Bigfoot sightings, because, truth be told, the Jerry Crew story is not about a sighting. It is a footprint find only.

Back to the Source When researching the Bluff Creek 1958 events, one has to dig back to the original news items—some of which have been reprinted in Roger Patterson's self-published book, *Do Abominable Snowman of America Really Exist?*—to the comments and hints in Ivan T. Sanderson's *True* magazine articles and his book, and also to the rather comprehensive treatment to be found in Marian T. Place's *On the Track of Bigfoot*, the first five chapters of which are concerned exclusively with the Crew drama.

What's incredible about the Place account is the depth of texture she brought to the Crew incident. Marian Place tells us, for example, what Jerry Crew was wearing (khaki work pants and shirt, thick-soled shoes, and an aluminum hard hat) when he found the first footprints, the essence of conversations Crew had with Wilbur Wallace (the construction foreman and brother of Ray Wallace), and the chronology of events that unfolded at the Bluff Creek work site. Marian Place acknowledges the *Humboldt Times* "RFD" columnist and editor Andrew Genzoli as her primary source.

The Chronology Examining the best original sources, this is how the events apparently transpired. Let us take a quick, Spartan journey through the events leading up to the discovery of "Bigfoot."

During the spring of 1957, construction begins on the Bluff Creek, California, road. Ray Wallace is the contractor, and his brother Wilbur is the foreman. They hire thirty men, including some Hoopa Indians who are experienced loggers. By the summer, Wilbur Wallace would later report at the end of 1958, something threw around fifty-five-gallon, metal oil drums at the Bluff Creek work site. By the winter of 1957–1958, only ten miles of progress has been made on the Bluff Creek road. Work is halted by cold weather.

Early spring, 1958, some hoax tracks are left in the Mad River area, near Korbel, California. When the Korbel tracks are discovered, some people think it might be a bear. This is another Wallace work site. During the spring of 1958, old and new hires continue the work on the Bluff Creek road. One of the new men is Gerald "Jerry" Crew, a man so deeply involved in family and community activities he drives home every weekend.

Ten more miles are cut into the forest. The route they are building is angling upward across a face of a mountain. On August 3, 1958, Wilbur Wallace would tell investigators later in the month, something threw a seven-hundred-pound spare tire to the bottom of a deep gully at the Bluff Creek work site. On August 22, at quitting time, Jerry Crew is the last to depart. He is a fourth of a mile deeper in the woods than anyone else. He then drives the two and a half hours home to Salyer for the weekend.

During the following week, when he comes to work on Wednesday, August 27, Jerry Crew discovers giant, manlike footprints around his bulldozer. He is so upset—even though his first thought is that someone is pulling a prank—that he finally decides to tell Wilbur Wallace, the foreman and brother of the contractor, Ray Wallace.

On September 21, 1958, Mrs. Jess Bemis, wife of one of the Bluff Creek work crew, writes the *Humboldt Times'* Andrew Genzoli, editor and author of the "RFD" column. She tells of her husband's tales of "Big Foot." Her letter is published on this date. On September 25, Genzoli publishes an 1886 story, thus giving some historical background for the hairy-giant stories. Late in September 1958, newswoman Betty Allen writes a column calling for a plaster cast to be made of the enormous prints being found. (Allen would mention to researcher Don Davis that non-Indians in the Klamath area had been using the word *Bigfoot* for these track-makers years before 1958. Allen had collected accounts, talked to natives, interviewed witnesses, and really introduced her editor Genzoli to the idea of running the Bigfoot letters and stories. Allen's role in the birth of Bigfoot in America has largely been neglected. Craig Heinselman's *Hominology II* carries the late Don Davis's never-before-published article on Betty Allen.)

On October 1 and 2, 1958, Jerry Crew sees more tracks. Two workers quit. Wilbur Wallace allegedly first leads brother Ray to the tracks. On October 3, Jerry Crew makes plaster casts of the big tracks after learning how to from his friend Bob Titmus, with help also from Betty Allen. Crew says he wants to cast them to stop people from ridiculing him. On October 5, 1958, Andrew Genzoli writes and publishes in the *Humboldt Times* his now famous article detailing the reports of "Bigfoot"—complete with the photograph of Jerry Crew holding a "Bigfoot" cast. His story is picked up worldwide by press services. This is the birthday of the widespread use of the term *Bigfoot*.

By mid-October 1958, Ray Wallace hires Ray Kerr and Bob Breaezle. On October 12, Ray Kerr and Bob Breaezle say they encountered a Bigfoot on an area road, catching its enormous giant, hairy body in their headlights. On November 1, 1958, Bob Titmus casts more prints at Bluff Creek and shows them to John Green, René Dahinden, and eventually to Texas millionaire Tom Slick. In November 1958, Tom Slick funds the on-site Bigfoot investigations of Bob Titmus, Ivan Marx, and others. During most of 1959, the Pacific Northwest Expedition of Slick's conducts searches for Bigfoot. Ivan T. Sanderson gets deeply involved.

The Sanderson Investigations During 1959, zoologist Ivan T. Sanderson drove about in a station wagon, touring the country for a planned book on America's ecology. He used the opportunity to do some investigative work on interesting unexplained phenomena, as well, including the reports he had heard from the previous year of a "Bigfoot" in California. Sanderson was one of Texas oil millionaire

Thomas B. Slick's private consultants on matters related to the Yeti investigations in Nepal and, after 1958, the so-called Bigfoot question in the Pacific Northwest of the USA and Canada. Therefore, in those multiple roles, Sanderson found himself in August 1959 talking to many of the early individuals involved in the Crew story. He stayed at a motel in Willow Creek for a little over a week, looking over the large files of Betty Allen, and interviewing witnesses she would bring to him to meet. Sanderson was expected to make candid assessments of what was taking place to Slick. Sometimes, however, what he discovered was screened through his old friend anthropologist George Agogino.

In 1991, Agogino told me he had discovered some long-lost letters from his and Sanderson's time as Slick consultants. One I found particularly interesting was dated February 21, 1960, from Sanderson to Agogino. Sanderson had decided to detail for Agogino some items he did not wish to share with Tom Slick, openly spelling out several concerns about "various small items in the past." About these "Bigfoot affairs," as Sanderson termed them, he noted, "There were several people that we met and interviewed in Willow Creek who impressed us very favourably indeed; notable among these were Betty Allen the newsgal (she is a grandmother and a dear), Jerry Crew, and his nephew. There were certain people who did not." Although Sanderson felt that some of the people were kind to them, but he was, nevertheless, troubled about several people, including, for example, an unnamed motel owner. Sanderson appeared to have the most reservations about Ray Wallace.

Ray Wallace   Ray Wallace is a routinely underexamined figure in the original Bigfoot drama. Here, then, is the Wallace story, up until his death at the end of 2002. A trickster in the field, Wallace was ignored or disregarded in his later years as "a noted creator of questionable cinematic Bigfootage." Wallace said he had seen UFOs two thousand times, Bigfoot hundreds of times, and had, since the early days, claimed to John Napier and others that he had film footage of Bigfoot a year before the Crew footprint finds. To the dismay of Tom Slick and Peter Byrne, Wallace insisted in 1959 that he had captured Bigfoot, but when Slick put down some money, Wallace failed to produce a Bigfoot. Wallace told critic Mark Chorvinsky that he was the one who told Roger Patterson where exactly to go on Bluff Creek that fateful day in 1967 when Patterson finally captured Bigfoot on film. Of course, few Bigfoot researchers believed Wallace's claim. As Chorvinsky points out in his Wallace articles, Ray Wallace said he had many films of Bigfoot, which he floated around as "new" pictures of Bigfoot to various researchers until someone took the bait. For example, a dozen years ago, Wallace's alleged photos of Bigfoot looked amazingly like someone's bad idea of a version of the "Patterson Bigfoot," asleep on a log. It was an obvious hoax.

Wallace was mixed up in all sorts of debatable matters, from flying saucers to fake Bigfoot prints. Rant Mullens, hoaxer extraordinaire, said he would make giant, carved wooden footprints and give them to Ray Wallace, who would prepare Bigfoot casts for display.

Wallace's involvement in the 1958 case is spelled out in Sanderson's published work: "Jerry Crew found the first evidence of the 'Snowman,'" stated Sanderson calmly near the beginning of his retelling of the famous 1958 encounter in his 1959 *True* article. "Jerry was an older member of the crew employed by a Mr. Ray Wallace, subcontractor to the firm Block and Company, which had contracted with the Public Works Department on behalf of the National Parks Service to build the road." Sanderson goes on to tell us of the circumstances of the incident. Crew left for the weekend to be with his family and, upon returning, discovered the first footprints. "His [Crew's] first reaction was to consider them a hoax. Crew had heard of similar tracks found by another road gang working eight miles north of a place called Korbel on the Mad River earlier in the year, and his nephew, Jim Crew, had also mentioned having come across something similar in this area. Being a practical, matter-of-fact person, he felt considerably annoyed that some 'outsider' should try to pull such a silly stunt on him." What Sanderson does not tell us, perhaps because he did not know, is that the Mad River crew was also working on a Wallace subcontract.

Andrew Genzoli would write in a follow-up article on October 14, 1958, in the *Humboldt Times,* that a "Mrs. Paul Keesey of Pepperwood, reminded us of a hoax played in the woods country. She wrote: 'I have read with interest the articles on the huge prints. I recall eight years ago, when up around Trinidad on one of the logging roads, they had a similar thing happening. This was told to me in my restaurant at Bella Vista hill by several truck drivers. When they investigated, it turned out to be the work of a prankster.'"

In the same issue, the paper interviewed one of the Wallace brothers about the new sighting by two men Ray Wallace had just hired. Then the paper noted, "The chat with Wallace also brought out in vehement terms that he is more than slightly perturbed over accusations allegedly made by the Humboldt sheriff's office that he has perpetrated a hoax on his own construction job. 'Who knows anybody foolish enough to ruin his own business, man?' Wallace asked. He referred to the fact that about fifteen men reportedly have quit their jobs on the project since sightings of the giant footprints. 'I've got three tractors sitting up there without operators, man, and the brush-cutting crew has all quit. It just doesn't make sense.'"

With a contract to do the work, Wallace would not, of course, have had to pay those who left. But would not the work have had to be finished? Was he worried about a deadline? How would Ray Wallace have benefited from these events?

The Wallace brothers keep turning up in all of the stories associated with the Jerry Crew footprint finds of 1958. Sanderson would write, for example, "A number of other things had happened. Most notable among these was the reappearance of Bigfoot the night

before the contractor, Ray Wallace, returned from a business trip."
Likewise, it is Wilbur who is the source of the tales of the huge oil
drums and truck tires being tossed around. The two people who saw
the Bigfoot in a road were both Wallace hires, specifically looking for
Bigfoot. Jerry Crew was hired by Ray Wallace and bossed by Wilbur.
Chorvinsky would tell me during the mid-1990s that he was afraid to
outright claim that Ray Wallace did anything, because he was scared
that Wallace would sue him. Wallace appeared, however, to be very
willing to place himself in the middle of all of this and seemed to have
links to many events in the early Bigfoot days.

This is not to say Ray Wallace or his brothers are responsible
for the hundreds of years of hairy-giants-in-the-woods stories, of
course, but perhaps they wished to take advantage of the already
available history of sightings and footprint finds for their own ends.
Robert Pyle writes in his book, *Where Bigfoot Walks,* "There are
those, in fact, that believe that Ray [Wallace] began the entire series
of modern northern California episodes himself."

But why?

Follow the Money It is an axiom in historical investigations that
much can be learned from examining the
financial motives in any complex event. What
seems to be occurring is not necessarily what is happening, and clues
are often visible only at a deeper level, revealed by following a money
trail. Watergate, Iran-contra, Whitewater, even the Al Qaeda investigations, have all turned on the money issue.

Bigfootgate? Bluff Creek? Even in 1958, people were appre-
hensive about the early reports and were wondering where the
money led. In Sanderson's February 21, 1960, letter to Agogino, he
lays out his doubts. Sanderson told Agogino that after Sanderson's
True article was published, he received a letter from a man who was
rather convinced that something real was there: "But along the line,

he now gives full details of the Mad River sighting and tracks of 1957, and mentions casually that the road there was also being built by Ray Wallace. Then I get another letter addressed to me, care of *True*, from a lady who owns a motel in southern Oregon, which tells me that she had another Wallace brother and two other men, whom she named, living with her all the winter of 1958–59, who used to spend much time sitting out on the porch and doing some drinking. She reported that she had overhead them (as her office was next door) having a terrific laugh over the Bigfoot business and describing in detail how Ray Wallace had made them with their, and others', assistance by making imitation 'feet,' weighing them, and then being hauled up and down the slopes (by the new road) by means of the cables they used for clearing the logs out of the way."

Elsewhere in the letter, Sanderson commented, "First, almost everybody who did not believe the tracks were made by an unknown living entity seemed to have the same idea. This was that Ray Wallace made them. The reason—that he was a great 'funster.' It was also hinted that he was falling down on his contract and wanted some reason to go to the contractor (he was the subcontractor) and say that he could not fulfill his quota, and that the best way was to demonstrate that he could not get labor to go there or stay there."

Federal contracts can be changed, no-cost extensions can be granted, and a variety of waivers can be allowed—with good reason. The Wallace Construction Company worked through the Block and Company firm to build the Bluff Creek road for the Public Works Department on the behalf of the National Parks Service. Granite Logging Company has been mentioned as the employer of Jerry Crew, who is said to have been working for the Wallaces. The Mad River work site, another one being cleared by the Wallace Construction Company in 1957–58, had experienced giant hoax tracks earlier, but no one had dug deeper into that story after the Crew report received international headlines.

Nevertheless, late in 1958, due to the hysteria created by the Bigfoot prints at the Bluff Creek work site, two workers quit, and then fifteen, and finally rumors flew that everyone quit. Within a decade, the Bluff Creek logging road would be abandoned because floods would wash it out too often.

Unfortunately, the behavior of Ray Wallace from the 1950s to his death didn't give much hope that some of the early suspicions about him were wrong. Sadly, Wallace's background presence in the Crew incident and in other events of that time has mostly been ignored in the attempts to get at the root of the Bigfoot question.

I attempted to interview Ray Wallace three times about these suspicions and give him a chance to respond. His wife would not allow me to talk to him and rebuffed me every time.

Who would have carried out part of the 1958 Bluff Creek spoof? All evidence points to Ray Wallace and his brothers. Chorvinsky's and others' insights into Wallace's behaviors, the revealing Sanderson-Agogino letters, and the logic of the possible use of weighted "feet" and tree cables all make sense.

Ray Wallace even told us, indirectly, that he did it. Wallace admitted to using fakes. He admitted to using Rant Mullens's false Bigfoot wares in the past. Where do Wallace's tales end and his half-truths begin? In the 1960s and 1970s, as evidenced in letters he wrote to people like Jerry Clark at *Fate* and Jim McClarin at *The Manimals Newsletter*, Wallace told anyone who would listen that "Big Foot" was guarding caves full of gold. Additionally, Wallace was telling people something else that everyone overlooked just as quickly: that he had fake Bigfoot prints made for his use at Bluff Creek in 1958.

In an incredible letter signed by Ray Wallace, he wrote, "When I was building a road on Bulf [*sic*] Creek this one old Big Foot used to peer from behind those giant fir trees and watch my bulldozers build road up the rough terrain along Bluff Creek. . . . When the bear

hunters come [*sic*] into the Bluff Creek area to chase the Big Foot with their hounds we never saw Big Foot any more, after this had went on for about two months. I told some bear hunters that I was making those big tracks, they asked to see what I was using to make them with, when I couldn't show them anything they kept right on chasing the big foot's [*sic*] with their hounds, which really made me mad, I had some Indians working there for me and they told me many stories about the Indian-devil during noon time, About [*sic*] how he wasn't mean any more. . . . I could see that the bear hunters wasn't [*sic*] going to stop chasing the big foot unless I could show them how I was making the tracks, so I wrote a letter to a friend of mine . . . who used to build donkey sleds, and heel loading booms that we used in our logging operations while we were in Oregon. This was a professional broad axe man, in his younger years he used to hue boom [*sic*] sticks for ships, just as smooth as if they were done by machine. I told him that I wanted a set of feet hued out of some kind of soft wood so I could show the bear hunters how I was making the big trackes [*sic*]. . . . I run [*sic*] into all kind [*sic*] of trouble trying to keep Big Foot from being killed by hunters. Some of the bear hunters went to Eureka and told the sherriff [*sic*] that I had a pair of feet made of wood and was making Big Foot tracks. Then the sheriff sent a Deputy out to bring me into town to talk to him. I tried to get my attorney to sue Humboldt county sherriff [*sic*] for a Million dollors [*sic*] damage suit. But he wouldn't as he said the sherriff [*sic*] was a good friend of his. I still have the set of wooden feet that I paid fifty dollars for."

Looking closely at this Wallace "confession," his "Save the Bigfoot" rationalization appears to be an invention to put some spin on his scheme's being temporarily exposed by the sheriff's office. He mentions the sheriff's office questions in his letter to McClarin and we know it is, indeed, a public fact from an October 14, 1958, *Humboldt Times* article, which noted that the Humboldt sheriff's office was investigating Wallace because he might have "perpetrated a hoax on his own construction job." The key is the public revelation of Wallace allegedly creating Bigfoot hoax prints, which must be rationalized by Wallace.

Of course, Ray Wallace always fashioned some seemingly reasonable excuse for his behaviors. This piece of logic, thus, is the hook to convince outsiders that Wallace may actually have created a hoax for the reasons he notes, but that is hardly the end of the Wallace tale. While one segment of the hoaxing may sound logical, if we then note that Wallace went on in his letter to tell Jim McClarin that the rationale behind his wanting to save the Bigfoot is to follow the beasts and find the caches of gold they guard, you begin to understand why people have come to expect so little from Wallace statements.

So could the milestone 1958 Bigfoot affair be partially based on an elaborate prank? Perhaps the scenario went something like this: Wallace and his brothers, through "funster demeanor," place large footprints in a series of his work sites for years in California, Oregon, and Washington. These jokes are viewed as harmless pranks, silly incidents of no concern to his men, other than as "after-work" distractions and to goat a new man. Sometimes one of the brothers uses the workers' reactions to the stories or the prints to explain work slowdowns or stoppages to his contractors. Perhaps it is a way to keep some control of Indian workers, who tell tales of forest cannibals and Indian-devils. Then, in 1958, a churchgoer named Jerry Crew, who does not enjoy the ridicule, takes the matter seriously and obtains "proof" in the form of a footcast when he sees some of the tracks. The folly is a complex combination of real history, actual Bigfoot experiences, authentic Bigfoot tracks, a funster, federal contracts, and an honest construction worker. Then in a burst of publicity, Bigfoot is born.

It may never have happened had not an innocent Bob Titmus shown up before the massive publicity of 1958 and taught Jerry Crew how to make the first Bigfoot plaster casts. These casts would then be instrumental in stimulating *Humboldt Times* editor Andrew Genzoli to publish the first illustrated Bigfoot article, complete with a photograph of Jerry Crew in a buttoned-down, striped shirt holding his incredible cast. The rest is Bigfoot history.

Sasquatch author and researcher John Green, in a 1995 *Anomalist* rebuttal to my initial Wallace-as-hoaxer suggestion, says he would not be surprised if Wallace had found tracks at his work sites. "Wallace was, after all, building roads in 'Bigfoot' territory, and that is the situation in which such tracks most frequently showed up in northern California, whether on a Wallace contract or someone else's, and that continued to happen long after Wallace packed up and moved to Washington. . . . There is, however, pretty convincing evidence that if anyone faked all those tracks at Bluff Creek in 1958, it couldn't have been Ray Wallace. The evidence for that is the pathetic quality of his repeated attempts to fake such things since that time. Or are we supposed to believe that changing from a master hoaxer into a laughingstock was all part of his ingenious plan?"

I agree with Green. Bluff Creek was, and continues to be, visited by real Bigfoot. But perhaps a little bit more was going on in 1958.

We heard more Wallace tales when he died of heart failure at the age of 84 on November 26, 2002. "Ray L. Wallace was Bigfoot," Wallace son Michael told Bob Young of the *Seattle Times*. "The reality is, Bigfoot just died." A photograph accompanying the story showed nephew Dale Lee Wallace posing with alder-wood carvings of giant feet he said Wallace used in 1958 to create Bigfoot. The media went wild. Many hastily written stories declared that Wallace had placed fake footprints throughout the Pacific Northwest and that the whole Bigfoot phenomenon was a hoax. Some stories even implied that Mrs. Ray Wallace had worn a costume to play the Bigfoot filmed by Roger Patterson in 1967 (see next chapter), even though Michael Wallace had told reporter Young that his father had nothing to do with the Patterson-Gimlin film. The news flap worked in a vacuum, neglecting not only the Native traditions and pre-1958 history of hairy giants and Sasquatch, but a small detail of considerable importance as well. It turns out the Wallace-owned carved feet do *not* match the first Crew casts! But these newly revealed fake feet exactly match the 1960 Bluff Creek tracks, for example, found by Steve M. Matthes, which he declared hoaxes in his 1988 book *Brave and Other Stories*. Yes, Wallace appears to have placed prank footprints near some of his California work sites from 1958 through the 1960s. It's sad that he had to resort to hoaxing to express his belief in the real Bigfoot.

It seems to me that a prank elevated to the level of a national story is merely one of those quirks of history that have little or nothing to do with the quality of the mischief. Who could have known that another incident that might have begun as a prank, the "discovery" of the Piltdown Man, would live on in histories for so long.

The important question, of course, is, does it matter that the original 1958 Bigfoot incidents may have been to some extent based on a prank? After all, weren't tales of these large, hairy creatures around for years before? Bigfoot chronicler Andrew Genzoli summed it up with these words: "Bigfoot is a story you can take or leave. To me, Bluff Creek's Bigfoot is a wonderful legend. Monster or myth, he has stirred the minds of men."

Skeptics and debunkers who use these speculations and evidence for a prank to strengthen their case that *all* Bigfoot reports are hoaxes will be missing the point. While a prank may have occurred, good Bigfoot evidence is abundant.

Bigfoot might have been named something else if a different case, such as one from the Hoopa First Nation of an *Oh-Mah,* had received the first wave of massive publicity. But events did not unfold that way. The reports and sightings of *Bigfoot*—that very American word—are now part of the landscape of America's hidden zoology.

7 Bigfoot Filmed

Thousands of miles of footprints. Hundreds of years of traditions. Scores and scores of close, firsthand encounters. Then in 1967 the next piece of the puzzle fell into place—an actual filmed representation of what scared individuals had reported seeing. And it occurred before the era of video and digital cameras, and before the existence of consumer photo-manipulation software such as Photoshop. The story would bring us back to the birthplace of Bigfoot.

Back to Bluff Creek Roger Patterson, an expert rodeo rider, did not realize what he was doing. He had picked up a copy of the December 1959 *True* magazine. In that issue, he found and read Ivan T. Sanderson's article "The Strange Story of America's Abominable Snowman," and it changed his life forever. He became passionate about Bigfoot. More than that, he became obsessed. From his home in Yakima, Washington, he created a little organization, the Northwest Research Association, and in 1966, he penned a little book, *Do Abominable Snowmen of*

America Really Exist? It was a collection of other people's articles and a few of his own thoughts and words on the mystery. Next Patterson wanted to make a documentary film about Bigfoot. And to do that, he decided, in October of 1967, to follow up on reports he was hearing of new tracks being found back in the Eden of Bigfoot, Bluff Creek.

Patterson decided to make the journey there with associate Robert "Bob" Gimlin, a part Native–American outdoorsman. First Patterson rented a Kodak K200 16mm cine camera from Sheppard's Drive-In Camera Shop, in Yakima, for the trek. On October 18, 1967, the shop's owner reported to local authorities that the camera was overdue. Roger Patterson was so busy searching; he'd forgotten to return the camera on time. As the two men were riding in the Six Rivers National Forest that memorable day of October 20, 1967, they filmed the trees, each other riding their horses along the trails, and other background material that would be useful in their proposed documentary. Finally, early in the afternoon, Patterson and Gimlin rounded a bend and spotted a large, upright creature on one of the creek's sandbars. The dark, full-figured creature was covered with short hair (even on its large, pendulous breasts) and possessed a sagittal crest (a bony ridge on top of its head).

Patterson's small Welsh pony smelled the creature and reared, bringing both pony and rider to the ground. But Patterson got up, grabbed his camera from the saddlebag, and while running toward the creature, took twenty-four feet of color film with the rented 16mm handheld Kodak movie camera. The creature walked steadily away into the forest, turning its head once toward the camera. Gimlin, meanwhile, remained on his horse, a rifle in hand, fearing his friend might be attacked.

Bob Gimlin told John Green in a taped interview that the horse Bob was riding did not cause him any problem and the others had run off. At one point Bob did dismount his horse with his rifle in one hand and the reins in the other, but the Sasquatch was walking

away and he did not point the rifle at it. Gimlin was quoted in the 1990s, on the *X-Creatures* Bigfoot documentary, as saying, "I had a .30-06 loaded with 180 grain bullets, and if that creature would have turned and rushed me, I would have shot it."

The Bigfoot quickly disappeared into the woods. The men tracked it for three miles, but eventually lost it in the heavy undergrowth. Patterson and Gimlin immediately took footcasts of the series of ten footprints—fourteen and a half inches long by six inches wide—found in the sandy, blue-gray clay soil. Nine days later Bigfoot trackers such as Bob Titmus recast several of the footprints that the Bigfoot had left that day.

Similar footprints found here over the years had drawn the two men from Yakima, Washington, to the area, and now they had 952 frames of color film to support the existence of this six-to-seven-foot-tall, five-hundred-to-seven-hundred-pound creature. While scientists who have examined this footage remain divided on its authenticity, to date no firm evidence has surfaced to cast serious doubts on the film, or the events that produced this incredible footage of a Bigfoot.

Patterson and Gimlin Talk to the Media

Roger Patterson and Bob Gimlin were immediately overwhelmed by requests for interviews; Gimlin declined most of them. Researchers have scanned these news articles through the years to get some idea of how these two felt about their encounter. The best of these interviews, courtesy of John Green and never before published, was a radio dialogue conducted in Vancouver, Canada, in November 1967, by open-line host Jack Webster. He spoke to Roger Patterson and Bob Gimlin right after the first showing of the film to Vancouver media and scientists from the University of British Columbia and the British Columbia museum.

WEBSTER: I've been interviewing eyewitnesses of Sasquatch sightings, Sasquatch themselves, since 1954, and I might as well tell you that this is the first time I've been what you might call really impressed. I saw the film taken by Roger Patterson and Bob Gimlin near Eureka, California, on Friday afternoon the twentieth of October, and I'll tell you it's like a personal eyewitness of a flying saucer, a personal one. Roger was kind of excited, but it shows quite clearly a huge, humanlike, fur-covered creature striding along a creek bed in a most distinctive manner. I think you can say honestly from the film that the creature is female. When it turns sideways, you can see the mammary glands, and the hips appear to be massive thickness right through. My immediate reaction was, you know, it's a phony, and then I began to think about it and, you think, if that's wearing a costume, it's a most unusual costume, there's no sagging, no bulging, no nothing, and then the footprints are there, the actual footprints of this creature in the Bigfoot country are deep, so the creature must be a heavy creature unless it's a very tall man carrying a hell of a . . . a great deal of lead weight around his shoulders. However, here's the man who took the picture, Roger Patterson from Yakima.

Now, Roger, what took you to that place, and precisely where was it, and why did you go there?

ROGER: Well, first of all, the reason that we were in this place was that I'd been filming a documentary on this thing for the past eight months or so and I'd been going to areas interviewing people that have seen these creatures, other than myself now, and we went to this particular area because a month before this they had found three different sets of tracks up in that area.

w: Now come back to yourself. First of all, you showed some routine film of your packhorses, didn't you?

r: Right.

w: Now what were you doing filming at that particular time on the packhorse trip?

r: Well, we hadn't taken any and I thought right of that particular area there, before, and it was a beautiful area right in there, there was some of the—

w: You were just taking odd shots, then?

r: We were just taking some shots of the scenery and of myself and Bob and—

w: All right, just jump to what you first saw that made you excited.

r: Well, we rounded a bend in the road—

w: You were walking?

r: No, we were riding.

w: Riding on horses.

r: Riding on horses.

w: Where was your camera?

r: My camera was in my saddlebag, on the left-hand side.

w: And who was "we"?

r: Bob Gimlin and myself.

w: Bob's right here, right?

r AND BOB: Right.

w: So you're riding on the horses, your camera's in the saddlebag, you came around the bend, and then what happened?

r: All of a sudden I caught something out of, glimpsed, out of the corner of my eye, and my horse immediately reared on me and I was,

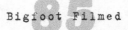

I tried to pull him down, and at this instant after I seen the object to the side I wasn't able to see it again for a little bit. My horse fell with me, I probably pulled him half-over, and as he got up, I was able to get up and control him until I went around the other side and got the camera out of the saddlebag and I turned my horse loose and was able to start shooting and I yelled—

w: Now just a minute, you turned your horse—you got off your horse and turned it loose . . .

R: Right. Well, my horse was nowhere—I was already off my horse; I was on the ground underneath him.

w: Okay, you got your camera, turned your horse loose.

R: Right.

w: Then you looked up and what did you see?

R: That's when I seen this, this creature, about one hundred and twenty feet away, and she was, at that point, had just turned around and was just going up the bank, this small bank over there and I started running and trying to get a shot of her and I yelled at Bob to cover me.

w: Where was Bob . . . where were you then, Bob, Bob Gimlin from Yakima?

B: I was directly behind Roger, mounted on the horse that I was riding on and . . . also when this creature . . . we sighted this creature, my horse frightened kind of too but he was an older, seasoned horse and I controlled him quite well because I stayed in the saddle, and I did cover Roger the time he told me to cover him and I—

w: What do you mean "cover him"?

B: I took my rifle from the scabbard in the saddle and in the event

that this creature would attack, I thought that I could protect him somewhat.

w: Did you have your eyes on the creature all the time?

b: Most of the time, when I didn't have them on the ground where I had to . . . trying to control the horse kind of, it was a little bit unlevel and—

w: What was the creature then doing, when you first saw it?

b: When I first saw it, it was standing, looking straight at me.

w: Face on?

b: Face on.

w: Describe it to me, Bob.

b: It was a large, hairy creature with arms that hang down beside its, you know, far down on its sides, below its knees, and it was quite—

w: Do you agree with that?

r: No, I think Bob's a little excited here, I don't believe they were below the knees, they were above the knees.

w: But they were well down on the sides, weren't they?

b: Way down, right.

w: And I could see that on the film tonight, they were well down on the sides.

b: And she was heavy, although I had no way of estimating her weight at that time, and only guessed at it since then, but she turned and she stood there for an instant, then she turned and started up over this bar . . .

w: Now, when you looked at it, describe her physically to me. Was there any shred of clothing of any kind?

b: No clothing at all on this creature, it was covered with hair only, except around the face and nose. The nose was bare and around the cheeks were bare.

w: What kind of nose did it have?

b: It had a broad, flat nose.

w: Like a gorilla's nose with the open nostrils?

b: No, no, not like that, the nostrils you could not see down.

w: Would you agree with that, it had a human-type nose?

r: That's right.

w: What about the lips?

b: The lips I never really noticed that much at that particular time, when she was face on to me, because she just stood there for an instant and turned and walked away, started walking away.

w: Any sound at all?

b: No sound that I heard.

w: Now what about the physical characteristics, her figure?

b: She was kind of slumped, and very heavily through the . . . well, her entire body was heavy, and—

w: Were the breasts visible?

b: They were visible.

w: Were they covered with hair?

b: They were covered with hair.

A Look Back

w: Now, the proportions of the body. Was it like a giant human?

r: Yes, it seemed to be, to me, more like a giant man except it had breasts. This is one thing that . . . that her characteristics . . . and the anthropologists and zoologists this evening brought this out, it seemed to me more like a huge man, she . . . in other words she didn't have a narrow waist and a big set of hips like we think of as a woman.

w: And when it strode away from the camera, it walked very much like a huge big man, didn't it?

r: Well, it did. However, I would make the estimate that, or the judgment I might say, that a female of this kind wouldn't look very femalish under the environment that you maybe would have to . . .

w: Bob how did you feel when you saw it . . . you think someone was pulling a gag on you?

b: No, not really, it was, it was surprising, and we talked about these things many times, and actually talked what we would do if we happened to see one. . . .

w: Now before we finish the chase . . . you had your rifle out of the scabbard, what kind of rifle was it?

b: Thirty-aught-six [.30-06] rifle.

w: You can use a rifle, obviously.

b: Yes, I can, I've grown up—

w: It would be worth a hundred thousand dollars cash to you if you had raised that rifle and shot this creature. You must have known that.

b: I don't believe I could do it.

w: Even if you just wounded it.

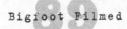

B: Well, I, like Roger said—

R: That would be a mess.

W: A mess?

R: A mess. . . . Both Bob and I, we had agreed that we will not shoot one of these creatures, and if she would attack us, whether we would be protecting our lives, I think that we would have to fear for our own lives if we were to wound one and make a total mess out of something like—

W: Right, so finally—I'm back to Roger Patterson again—when you got your camera steadied, did you stand still and take the pictures I saw, or did you follow it on foot?

R: I followed it on foot, because this was the only way that I had, I, I viewed the situation of course at the time and I could see her moving away from me and I knew Bob was there, and I thought if I'm ever going to get any pictures, I'll have to do it now, and I ran, as best I could, and trotted—

W: How close did you come, at the closest?

R: Well, I think we were closer when we first seen it than at any other time, don't you, Bob?

B: No, I disagree with you there, I believe just immediately after we got across the creek we were probably closer to her at that time than we were when we first sighted her, because she had her back to us at that time and . . . or at least I was closer, because I ran a little further up on the horse, I was moving pretty fast and I got him finally across the creek, so I believe at that time when I crossed the creek, I was the closest I ever was to her and I believe it was about ninety feet at that time.

w: Now, Roger, how far did you . . . oh, by the way, did you notice the colors of the palms of the hands there, were you close enough for that?

r: Oh, I was, but I never noticed.

w: Now, how far did you follow her?

r: I really didn't follow her any much further than when my camera run out of film and I knew that it was out, and Bob got on his horse and went after her then, and from that point he seen her more than I did, I never seen her again. . . .

w: How far were you able to follow her?

b: I watched her until she went up the road about three hundred yards, and she went around a bend in the road and that was the last I seen of her.

w: Now, after all this too dreadful excitement, what did the pair of you do? Here you've, after all these hundreds of years of rumors and sightings and all the rest of it all up and down the Pacific Northwest and Michigan and Wisconsin and everywhere else, what did you do when you're standing there, you've recovered from the shock, with a camera full of film? I mean, just tell me precisely what you did at that time. What did you say to each other?

r: Well, I, when Bob come back, I yelled to him and I said, "Bob, come back," because at this point my horse was I didn't know where and the packhorse was gone, my scabbard, and my rifle was in the scabbard, on the horse, and the tracks before, down in there that we had heard about, were in a set of three, and there was a bigger one there, and I thought that possibly there was a male in close in—

w: You were getting nervous.

R: I was getting nervous.

W: You were on foot there without the rifle.

R: I was on foot without anything, and I yelled to Bob to come back and we would think the thing over and—

W: Was that just about the time you broke off the chase, you might say?

B: Right, that was, when I last seen her go round the curve. And at that time I went back and proceeded to gather up Roger's horses, his horse that he was riding and the packhorse, and after—

W: Then what?

B: After chasing them up and down the road for a little while and finally catching them, well, we talked it over and I said I'd check around and see if maybe that I could find some tracks where she had come into this area and possibly sight the other one, so I took the camera while he gathered up his stuff and—

W: You scouted around for a while, did you? Well, when did you . . . were you able to identify specifically the tracks you had made while you were following her?

R: Yes, because immediately after we went across the creek and immediately after I called Bob back, we looked at the tracks and they were, the tracks were there.

W: These are the tracks we saw in the movie tonight.

R: That's right.

W: The tracks for which you have the plaster casts tonight.

R: Right.

W: How come you had plaster casts with you . . . plaster with you?

R: We didn't have plaster, 'cause we went, we had to go back to the—to the truck and get plaster and come up and cast them.

W: How long would that take you, to leave the scene, go back to the truck, and come up again?

R: We were at that point about two, what, maybe two miles from that area then?

B: Not two miles, I'd say. By the road it was just about an even two miles, across the hill that way it was a little shorter but we went—

W: Now, okay, so you then gave up . . . you took the plaster tracks. . . . How deep were these tracks by the way, in inches? . . . Inch and a quarter or . . . ?

B: Some of them were down as far as three and a half inches deep into the softer soil. These particular ones we took here were, weren't quite so deep because they were flatter tracks.

W: All right now, many of the zoologists that were people you consulted, have they given you any idea of the weight of this creature? The height or the weight?

B: They did on the height, measuring by the soles of those feet, in the picture, and they estimated the height to be approximately six foot nine inches.

W: What was the length of the stride?

R: Just pardon me, this was estimated on a fourteen-and-a-half-inch, excuse me, a fourteen-inch track, and these tracks were fourteen and a half inches, which would, would add quite a considerable bit. . . .

W: What was the stride cadence? I believe that's the proper technical description.

R: She averaged a forty-one-inch stride, somewheres thereabouts. She was taking—she took up to a forty-six-inch stride.

W: So that was three feet five to . . . twelve threes are thirty-six, twelve fours are forty-eight . . . three feet five to three feet ten.

R: Yes.

W: My goodness gracious me. Of course this . . . There must be lots of them around there, I mean, whatever were they doing down by the creek?

R: Well, there were fish in this creek, we didn't fish it but we seen them jumping, and I . . . I can only surmise what, she was either drinking or possibly trying to catch a fish in the creek.

W: Any sign of feces as a result of that, feces around, any other tracks of the animal?

R: No, there was no, no, no droppings at all.

W: That's the word I was looking for. Well, now what? You going to sell this film to the highest bidder?

R: Well, we're just having to . . . we haven't made any definite plans, but I would imagine that we will, will in future probably sell it.

W: How can you afford to take all this time off to go down . . . oh, no, well, first of all, how long have you been looking for Sasquatch, live Sasquatch?

R: Well, off and on, for about seven and a half years, but the last four years I've made much more of an effort than any other time.

W: You're financially independent?

R: Well, somewhat.

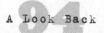

w: In other words you can go out for this kind of caper without suffering too much financially.

r: Well, it's been tough.

w: Why has nobody ever found any bones of these Sasquatch, down in that Bigfoot country where they have been reported so many times?

r: Well, not only down in that country but there's been tracks all over the Northwest and Canada, as you well know in Canada, but they seem, I think anyway . . . this maybe doesn't agree with all the fellows that's been involved in this . . . but they seem to dwell primarily in the rain forest or they can get to the rain forest fairly easy, and bones in this type of climate, in the rain-forest climate, don't last very long.

w: Do you realize, Bob Gimlin and Roger Patterson, that people are going to say you're total nuts? You know that, don't you? You're going to be held up to ridicule by some people.

r: Well, I've taken quite a bit of this in the past and it doesn't surprise me. I know they're there, and I know that we're going to get one in the next possibly five to ten years or maybe sooner, and when we do, I think there's going to have to be many people and also scientists maybe eat a little crow.

w: You said they are vegetarians, eh?

r: I don't think that they're solely vegetarians.

w: Do you think they go for fish, like bears go for fish?

r: I think that they, they will eat what they have to, to keep alive, and in some areas if they can get enough vegetation, they—

The tape John Green has of the radio interview, a partial fragment, ends abruptly there.

The Analyses, Doubts, and Affirmations Begin

Capturing the fleeting sight of a seven-foot, apelike creature retreating into the northern-California wilderness, the Patterson-Gimlin Bigfoot film is among the most renowned artifacts in the field of hominology. The footage has achieved iconic status even among the public at large and forms the foundation of many Bigfoot hunters' beliefs.

As soon as Roger Patterson began to show it, the footage created controversy. That he had written and self-published his book, *Do Abominable Snowmen of America Really Exist?* (1966) and had set out to film a documentary about sightings of Bigfoot counted against the film's reality, in the eyes of many.

Patterson and Bob Gimlin said they had, at first, spotted the huge, dark-furred, bipedal creature hunched over in the middle of a creek. The beast then rose to a full height that Patterson estimated at seven feet four inches. But a filmed analysis by John Green of the exact site, using researcher Jim McClarin as a stand-in for Bigfoot, showed the creature may have been only six feet six inches tall. Patterson's excitement may have caused an overestimate of the height.

Patterson and Gimlin came upon a number of footprints, fourteen inches long and five inches wide, and they preserved them in plaster casts. Primatologist John Napier pointed to what he thought to be physiological inconsistencies in the footprint casts between the height of the creature and the length of its stride as shown in the film. Down through the years other anthropologists such as Grover Krantz and Jeff Meldrum have stated that the footprints actually support the film. Krantz also demonstrated that the human walk involves the locking of the knees. But this filmed Bigfoot does not lock its knees; this would be extremely difficult for a hoaxer to do and yet look as smooth as this creature's walk. If the creature was a fake, it was clearly a remarkably skillful one.

In the ensuing decades, the 952 frames of Patterson's Bigfoot film have been submitted to all manner of examination and analysis. Because of its apparent breasts, the creature has been classified as female (nicknamed Patty by Bigfoot insiders). Theorists have extrapolated descriptions of everything from its psychological bearing to its eating habits on the basis of its behavior in the film. Minutiae of the creature's physiognomy, such as the exact way in which it moves its neck, and its unusual method of distributing its weight as it walked, have led many to conclude that this could not be a man in a suit. But many others feel just as certain that Patterson's Bigfoot was a fake. They argue that, being established in the "Bigfoot business," Patterson stood to profit from fabricating film footage of the creature. As a result, many have tried to discredit the film.

The Chambers Affair

The only known source of high-quality costumes and makeup in 1967 was the movie special-effects industry, and circumstantial evidence that this Bigfoot came from Hollywood was floated around for years. After "in-depth" investigations and interviews, skeptical researcher Mark Chorvinsky found in the 1980s and early 1990s that the consensus among movie special-effects professionals was that the film depicted a prankster in a skillfully crafted costume. In fact, many stated that the falsity of the Patterson film has been common knowledge in the industry for years. The makeup artist most frequently associated with the Bigfoot film was John Chambers, a legendary elder statesman in the field of monster-making.

During his thirty-year career, Chambers worked on several movies and television shows, including TV's *The Outer Limits, The Munsters, Lost in Space,* and *Mission: Impossible.* Chambers was responsible for putting the pointy ears on *Star Trek*'s Mr. Spock. His makeup and prosthetics film credits include *National Lampoon's Class Reunion* (1982), *Halloween II* (1981), *The Island of Dr. Moreau* (1977),

 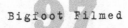

Ssssss (1973), *Battle for the Planet of the Apes* (1973), *Superbeast* (1972), *Conquest of the Planet of the Apes* (1972), *Slaughterhouse-Five* (1972), *Escape from the Planet of the Apes* (1971), *Beneath the Planet of the Apes* (1970), *Planet of the Apes* (1968), *The List of Adrian Messenger* (1963), and *Showdown at Boot Hill* (1958).

John Chambers is most famous, however, for designing the anthropoids in the original *Planet of the Apes.* Chambers recalled how he spent hours at the Los Angeles Zoo doing research when he worked on that movie in the 1960s. "It was the best way I could think of for capturing the elastic facial expressions of the apes," he said in a 1990s Associated Press interview.

Chambers's preparation led him to develop a new type of foam rubber that was easier to work with than the material commonly used at the time. He also created facial appliances that could be attached to actors' faces to form primate features. His innovative, highly articulated ape masks won him an Academy Award in 1968. For his efforts he became only the second makeup artist to receive an honorary Academy Award. A competitive category for makeup was established in the 1980s.

All the fingers in Hollywood pointed to Chambers as the man behind the Patterson-Gimlin film. Chorvinsky reported that although none of the makeup professionals he spoke with had first-hand knowledge that Chambers had created the Patterson Bigfoot, it was widely accepted that he was responsible for it, or that Chambers was the only artist at the time skillful enough to have crafted such a costume. But as the thirtieth anniversary of the Patterson event approached, Chambers, who was then residing in a Los Angeles nursing home in frail health, told interviewers that he had had nothing to do with the Bigfoot seen in Patterson's film.

In October 1997, new reports surfaced that Chambers had concocted the creature. But they were merely the Chambers story recycled. This time, movie director John Landis stepped forward to "verify" what he said had been known among Hollywood makeup artists for years: that the Patterson-Gimlin footage from Bluff Creek, California, was using a John Chambers–created suit.

Typical of the headlines was the one that appeared in London's *Sunday Telegraph* for October 19, 1997: "Hollywood admits to Bigfoot hoax." The article, timed to the thirtieth anniversary, reads in part:

> A piece of film, which for thirty years has been regarded as the most compelling evidence for the existence of Bigfoot, the North American "abominable snowman," is a hoax, according to new claims. John Chambers, the man behind the *Planet of the Apes* films and the elder statesman of Hollywood's "monster-makers," has been named by a group of Hollywood makeup artists as the person who faked Bigfoot. In an interview with Scott Essman, an American journalist, the veteran Hollywood director John Landis revealed "a makeup secret only six people know." Mr. Landis said: "That famous piece of film of Bigfoot walking in the woods that was touted as the real thing was just a suit made by John Chambers." He said he learned the information while working alongside Mr. Chambers on *Beneath the Planet of the Apes* in 1970. . . . Howard Berger, of Hollywood's KNB Effects Group, said it was common knowledge within the film industry that Mr. Chambers was responsible for a hoax that turned Bigfoot into a worldwide cult. Mike McCracken Jr., a makeup artist and associate of Mr. Chambers, said: "I'd say with absolute certainty that John was responsible."

But the gulf between the news reports (Scott Essman is an associate and friend of Chorvinsky's and was merely promoting the Chorvinsky line of thought) and reality appeared to be quite wide. At 1 P.M. on Sunday, October 26, 1997, California Bigfoot researcher Bobbie Short interviewed Chambers, who was active and alert in his

Los Angeles assisted-care room. The makeup artist insisted he had no prior knowledge of Roger Patterson or Bob Gimlin before their claimed Bigfoot encounter on October 20, 1967. He also denied having anything to do with creating the suit, notwithstanding contrary claims passing through the Hollywood rumor mill. Chambers went on to say he was good but he was not good enough to have fashioned anything nearly so convincing as the Bluff Creek Bigfoot.

The appearance of the Patterson-Gimlin footage in 1967 led many skeptics to think Chambers was the creator of the fully haired, upright primate in the film. Critics of the Bigfoot film's debunkers would later point out that the original *Planet of the Apes* costumes were not even full-body suits, but mostly rigid facial and upper-torso gear.

Intriguingly, for some years, it is the well-known movie director John Landis who has claimed that Chambers not only made the Patterson suit but helped shoot the film. For just as long, people have pointed to Landis as the one from whom they heard the story, not Chambers. But Chambers himself says the only Bigfoot he made was the Burbank Bigfoot, a large stone prop intended to imitate a real Bigfoot-like creature and used for a carnival tour.

By Chambers's own admission, as noted, he said he "was good but not that good" enough to have made anything nearly as convincing as the Bigfoot seen at Bluff Creek on October 20, 1967. Chambers never really bothered to set the record straight and was instead driven by his ego to let people believe he "might" have been so clever as to produce the Patterson Bigfoot film. Many of those with whom he worked assumed he had hoaxed Roger Patterson. He had not.

Hollywood stories are seldom happy ones, and John Chambers's was no exception. Lives there consist mainly of a spiking need for importance that creates half-truths and makes Hollywood the rumor mill it is known to be. In this environment the Chambers-Patterson rumor has survived and grown, mushrooming into wild ·

allegations and innuendo. Much that has been written about this episode is based on what "people" thought, with no factual basis except the sly grin of an ego-driven man. Chambers was a giant in his time, but his ego ran away with itself and the rumors mounted with wings of speculation over the years, which has sent the Bigfoot community into a tailspin. The Chambers rumor is merely another pathetic story out of Hollywood, a sad commentary that has nothing to do with cryptozoology.

John Chambers died of diabetes complications on August 25, 2001, at the Motion Picture and Television Fund retirement home in Woodland Hills. He was seventy-eight. His obituaries mentioned, in passing, his whispered role in the history of Bigfoot. John Chambers's name will forever be linked to Bigfoot, no matter the truth behind the rumors.

Intriguingly, one of Chambers's few roles as an actor was in a 1971 movie about a California Bigfoot that terrorized coeds. John Landis, who also played the film's very thin Bigfoot, directed the film, called *Schlock*. Chambers played the National Guard captain in the film. Chambers's student Rick Baker, who one day would create Harry, the Bigfoot in *Harry and the Hendersons,* did the makeup and created the Bigfoot in *Schlock*.

Outfoxed by Hype? On December 28, 1998, the Fox Television Network promised to expose "the greatest myths on Earth" in their special "World's Greatest Hoaxes: Secrets Finally Revealed." One segment of the documentary involved the famous Patterson Bigfoot film. It began with attempt to assassinate the character of Roger Patterson, calling his 1967 film of Bigfoot an "elaborate hoax." The Patterson debunking was presented in the milieu of some rather obvious "filmed Bigfoot" hoaxes, almost in an attempt to spoil the one good apple by association with many bad ones.

The Fox assault continued with the appearance of UFO skeptic Kal Korff on-screen, saying that after extensive analysis he thought the Patterson film was a fake because it had a distinctive dark line down the back—exactly in the place that a constructed suit would have one, he said. Trying to sound as if he knew something about animals, he made some outrageous statements about how nothing in the animal world has anything like this on its body.

Sorry to say, but Korff appears never to have seen my uncle Wilson's hairy back on the beach in Florida. Or has Korff not even seen a gorilla in a zoo? Primates naturally have a line down their back, as do dogs (an extreme example, of course, being the Rhodesian Ridgeback) and lots of other animals. That's how we are "made."

Within hours of the broadcast of the program, famed California Bigfoot researcher Bobbie Short had interviewed an associate of hers at the San Diego Zoo. As the zoo employee pointed out, the San Diego Zoo's gorillas have a very visible line (crease) down the center of their back, following the direct alignment of their spinal cord into the crease of their buttocks. The creature in the Patterson Bigfoot film has the same line. This line is the place where two large groups of muscles come together, and the hair there often looks darker in reality because there is more of it, or in certain lighting conditions because the crease is a slight depression.

The Fox special's most disturbing argument against the Patterson film, however, came through their interview with Clyde Reinke, identified as a "former ANE executive." ANE stands for American National Enterprise, a nature-film company that produced several semisuccessful nature films during the 1970s.

Reinke claimed that Roger Patterson was "on the payroll" at ANE, was a permanent employee, and was salaried there. He said that Roger Patterson was told to go out and film a Bigfoot. Patterson did this, allegedly, by filming Jerry Romney, a former ANE-associated insurance agent, dressed as Bigfoot. Finally, Reinke claimed that

ANE packaged the Patterson film with their nature films and made "millions" of dollars.

Little in what Reinke says, however, can be proven, and most of what he details can be questioned. The Fox special even cast doubt on their own story. They interviewed Jerry Romney, who says he never told Reinke he was the "man in the suit" and says he was not the Bigfoot in the Patterson film. He's not certain why Reinke has made these claims. In 1967, Romney was a trim and fit former basketball player. In 1998, he's a mildly heavy, older male. He carries some weight around his belly, and his 1998 physique somewhat matches the Patterson Bigfoot. The Fox special shows some footage of Romney walking along and compares it to the Patterson-Gimlin film, saying they correspond. But, of course, the Romney of 1998 is not the Romney of 1967!

There was little new here, however. Years before, in 1991, California researcher Peter Guttilla had interviewed Clyde Reinke, then a private detective living in Beatty, Nevada. For two hours during that interview Reinke weaved a convoluted tale of "his" alleged 1960s meetings with Roger Patterson and several other "coconspirators" for American National Enterprise. ANE, according to Reinke in these interviews, "cooked this thing up," meaning the Patterson-Gimlin Bluff Creek movie.

Reinke said he was "personnel director" for ANE in the mid-sixties, adding, "I signed Patterson's checks," but no canceled checks have been produced. No payroll receipts have shown up for either Reinke or Patterson.

Clyde Reinke also implicated the "Olson brothers," Dean and Ron, among others. Guttilla made contact with two of the surviving principals, including Jerry Romney, the former Brigham Young University basketball player Reinke claims was "the man in the suit." Guttilla says Romney completely denied it. Guttilla says that most claims Reinke made and other "leads" were "dead ends." Those are his words, not mine.

Meanwhile John Green, a man who has researched the subject since 1957 and is the author of the classic book *Sasquatch: The Apes Among Us* (1978), had this to say about the Fox claims in 1999:

> Roger Patterson had no part whatever in the original production of the ANE Bigfoot movie, although he and Ron Olson became closely associated later on. ANE started out in 1970 with the intention of getting a movie of their own, thinking that they could do so by a computer analysis of sighting and footprint reports which would tell them where to go with the cameras. I was retained by them for about a year and a half during which I organized a computer survey for them. They never followed through with the computer time—they didn't even have a computer of their own—but more than two hundred incidents were recorded on computer questionnaires, and I subsequently worked with the producer Dave Meyer in getting some of the interviews. All this is recorded in correspondence which I still have.
>
> Sometime in 1971, they decided to use the Patterson footage and negotiated movie rights with Roger Patterson. This, of course, is about four years after he got his film. They would no doubt have been wise to connect with Roger in the first place. They may even have tried to do so, but he had a different financial backer at that time, and as I said, they thought at first that they could get their own movie. There is certainly a hoax involved here, but not the one claimed by Fox. They are the ones who were hoaxed.

Perhaps Reinke has simply mixed up about the years and how Roger Patterson was involved. In 1971, ANE did produce a Bigfoot movie that used the Patterson film, entitled *Bigfoot—Man or Beast—A Rainbow Adventure-Film Report*. And if Patterson was a "photogra-

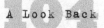

pher" for ANE in 1967, there is nothing in the record that documents his employment at that early date.

The Fox special was entertaining, biased, and controversial, but it missed destroying the Bigfoot legend by a wide margin.

The Continued Attacks

The Patterson Bigfoot film—the Zapruder film of cryptozoology—found itself under full assault as the century ended.

On January 11, 1999, a news release bounced across North America, appearing in local papers and such national outlets as *USA Today,* proclaiming that the final "proof" of a hoax had been discovered—that an object hanging from the Patterson Bigfoot's fur resembled a metal fastener.

"When the guy in the suit turned to look at the camera, it probably snapped loose and dangled from the fur," self-proclaimed Bigfoot expert Cliff Crook would tell reporter Joseph Rose. "It's a hoax. Why would Bigfoot be wearing a belt buckle?"

Bigfoot Central's Cliff Crook of Bothell, Washington, and Chris Murphy of Vancouver, Canada, were quoted as saying that enlargements and "computer enhancements" of the film's frames revealed an object hanging "from" the Bigfoot in one frame of the film. When people hear "computer enhancement," they usually think of NASA or the CIA, but a little digging would quickly reveal this media characterization was far from reality.

Murphy divulged that first he used screened photographs of the Patterson film found in a 1980 book (*Manlike Monsters on Trial,* edited by Marjorie Halpin and Michael M. Ames). Photo experts would later point out that the "noise" in a printed photo from the film, as opposed to the frames examined in the film, would be much greater and have much more chance of containing false information. Anyway, Murphy says he photocopied this photograph for a class project of his son's in 1995 and began questioning the film's validity after discovering an aberration when, using a computer, he zoomed in tighter and tighter on the frames, finding what appears to be a glimmering ornate latch in the shape of a bottle opener.

The big problem is that others can't see it.

Local Sasquatch club leader Ray Crowe summed up the feelings of a lot of people in the know when he said, "It's like picking a sheep out of the clouds. They've blown up the images beyond the size of recognition. So, they can pretty much see anything they imagine."

Steve Armstrong of Tampa, Florida–based Pegasus Imaging told reporter Joseph Rose he believes the film is such that it wouldn't capture an image of something as small as a buckle. And then there's the bit-mapped nature of digital compression and enlarging. "Zoom in on an image too much, and you get a lot of blocky artifacts," Armstrong said.

The result, said Jennifer Polanski of Adobe Systems, might be "a blob" that looks something like a belt buckle. Even with Adobe's popular Photoshop software, it's hard to see how someone can take a faraway figure like that in the Patterson-Gimlin film and zoom in on a metal fastener, she told me.

While Patterson died years ago, Gimlin, sixty-seven, still lives in Yakima. He dismisses the rumors in a 1999 interview as "wacko." "I was there. I saw [Bigfoot]. The film is genuine," Gimlin said to reporter Rose. "Anybody who says different is just trying to make a buck."

The critical blitz didn't end there. During mid-January 1999, at Yakima, rumors began circulating that the late Roger Patterson had paid a Hollywood costume designer to make the suit and paid a big "Yakima Indian" to wear it, and now the owner of the suit had hired a local attorney to bring it out of the closet for the world to see. Finally, late in January, mostly through reporter David Wasson of the *Yakima Herald—Republic,* the story broke with the headline "Bigfoot Unzipped—Man Claims It Was Him in a Suit."

Sparked by the "revelations" of the "fastener" story of Cliff

Crook–Chris Murphy, Zillah attorney Barry M. Woodard confirmed to Wasson that he was representing a Yakima man who said he wore the elaborate ape suit in the Patterson-Gimlin film, and that his client had passed a lie-detector test to prove it.

Wasson would write, "Woodard described the man only as a fifty-eight-year-old lifelong resident of the Yakima Valley who approached him a few months ago after a network news program called questioning authenticity of the 1967 film. The man wanted help negotiating a deal for rights to his story . . . as well as to explore any legal issues he might face as a result of his involvement in the hoax."

Attorney Woodard provided a statement from retired Yakima police officer Jim McCormick, a certified polygraph examiner who administered a lie-detector test on Woodard's client. Results of the seventy-five-minute examination showed the man was telling the truth when asked about having worn the Bigfoot suit in the 1967 film, McCormick wrote.

Why weren't they coming quickly forward with a name and details? Money reasons. Woodard's client supposedly wanted to sign a contract with the tabloid *Sun* before releasing any further information. But late in February 1999, a planned news conference never happened. Reports began to circulate that the fifty-eight-year-old, six-foot-tall man who now weighed two hundred pounds would be the laughingstock of a news conference when asked to demonstrate how thirty years earlier he was able to portray the special gait of a fifteen-hundred pound, six-and-a-half-to-seven-foot-tall Bigfoot. A year later, then two, now four, and no more news of this "exposé" has surfaced.

Why would there be so many attacks on the Patterson-Gimlin film at that moment in history? The reason is simple: money.

Follow the Imagined Money

The rights to the Patterson film were at a crossroads at the end of the twentieth century. Two people owned the rights to the Patterson film in 1999. They were Roger Patterson's widow, Patricia, and René Dahinden, the colorful Canadian-based, Swiss-born Sasquatch hunter who has been involved in tracking down Bigfoot since 1956. But Dahinden had cancer and would sadly pass away in 2001, and as his friends would say, "The vultures were circling."

Simply put, Pat Patterson owns the film (motion-picture) rights to the Patterson film, and Dahinden had the still-picture rights. They shared some video and CD-ROM rights. Pat Patterson has only been marginally interested in Bigfoot for years, but was getting more and more interested again. She now has a Web site and is mentioned more and more in discussions about the film. Dahinden, dealing with his painful cancer, did not enjoy spending his last days fighting Web masters stealing the photograph for their sites or dealing with the hoax claimers.

Dahinden had already been offered several thousand dollars, but he was angry, not in any mood to negotiate the rights to anyone. It is easy to see why he got so upset during 1999.

One way to undermine the financial worth of the Patterson film, of course, is to claim it is a hoax. If the film then becomes "spoiled" property, would it not be worth less on the open market? This is the kind of question that was going through the heads of Bigfoot researchers and Dahinden in those days, as everyone looked a little bit deeper into the newest "Patterson film is a hoax" articles in the papers.

For example, Chris Murphy, a stamp collector and investment manager living in Canada, first pushed the "fastener" tale. Interestingly, Murphy has a short history of interest in Bigfoot—of less than a decade. But during this time, he allegedly quickly sized up the field and approached René Dahinden, who has never made much money on the sale of his stills from the Patterson film, and asked about becoming Dahinden's promoter and manager.

Many people knew Dahinden as strong-willed and sometimes difficult to work with. After all, he was partially the model for the obsessed foreign-born Sasquatch hunter in the movie *Harry and the Hendersons,* and anyone who has seen that fictional film will recognize some of the nonfictional traits of Dahinden. But Murphy persisted and began to work with Dahinden. Murphy republished the 1966 Patterson book, distributed some books on the Snowman from Russia, and published a book on Bigfoot articles. He helped Dahinden get organized and developed a series of large-format prints of the frames from the Patterson film. But then he allegedly decided to publish a book on "Ohio Bigfoot" with a couple of little-known local researchers. Then to René Dahinden's great disappointment, Murphy wrote some things in the book as if Murphy were an expert on the Patterson film, even including some "enhancements" from the film where Murphy saw some baby Bigfoot in some of the frames. This was too much for Dahinden. Tempers grew between the men and they parted ways.

Then there is Cliff Crook, who was a decades-old rival of Dahinden's and the other nonfictional person depicted loosely in *Harry and the Hendersons.* He was a mild-mannered Bigfoot-studies participant from Washington State. Director of the self-styled Bigfoot Central, Crook is a true believer, having seen Bigfoot when he was just a teenager in 1956. But Murphy apparently fished around for someone to hook up with, to push his "fastener theory" with, and then found Crook. Together they attacked the Patterson film—which most of the public did not realize was certainly an indirect attack on René Dahinden (more than on Pat Patterson).

The story unfolding in Yakima appeared to be more of the same. News reporter Dave Wasson was quick to note in his reports

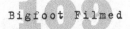

which individuals owned what with regards to the Patterson film. He mentioned the money trail but missed that contemporary elements were jockeying for position.

The truth of the matter is that not much money has ever been made from the Patterson film, but it certainly looks as if with anger, feuds, a looming death, and contract battles ahead, the *true* worth of this film—that it shows an undiscovered species of hominoid—was being forgotten.

Patterson-Gimlin Film Today

The case is far from being closed. Most Bigfoot experts, including John Green, Jeff Meldrum, as well as the late René Dahinden and late Grover Krantz, hold that the film is valid footage of an unknown primate. A $75,000 study by the North American Science Institute concluded that Patterson's filmed Bigfoot is authentic. The NASI's computer-enhancement analysis suggested that the creature's skin and musculature are what one would expect to find in a living animal, not in a hairy suit, however innovatively it was constructed.

The tantalizingly curious nature of the Patterson-Gimlin footage verifies for all time the need for more evidence and future searching. After all, the footage reinforces the notion that this creature is walking away from, not toward us, inviting us to follow.

8 Frozen Man

A film is one thing. A body is quite another. The year 1967 also brought to light what appears to a specimen of a kind of Bigfoot. It began with a mysterious millionaire who was debating what to do with a frozen hairy hominoid that had fallen into his hands. The owner of the Minnesota Iceman, as it would soon be called, wanted to display this frozen Bigfoot-like beast to see what people's reaction to the "missing link" would be. As the story would develop, the true owner did not wish to be "the one" to undercut the truth of biblical creation. How could this be accomplished without "scientists" getting the specimen? A plan was hatched. The body would be shown around Middle America, from one rural town's stock shows to the next, off the beaten track, and out of the limelight. No one would notice and the mystery owner could gauge public reaction. But then a series of events began to unravel the plot.

During the autumn of 1967, college zoology major Terry Cullen spotted an extraordinary exhibit in Milwaukee—a fresh, apparently authentic corpse of a hairy, manlike animal. For twenty-five cents people could see the "man left over from the Ice Age" that exhibitor Frank Hansen kept frozen in a block of ice inside a refrigerated glass coffin.

After trying unsuccessfully during 1967 and 1968 to interest mainstream academic anthropologists, Cullen alerted Ivan T. Sanderson, a naturalist and author of the successful book *Abominable Snowmen*. Sanderson's houseguest in New Jersey at the time was none other that the Belgian cryptozoologist Bernard Heuvelmans, author of *On the Track of Unknown Animals*.

What everyone wanted to know was, why hadn't anyone noticed this thing before? After all, the body had been on public exhibit for almost two years in Minnesota, Illinois, Wisconsin, Texas, Oklahoma, and other states. Why hadn't anyone spotted it before Cullen? Sanderson answered such questions this way: "Just how many people with proper training in any of the biological sciences (including medical practitioners and students) go to such shows? If any do, how many are trained physical anthropologists or primatologists? How many have ever heard of the ABSM [abominable snowman] search? The answer is: practically nobody who attended the exhibit."

After hearing from Cullen on December 12, 1968, however, Sanderson invited Heuvelmans, and the two immediately traveled to see firsthand what Hansen was showing at fairs and shopping centers across the American Midwest. For three days, from December 16 through 18, 1968, Sanderson and Heuvelmans examined the creature in Hansen's cramped trailer. The specimen was an adult male with large hands and feet. Its skin was covered with dark brown hair three to four inches long. The creature had apparently been shot through one eye, which dangled on its face, but it also had a gaping wound and open fracture on its left arm. Smelling putrefaction where some of the flesh had been exposed from the melting ice, the two concluded that the creature was authentic. They could hardly believe what they saw.

A Look Back

Heuvelmans described it this way in the *Bulletin of the Royal Institute of Natural Sciences of Belgium:*

> The specimen at first looks like a man, or, if you prefer, an adult human being of the male sex, of rather normal height (six feet) and proportions but excessively hairy. It is entirely covered with very dark brown hair three to four inches long. Its skin appears waxlike, similar in color to the cadavers of white men not tanned by the sun. . . . The specimen is lying on its back . . . the left arm is twisted behind the head with the palm of the hand upward. The arm makes a strange curve, as if it were that of a sawdust doll, but this curvature is due to an open fracture midway between the wrist and the elbow where one can distinguish the broken ulna in a gaping wound. The right arm is twisted and held tightly against the flank, with the hand spread palm down over the right side of the abdomen. Between the right finger and the medius the penis is visible, lying obliquely on the groin. The testicles are vaguely distinguishable at the juncture of the thighs.

Sanderson and Heuvelmans nicknamed the creature Bozo. Later Sanderson would write about it in the May 1969 issue of *Argosy:*

> Bozo's face is his most startling feature, both to anthropologists and anyone else—and for several reasons. Unfortunately, both eyeballs have been "blown out" of their sockets. One appears to be missing, but the other seems (to some, at least) to be just visible under the ice. This gives Bozo a gruesome appearance, which is enhanced by a considerable amount of blood diffused from the sockets through the ice. The most arresting feature of the face is the nose. This is large but only fairly wide, and is distinctly "pugged," rather like that of a Pekinese dog—but not like

that of a gorilla, which actually doesn't have a nose, per se. The nostrils are large, circular and point straight forward, which is very odd. The mouth is only fairly wide and there is no eversion of the lips; in fact, the average person would say he had no lips at all. His "muzzle" is no more bulging, prominent, or pushed forward than is our own; not at all prognathous like that of a chimp. One side of the mouth is slightly agape and two small teeth can be seen. These should be the right upper canine and the first premolar. The canine or eye-tooth is very small and in no way exaggerated into a tusk, or similar to that of a gorilla or a chimp. But—to me, at least—the most interesting features of all are some folds and wrinkle lines around the mouth just below the cheeks. These are absolutely human, and are like those seen in a heavy-jowled, older white man.

Although Hansen wanted the discovery kept quiet, both Heuvelmans and Sanderson wrote scientific papers on the creature within the year. Heuvelmans named it *Homo pongoides*. Sanderson, who was a well-known nature personality on TV, mentioned the Iceman on the *Tonight Show with Johnny Carson* during Christmas week of 1968. Bozo was out of the bag.

The body then disappeared under mysterious circumstances. U.S. Customs became involved when Frank Hansen exhibited the carcass in Canada. During one of these border crossings Hansen said he had replaced the original with the model made in Hollywood, and Customs let him go back to Minnesota. Had Hansen made up the story of the model to get it through Customs? Was he still showing the real thing? Or did the switch take place when the FBI came around Hansen's place in the following days? We will never know.

Anthropologist John Napier, then of the Smithsonian, interested Smithsonian president S. Dillion Ripley in trying to relocate

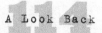

the original carcass for official study. When the Smithsonian Institution got involved, Hansen explained that the creature was owned by a millionaire and declined to have it examined further. Later, sometime after February 1969, Ripley wrote to J. Edgar Hoover, asking him to get involved. Hoover was not helpful or interested. He said that as there was no violation of a federal law, the FBI would not officially pursue the matter.

In any case, at some point, the model replaced the original, with various Hollywood makeup artists claiming to have created the Iceman. How do we know that a model replaced the original body? Thanks to photographs of the traveling exhibit that Mark A. Hall and I took, Sanderson and Heuvelmans would later be able to enumerate at least fifteen technical differences between the original and the replacement. They held these in secret in order to differentiate a model from the real thing.

I saw the "exhibit" at the Illinois State Fair in 1969. I wondered at the time whether this was the real thing or the copy. I photographed it extensively and sent copies of those photos to Ivan T. Sanderson and Mark A. Hall. From those photos, Sanderson told me I had seen a copy. Mark A. Hall in Minnesota had a similar experience in 1969, photographing Hansen's exhibit as it traveled around the upper Midwest, and exchanging those photos with me and Sanderson. Hall would later go on to be director of Sanderson's Society for the Investigation of the Unexplained and become the main chronicler of the Minnesota Iceman mystery.

The Mystery Continues — Some skeptics have shelved the Minnesota Iceman as a joke, a carnival display to fool people. But the Iceman was never a "carnival" exhibit. Carnivals have a certain reputation, personnel, and level of exhibitions. The exhibition milieu in which the Minnesota Iceman was shown was not that of a carnival. Throughout the Midwest, in the 1960s and 1970s, the Minnesota Iceman was shown at stock fairs, state fairs, and shopping malls. Hansen had also shown antique tractors in these shows. He was not a "carnie." The elitist practice of labeling the Minnesota Iceman a "carnival exhibit" is a way to immediately diminish the possible significance of this evidence even before another word is spoken.

Some of this evidence has never seen the light of day—especially in English. Early in 2000, French researchers Jean Roche and Michel Raynal reminded the cryptozoology world that Bernard Heuvelmans's detailed color slides of the Minnesota Iceman had never been published. Remarkably, much of Heuvelmans's work on the Iceman remains outside of an English-language readership as well. Bernard Heuvelmans and Boris F. Porchnev, in *L'Homme de Neanderthal est toujours vivant* (Paris: Librairie Plon, 1974), wrote a single-spaced, five-hundred-page technical overview of the Minnesota Iceman that should have been translated into English years ago. It has not.

The Smell of a Mystery

One of the pieces of evidence in support of the reality of the Minnesota Iceman is the smell of rotting flesh that Heuvelmans and Sanderson mentioned in their discussions of the Iceman. Here's how Sanderson noted it: "Let me say, simply, that one look was actually enough to convince us that this was—from our point of view, at least—'the genuine article.' This was no phony Chinese trick, or 'art' work. If nothing else confirmed this, the appalling stench of rotting flesh exuding from a point in the insulation of the coffin would have been enough." Debunkers have said this is an old "carnie" illusion, wherein one puts a piece of old meat underneath the exhibit, discouraging people from staying long, so that more people can get in. But it's not such a simple matter with the Minnesota Iceman.

The entire putrefaction episode is well summarized in Hall's book *Living Fossils:* "In the course of the inspection Heuvelmans touched a hot lamp to the top pane of glass, causing cracks in it. The result was the smell of putrefaction came through the cracks." The smell was the result of an accident during Bernard Heuvelmans's close-quarters examination, not the result of something that Frank Hansen could ever have foreseen.

When I saw the model in exhibition in 1969, there was no smell manufactured to distract or fool people. The Minnesota Iceman was exhibited in a glass coffin, as was the original, with no smell coming from the exhibit. If this was a faked model that was supposed to reek with reality, more than ever a manufactured smell would have been called for in such a showing.

What Is the Minnesota Iceman?

Ivan T. Sanderson and Bernard Heuvelmans disagreed over the exact nature of the Iceman. Heuvelmans's scientific paper of his description of this new form of living Neandertal, which he named *Homo pongoides* (i.e., "apelike man"), was published in February 1969, in the *Bulletin of the Royal Institute of Natural Sciences of Belgium*. Few anthropologists today have read it, of course.

"For the first time in history," wrote zoologist Bernard Heuvelmans, the Father of Cryptozoology, "a fresh corpse of Neanderthal-like man has been found. It means that this form of Hominid, thought to be extinct since prehistoric times, is still living today. The long search for rumored live 'ape-men' or 'missing links' has at last been successful. This was not accomplished by expeditions to faraway places and at great expense, but by the accidental discovery, in this country, of a corpse preserved in ice. . . . This specimen is a contemporary representative of an unknown form of Hominid, most probably a relic of the

Neanderthal type. The belief, based on strong testimonial evidence, that small, scattered populations of Neanderthals survive has been held for years by some scientists, mostly Russian and Mongolian."

In Sanderson's 1969 paper for the Italian scientific journal *Genus,* he wrote that the Minnesota Iceman "most certainly should not be assigned to the Neanderthals race or complex."

Several notable Heuvelmans followers disagree with Sanderson, of course. One is the recently murdered Jordi Magraner, a French-Spanish zoologist who did fieldwork in north Pakistan and Afghanistan during the 1990s in search of the local wildman, the *Barmanu.* He collected more than fifty firsthand sighting accounts, and all eyewitnesses recognized the reconstruction of Heuvelmans's *Homo pongoides.* They picked out *Homo pongoides* as their match to *Barmanu* from Magraner's ID kit of drawings of apes, fossil men, aboriginals, monkeys, and the Minnesota Iceman. Magraner agreed this may be a Neandertal. Of course, this only proves the *Barmanu* looks like *Homo pongoides,* not that it is a Neandertal.

Helmut Loofs-Wissowa, an anthropologist at Australian National University, also thinks Heuvelmans was correct. He too points to the Neandertals, represented by the Minnesota Iceman, as the source of relict populations of wildmen he has studied in Vietnam. Loofs-Wissowa's creative work links the semi-erect penis of *Homo pongoides* with what he sees as Paleolithic cave art and other evidence he connects to Neandertals. His scholarly considerations are worthy of a close reading by all interested in this question.

Mark A. Hall, after being close to the investigation for the last quarter century, is not bothered by the assignment of *Homo pongoides* to the Asian examples that these scholars have focused on. He merely thinks they have the wrong fossil ancestor linked to the accidental American, the Minnesota Iceman. Hall considers the more proper prehistoric candidate to be *Homo erectus.*

The Iceman appears to be an *accidental,* in other words, not of

local origin. Heuvelmans theorized the Iceman was a Neandertal who had been murdered in Vietnam during the war and smuggled into the United States in a "body bag." Its *erectus*-like features, however, match quite well some of the reports coming out of Central Asia, within and just north of Pakistan. Hall questions the Iceman's supposed Vietnamese origin and alleged Neandertal affinity and today feels the original Minnesota Iceman was of south-central Asian *Homo erectus* origin, perhaps even a *Barmanu*.

Or Was It a Bigfoot?

We should also consider the possibility that the Minnesota Iceman was an example of the Eastern subspecies of Bigfoot.

Jean Roche, a French cryptozoologist and the author of *Sauvage et velus: Yéti, Sasquash, Almasty, Barmanou, Bigfoot,* tends to believe some of what Frank Hansen said about the origins of the Minnesota Iceman — that he had shot the creature during the 1960 deer-hunting season while he was staying in a small resort on the shores of the Whiteface Reservoir, at Aurora, Minnesota. He was hunting with Lieutenants Roy Aafedt and Dave Allison, and Major Lou Szrot, when the Iceman was killed.

Hansen reported that the Bigfoot he killed engaged in predatory behavior. As Roche points out in his 2002 theory, that was not known at the time of the peak Iceman media attention (1967–70), but it is well-known now, including the extensive records of these beasts in the Great Lakes area (e.g., Ohio, Pennsylvania, Wisconsin, Michigan, Minnesota) where Hansen said he killed the Iceman.

But clearly, Roche is careful, and he writes me, "Hansen has told several other stories about the case. But I believe he lied just in order to protect himself."

We may never know what became of the Minnesota Iceman. Until one of these mystery primates is discovered, we will not understand the true role the Iceman should play in the history of hairy-hominoids studies. But for now, we must accept that the enigma of the Minnesota Iceman remains as one of the most hotly debated episodes in hominology. And, indeed, it may belong in the classic Bigfoot file, after all.

9 Bossburg, Momo, and Other Flaps

After the remarkable film footage from Bluff Creek and the Minnesota Iceman episode, the feeling in Bigfoot circles was that "we are so close to catching this animal." Anything could happen next.

Bossburg What did occur was Bossburg, an event that
⬚⬚⬚⬚⬚⬚⬚⬚⬚ has had a long-term impact on the pursuit of Bigfoot in the Pacific Northwest. As British anthropologist John Napier would remark years later, Bossburg would have a "claim to fame" for producing some of the most complex and compelling tracks seen to date.

Bossburg is located in the extreme northeastern corner of Washington State, in Stevens County, a relatively easy twenty-mile journey from British Columbia, as the crow flies. Near Bossburg's town dump, a butcher named Joseph Rhodes had found the first tracks on November 24, 1969, and noticed that one foot of the set was "crippled," to use the description popular at the time. The word spread quickly among Bigfoot researchers. John Green told René Dahinden that Ivan Marx, formerly of the Tom Slick expedition, was in pursuit of a "crippled" Bigfoot. Dahinden called Marx, then took off for Bossburg before the end of November, apparently.

When Dahinden arrived, he found and covered one of the better pair of tracks. One clearly showed that the right foot that had made the track was deformed: it looked as if it had two bumps out to the side and only four toes showing. Using what he found available, a cardboard box, Dahinden casually preserved what many consider to be one of the best pieces of Bigfoot evidence ever found. Dahinden took pictures, cast it, and saw this was something unique.

Seven hundred miles away, in western British Columbia, taxidermist Bob Titmus, who had taught Jerry Crew how to cast the tracks at Bluff Creek in 1958, made his way to Bossburg. His behavior was curious to Dahinden, who wrote that Titmus "went out and bought an eight-pound slab of beef and hung it in a tree. I believe he was sitting out there at night in his panel truck, watching the meat, and thinking that if this thing was a cripple and was living off the garbage dump, when it came along, he would just grab it by the arse and throw it in the truck and run off home with it."

Another Bigfoot hunter, Norm Davis, had a similar notion and put out a bowl of fruit in the hope of nabbing the Bigfoot. Titmus left within three days. Then Dahinden shared Davis's trailer, and before long, the trailer was on Ivan Marx's land, and all three had combined resources.

On Saturday, December 13, 1969, after a significant snowfall, Dahinden, Marx, and a local man named Jim Hopkins were looking for signs of Bigfoot around Roosevelt Lake, where they found tracks. Boy, did they find tracks!

The series of tracks they discovered, in their number and clarity, remains one of the best footprint series ever revealed of Bigfoot in America. These men found and carefully counted 1,089 "clearly defin-

able prints," as writer Don Hunter would put it in his book, *Sasquatch*, with René Dahinden. These crippled tracks, wrote Hunter, "were, and are still, among the most convincing tangible evidence to be turned up in his [Dahinden's] years as a Sasquatch hunter. The left footprint measured 17 1/2 inches long, 6 1/2 inches across the ball of the foot, and 5 1/2 inches across the heel; the right one was 16 1/2 inches long, 7 inches across the ball, and also 5 1/2 inches at the heel. The right foot was deformed; the third toe was either badly twisted over or was missing, there being only a slight impression in the snow at its base; the little toe stuck out at a sharp angle; and the whole foot curved outwards and showed two distinct lumps on the outer edge."

The unusually long trail revealed much about the Bossburg "cripple" trajectory. The creature had followed the waterways (around the lake and from a river), crossed railroad tracks, and stepped over a five-wire fence forty-three inches high as it crossed a road. Then it rested, apparently, in a depression of the pine forest floor before going up a hill, then back down, where "yellow snow" showed it had taken a piss. In these days of DNA tests, we would all have thought about taking a sample of the obvious Bigfoot urine. But that was 1969, and these nonacademic, amateur Bigfooters did not. They missed a golden opportunity.

From there, the Bigfoot appeared to backtrack to near where it had come before, through some of the underbrush, and to an overhang at the river's edge. The trail of tracks, which Dahinden, Marx, and Hopkins followed upstream, finally vanished where the Bigfoot descended the river's bank into a rocky section where tracks would not show.

Dahinden photographed the tracks carefully and examined each print in the route seven times. They did not have many resources, so they kept some of the prints from the snow in Marx's freezer. These would later be discarded in a bout of frustrated Bigfooters' depression.

When tourists and their cameras descended on the area, the evidence was trampled and ruined. But the Bossburg flap continued. A U.S. Border Patrol officer found new tracks on the far side of the river, on December 18, 1969. The distinctive prints of the cripple foot could be seen, though a recent rain had mostly washed them out.

Dahinden pulled in some help from British Columbia friend Roy Fardell, and Roger St. Hilaire, a young San Francisco zoologist. The two were interested in establishing the validity of the prints— or discovering any fakery.

When I interviewed Roger St. Hilaire in 2002, he shared with me his memories of what he had found at Bossburg:

> I went to Bossburg twice, once in the winter 1969/1970 and again in the fall 1970.
>
> The alleged Bigfoot tracks found in the snow in Bossburg, WA, were all obliterated, except for one that had been covered with cardboard, when I arrived from California. This last remaining track was of the right (deformed) foot and the impression in the snow was somewhat distorted, presumably from repeated freezing and thawing. The track was close to the road just beyond a barbed-wire fence, which was about waist high. I could not determine from evidence available at the scene, or subsequently disclosed, whether the track was fake or real. Of course one probably cannot prove with absolute certainty that any track is a fake unless you catch someone in the act of creating a fake track. We all took pictures and later used the original casts of the footprints to make duplicates. Some Bigfoot researchers may have found enough evidence at the site to make conclusions, I did not.
>
> I know from my discussions with René, at the time, that he was very impressed with the thousand-plus alleged

Bigfoot tracks that he saw before I got there. I don't know if René may have changed his mind about the Bossburg tracks in later years. At the time I was with him in Bossburg, he was very excited about them and was convinced enough about the potential at Bossburg to support, out of his own pocket, the efforts of the Bigfoot hunters who worked with him.

Although the general feeling among our group was that the tracks were authentic, we (René, Roy Fardell, myself, and Dennis Jensen) all maintained a healthy degree of skepticism. We were looking for "hard evidence" of the existence of Bigfoot, and tracks in the snow were just not enough. We were also looking for any evidence that would prove that the tracks had been faked. We spent many weeks following up on leads and combing the banks of the Columbia River and the area around Bossburg on foot, by snowmobile, automobile, and sometimes by airplane, for any additional sign of Bigfoot. René was with us in the field almost every day, and I recall one day when he and I hiked about thirty miles and emerged from the bush long after dark. We found numerous lion, bobcat, coyote, deer, and other animal tracks in the snow during our excursions, but nothing related to Bigfoot.

By December 1969, the personnel hunting the Bossburg Bigfoot included Roger Patterson and his associate Dennis Jensen. Patterson would come and go, but Jensen, as chroniclers such as Dahinden and Napier would point out, would stay in Bossburg to "protect" the Patterson-lead pursuit. Ohio millionaire Tom Page's funding was in evidence with off-road vehicles, newfangled snowmobiles, and thorough air searches.

Dahinden, Patterson, Marx, Jensen, Fardell, St. Hilaire, and others held together as a loosely knit group of Bigfoot hunters through most of early January 1970. Then on the twenty-seventh the Joe Metlow–Bill Streeter affair occurred.

On that day Joe Metlow claimed he had found a cream-colored Sasquatch, discovered where it lived, and immobilized it in a cave. And he wanted the bidding to start. Patterson was being marginally funded by Tom Page and was on the phone with Page immediately. Page flew out, and the big split between the Patterson camp and the Dahinden camp began.

Page was willing to spend $35,000 initially for a Bigfoot, alive or dead. Then Dahinden got into the bidding and John Green came down to Bossburg. Green served essentially as a mediator between the two camps. The bidding had reached $55,000 for the Bigfoot. Page's helicopter was standing by at Colville airport to take the hairy primate away via his "Exercise Sasquatch-Retrieval." But Metlow's story kept changing. Don Hunter captured what happened next:

> René, by now back in Bossburg and in an apparent
> moment of truce with the Patterson team, paid a visit with
> Jensen to Metlow's home. Conversation was general and
> quite genial until Metlow casually mentioned that he had a
> Sasquatch foot in his freezer. The fur hit the fan again.
> René immediately offered $500 for one peek at the
> exhibit. Metlow raised him to $5,000. The excitement
> brought Dickie Davis to the scene, antennae quivering.
> Before you could say, "Bigfoot," Davis had a contract
> sketched out. It would include John Green to write the
> book, Bob Titmus to skin and dissect the foot's owner—
> presumably stashed in a cave somewhere above the snow
> line—and anthropologist Dr. Grover Krantz to introduce
> it to science. René was out, so was Patterson.

After a series of wild Sasquatch chases, following instructions left by Metlow, the Bigfoot hunters figured out there was nothing to

the claims and feelings grew raw in Bossburg. Lots of resources, funding, and energy had been wasted. The hunters left town discouraged, but more educated about human nature.

Ivan Marx Dahinden would keep in touch with Ivan Marx throughout 1970, and Ivan would always have an exciting new find—a new print, some even of hands, and *the 1971 film*. Tom Page told me that he flew back in, offering Marx $25,000 for the film, but it proved to be a hoax.

In *Sasquatch: The Apes Among Us*, John Green's chapter entitled "Ivan" is not about Ivan T. Sanderson, but concerns Ivan Marx. Green says that Ivan Marx, during the 1950s, was known as "the biggest, well, yarn-spinner in California." Marx was involved in Tom Slick's efforts in 1960; Marx's activities then are one of the major reasons that René Dahinden decided to leave that California search and go back to Canada.

After living in Burney, California, for years, Marx moved to Bossburg, Washington, by 1969. The famed Bossburg "crippled" Bigfoot prints started soon thereafter and continued until 1971, with Dahinden, Krantz, Green, Patterson, and others finding their way to Bossburg. Millionaire Bigfoot supporter Tom Page made an appearance. Peter Byrne appeared and reportedly put Marx on a $750 monthly retainer as a Sasquatch hunter when the 1971 film surfaced. But Byrne would soon identify where the film was taken and discover that the copy of the film he had been given was blank.

Marx's impact on the field cannot be ignored. I interviewed Ivan Marx in 1998. He was ill at the time. Is Marx's involvement in Bossburg overlooked or ignored? Could it be that Marx merely happened to be near when lightning, so to speak, struck Bossburg?

The zoologist Roger St. Hilaire reflected on Ivan Marx's involvement with these words:

As I remember, there was suspicion about the alleged Bigfoot tracks because of several reasons. The tracks were close to the road where they could easily be found. It appeared that some individuals stood to gain from a discovery of Bigfoot tracks in the area and the resulting publicity and potential funding for expeditions. Some of these individuals also had previous association with events related to Bigfoot. The tracks were in snow, and as I recall being told, went in one direction for a while and then reversed course ending up on surfaces which left no imprints; consequently, they could not be followed. How convenient! Just about every other animal track we found in that snow could be followed. I know René shared some of these suspicions.

My suspicions about the tracks were somewhat mitigated by the presence of the deformed foot. Why fake a deformed foot? It made no sense and I could not reconcile this issue. We were all really puzzled by the presence of the apparent deformity.

On one side, we have Napier, Krantz, and now anthropologist Jeff Meldrum, sensing the Bossburg prints are valid. On the other, we have Dahinden's opinions expressed in the Hunter/Dahinden book and in public about Marx and Bossburg. Green says simply in his 1978 book: "I tend now to write off the whole Bossburg episode to entertainment."

Legacy of Cripple Foot

What happened during those months in Bossburg is now, as they say, history. What remains are the left and right plaster casts of the Cripple Foot pair.

Grover Krantz, the late anthropologist who was one of the first academics to seriously consider the reality of Bigfoot, obtained

and studied the Cripple Foot tracks early in 1970. The casts he acquired were not the imprints from the 1,089 tracks series, however. Remember the tracks that René Dahinden covered with a cardboard box? The copies that Krantz received were of those two originals, found weeks earlier. And Krantz liked what he saw. Krantz made molds and studied them in some depth. These tracks have become extremely important. Incredible as it may sound, the Bossburg footprints are the one piece of evidence that changed Krantz from a Sasquatch skeptic to a Bigfoot believer. "Before I examined these prints, I would have given you ten to one odds that the whole thing was a hoax," he wrote in his 1992 book, *Big Footprints: A Scientific Inquiry into the Reality of Sasquatch*. "But there is no way that everything could have been tied together so perfectly in a fake."

The anthropologist John Napier also felt these tracks were genuine. He wrote in his book, *Bigfoot: The Yeti and Sasquatch in Myth and Reality* (1972): "Either some of the footprints are real, or all are fakes. If they are all fakes, then an explanation invoking legend and folk memory is adequate to explain the mystery. But if any of them is real, then as scientists we have a lot to explain. Among other things we shall have to rewrite the story of human evolution. We shall have to accept that *Homo sapiens* is not the one and only living product of the hominid line, and we shall have to admit that there are still major mysteries to be solved in a world we thought we knew so well."

The Grover Krantz–certified Bossburg prints are now known worldwide. Krantz sold them to many researchers, who have made copies that you can find on eBay today. Beginning in 2003, the company Bone Clones continued selling copies of the Cripple Foot prints through their catalog, on behalf of the Krantz estate (see Appendix B).

The reality of the Cripple Foot, an unfortunate name, which will live on, exists in the very nature of its unfortunate structure. As John Napier observed, "It is very difficult to conceive of a hoaxer so subtle, so knowledgeable—and so sick—who would deliberately fake a footprint of this nature. I suppose it is possible, but it is so unlikely that I am prepared to discount it."

The question that remains today is, was Ivan Marx merely lucky once and then attempted to stay in the limelight through hoaxes? Or was the Bossburg incident, from beginning to end, just an entertaining episode that should today be viewed as a cautionary tale? You be the judge.

Momo The largest Bigfoot flap of the early 1970s, was the Momo (MO Monster) series. It all began in July 1971, when Joan Mills and Mary Ryan were on a backwoods road, Highway 79, which runs north of Louisiana, Missouri. What they saw looked like a "half-ape and half-man" to them. Of course, the thing that upset them most was that it "made a little gurgling sound like someone trying to whistle underwater," according to Mills.

The real Momo scare actually began one year later, on Tuesday, July 11, 1972, at 3:30 P.M. on the outskirts of the city of Louisiana (pop. 4,600). Terry Harrison (age eight) and his brother Wally (age five) were playing in their yard, which sits at the foot of Marzolf Hill. The two boys had gone off by some old rabbit pens in the woods next to the Harrison property. Suddenly, their older sister Doris, who was inside, heard them scream and looked out the bathroom window. She saw something standing by a tree: "Six or seven feet tall, black and hairy. It stood like a man but it didn't look like one to me."

The Harrisons' dog got very sick shortly after the incident. Its eyes grew red and it vomited for hours, finally recovering after a meal of bread and milk.

That same afternoon Mrs. Clarence Lee, who lives half a block away, heard animal sounds: growling and "carrying on something terrible." Not long afterward she talked with a farmer whose dog, a recent gift, had disappeared. He wondered if the "monster" had

taken it. (Remember the recent case from Wisconsin mentioned in the first chapter? That Bigfoot was said to have an animal under its arm. Momo, as described by the witnesses in 1972, was flecked with blood, probably from the dead dog it had carried under its arm. Its face could not be seen under the mass of hair covering it, and it seemed to be without a neck.)

On July 14, Edgar Harrison and some members of his congregation sighted two "fireballs" soaring from over Marzolf Hill. At about nine-fifteen, Harrison heard something that sounded like a loud growl coming from near the metal water reservoir at the top of the hill. It got louder and louder and kept coming closer. "I wanted to wait and see what it was that was making this noise," he said. "My family insisted that I drive away, and so I drove down Allen Street across the Town Branch."

Late that evening, Harrison, along with several others, explored Marzolf Hill and came to an old building from which a pungent, unpleasant odor was emanating. Harrison subsequently described it as "a moldy, horse smell or a strong garbage smell." This was not to be the only time he encountered the odor—in the days ahead he would find it whenever he approached an area from which the strange noises seemed to be coming.

Around five o'clock the following morning, Pat Howard of Louisiana saw "a dark object" walking like a man cross the road near the hill.

On the twentieth, Richard Crowe (a reporter for Chicago's *Irish Times* and for *Fate* magazine) and Loren Smith went up the hill with Harrison for another look. Near the tree where Doris had seen the monster, Crowe wrote, "There was a circular spot in the brush where leaves and twigs had been stripped from the branches." Farther along, Crowe found evidence that someone or something had been digging in an old garbage dump, and not far away Harrison showed him two disinterred dog graves with the bones scattered about.

Higher up the hill they came upon two tracks some distance from each other. The first, over ten inches long and five inches wide, appeared to be a footprint; the other, five inches long and curved, was evidently the print of a hand. The prints had been made in hard soil (there had been no rain for ten days), and Crowe estimated that it would take a minimum of two hundred pounds of pressure to create such impressions.

Harrison led Crowe to an abandoned shack that Harrison thought might serve as a resting place for the monster. While they were there, Harrison's dog Chubby suddenly ran away; "then," Crowe wrote, "we smelled an overwhelming stench that could only be described as resembling rotten flesh or foul, stagnant water."

"That's him, boys!" Harrison exclaimed. "He's around here somewhere." They shone their flashlights through the surrounding trees but saw nothing. In the distance they could hear dogs barking furiously. (While the monster was about, dogs would refuse to go up the hill, but would run up and down the street, agitated.) Within five minutes the odor had subsided.

Harrison, Smith, and Crowe smelled it twice more before the night was over. On Friday, July 21, Ellis Minor, who lives along River Road, was sitting home alone around 10 or 10:30 P.M. when he heard his bird dog start to growl. At first, Minor thought the stimulus was another dog passing through the yard, but when the dog growled again, Minor snapped on his powerful flashlight and stepped outside—where he saw a six-foot-tall creature with long black hair standing erect. As soon as the light hit it, the thing turned around and dashed across the road, past the railroad tracks, and into the woods.

Late in July mysterious three-toed tracks made by something with an oval foot appeared on the Freddie Robbins farm eight miles south of Louisiana, Missouri. On August 3, just before dawn, Mr. and Mrs. Bill Suddarth, who farmed northwest of the town, heard a high-pitched howl in their yard, grabbed flashlights, and headed outside. In the middle of the garden mud they observed four tracks of a three-toed creature. Suddarth quickly phoned Clyd Penrod, a hunting buddy, who drove over to make a plaster cast of the best print. Penrod was puzzled by the whole affair.

"It was twenty to twenty-five feet from the tracks to anything else," he said. "I can't understand how they were made." They began nowhere and ended nowhere, and no other tracks were found anywhere else on the property.

The Suddarth prints were different from the ones discovered at the Robbins farm; these second prints were narrower, longer, and more perfectly formed. But both clearly showed three toes, not five.

Just Across the Border Momo was not the only monster to frighten Middle America that summer of 1972. In the extreme northwestern part of Arkansas, a state that borders Missouri on the south, the summer brought several reports of an imperfectly observed, vaguely described "creature." It first appeared, according to an article in Fayetteville's *Northwest Arkansas Times,* sometime in January, when on two occasions Mrs. C. W. Humphrey of Springdale heard dogs barking loudly, looked out the door of her trailer home, and saw a "creature" strolling on by. In the following months, several other persons in the neighborhood caught a glimpse of the thing, but only in the dark, and so they did not get a good look at it. Early in July, Pete Ragland shot at the creature with a .22 pistol.

Then, starting at ten-fifteen on the evening of July 20, the climactic events took place. Mrs. Humphrey, her three sons, and a daughter-in-law were sleeping when they were awakened by pounding on the trailer. Mrs. Humphrey quieted one of the children and went outside to find the cause.

There she encountered the "biggest-looking thing I ever saw"—something that alternately walked upright and crawled on all fours. Shortly afterward, Bill Hurst, who lives just south of the Humphrey residence, sighted the creature in his garden. It was staring at him with "two great big eyes." He was sure it was some sort of animal (others had thought it might be a huge man). When he yelled at it, it took off running.

The night of September 6, 1972, Barbara Robinson of Springdale called police to report that a prowler had peered through a bedroom window of her house. The policeman who investigated remarked that the prowler "had to be at least seven feet tall" since the window was that high and there was nothing in the immediate area on which he could have stood.

Was the Monster a Bigfoot?

Between 1967, with the Patterson-Gimlin Bigfoot footage and the commercial release in 1987 of *Harry and the Hendersons,* most people developed a set idea of what a Bigfoot looked like. Reexamining the cases from the 1960s and 1970s is a good exercise in clarification of what may really be out there.

In the decade before the Momo sightings, people were being visited by creatures that looked like the Missouri monster—huge, hulky, and with hair in their eyes. One series was from Sister Lakes, Michigan. The Cass County events of 1964, were quickly labeled the Monster of Sister Lakes by the papers. They involved sightings by migrant strawberry workers, the strawberry farm's owners, and soon, local residents. First seen in 1962 but kept mostly quiet, the Sister Lakes creature was described much like Momo, with little facial detail, a huge, hairy bulk, and shoulders disappearing into its neck.

Finally in May 1964, the Sister Lakes "monster" caused terrified fruit pickers to leave the fields. Then on June 9, one of the workers, Gordon Brown, and his brother clearly saw the thing in their car headlights—it looked like a nine-foot-tall, rigidly upright cross between a bear and a gorilla. The farmers Elevelyn and John Utrup also reported several encounters. On June 11, Joyce Smith fainted and Gail and Patsy Clayton froze in fear when these three thirteen-year-old girls saw the monster on a lonely road in Silver Creek Township. It merely turned and took off into the woods.

On August 13, 1965, a similar huge, dark creature with hair all over its body and face placed its arm in the car Christine Van Acker was sitting in with her mother near Monroe, Michigan. Panicking, they took off, and the image of the black eye that Van Acker received from the encounter was sent around the world by the wire services. The animal she drew was almost a mirror reflection of what would be seen less than a decade later in Louisiana, Missouri. Van Acker's drawing showed a bulky, hairy, bipedal beast with hair in its eyes. The image of Harry created by Rick Baker for the movies was not part of the equation yet, and these sightings were clearly showing something other than the Patterson Bigfoot.

When I began hunting for these elusive Momo-like creatures, discussions of Bigfoot in the East were still relatively rare. Over time, Momo and his mystifying kin grew to symbolize a specific geographic variety of Bigfoot in the East, which during those exciting times in the years 1960 to 1973 were known simply as "monsters."

And I was hot on their trail.

10 On the Trail in the Midwest

I grew up in Illinois and did many field investigations there in the 1960s and early 1970s. During this time, I heard what people claimed was a "Bigfoot" cry and I discovered some "Bigfoot" footprints. But I have never seen a Bigfoot—not in my four decades of searching. I've put the word *Bigfoot* in quotes with reference to my experiences, as Illinois gives us a good example of the differences between the classic Bigfoot of the Northwest, the shorter, more aggressive Eastern Bigfoot, and the much more apelike Southern Bigfoot, which is sometimes seen on the fringes of the Midwest and which I will discuss in detail in the next chapter.

One highlight of my field research came early on for me—the finding of decidedly anthropoid prints not far from where I lived. In the spring of 1962, I, along with my brothers Bill and Jerry, came upon apelike foot tracks in a dry creek bed (a side branch of Stevens Creek) near Decatur, in south-central Illinois. The best print from the series was about ten inches long, with a clearly visible, large opposed toe, the hallux, sticking out to the right of a left-foot impression. The dipping creek bed did not allow much movement on the part of this apparently upright primate, but about thirteen inches in front of one print was another partial footprint. The complete track is very much like those found throughout the South.

During this time I was also interviewing many local residents about the Bigfoot-like creatures they were seeing. For instance, I spoke to Steve Collins and Bob Earle, who had an encounter with a grayish creature in 1962. They saw it in Stevens Creek, just off of East Williams Street Road, Decatur. The monster stood upright in water, glaring at them. Its strange features, humanlike and animal-like at the same time, told them this was no bear. The beast then disappeared into the woods. Later, the witnesses told me it was "like no other animal" they had ever seen.

On September 22, 1965, the local newspaper, the *Decatur Review,* carried a sighting report, from four young people who were parked in a car at a "lovers' lane" area outside Decatur called Montezuma Hills, near Stevens Creek. They were sitting in the car when a massive, black, manlike shape came toward their vehicle. They rushed off in a panic, but after dropping off their dates at home, the two young men returned to the area for another look. As they searched around the same parking spot, they suddenly saw the monster again. It began to walk up to their car as though it was curious. The youths were too scared to get out, but even with the windows closed, they could smell the monster's terrible odor. They immediately left to get the police, and several officers made a thorough, but fruitless, search of the woods. The police on the scene said they had no idea what the young people had witnessed, but they were obviously frightened by whatever it had been.

Into the Bottomlands

While at Southern Illinois University, I dug up folklore and old news articles and also interviewed witnesses—old and new—of hairy-creature encounters. One series of sightings I looked into involved the round-headed Chittyville monster. In late July and August 1968, residents of Williamson County began noticing dogs barking loudly and "carrying on" at night. Then on August 11, 1968, at 8:30 P.M., Tim Bullock, twenty-two, of West Frankfort, and his girlfriend, Barbara Smith, seventeen, of Carterville, sighted a "creature" while riding northeast of Chittyville, near a wooded, bottomlands swamp, just three miles from the Big Muddy River. Bullock reported the creature threw dirt at them through the window. Smith saw it and started screaming. She described it as "huge"—about ten feet tall, with a head as large as a steering wheel. It appeared to be black, with a round, "hairy" face. They left the area and reported the incident to police. Bullock returned the next day and found a depression in the grass, as if a large animal had rested or slept there. A week later, the creature was seen again near Route 148, also near the Big Muddy River.

Farmer City Monster

Then in 1970, I looked into a new series of monster sightings. It all started in Marion County, where twenty-four hogs disappeared during the last three weeks of May 1970. In the three preceding months, there had been forty-four "hognappings" in the Salem-area farms. In the central part of the state near Farmer City, three sheep turned up dead in the early spring. Officials assumed it was all the work of "wild dogs"—until July 9, anyway. On that date Don Ennis, Beecher Lamb, Larry Faircloth, and Bob Hardwick, all eighteen years of age, decided to camp out on a wild, ten-acre, buffalo-grass-covered piece of land a mile south of Farmer City near Salt Creek. Their campsite, which I discovered was often used as a lovers' lane, was isolated. Before the night was over, they would realize just how isolated.

About 10:30 P.M., as they sat around the campfire, they heard something moving in the tall grass. When "it" moved between them and their tent, Lamb decided to turn his car lights on. The thing, with widely separated eyes gleaming at them, was squatting by the tent. It then ran off—on two legs. The young men left in such a hurry that Ennis, who had one foot in a cast because of a broken ankle, left his crutches behind.

Soon word about the Farmer City Monster spread. On Friday, July 10, more than ten persons said they had seen a pair of glowing eyes near the site of the first sighting. And on the twelfth and fourteenth, at least fifteen persons swore they had seen a furry creature in the same area. Witnesses I interviewed all said that it seemed to be attracted by the sound of loud radio music and by the light of campfires.

Police Officer Robert Hayslip of Farmer City decided to check out the stories. When he went out to the campsite/lovers' lane area early in the morning of July 15, between two and three o 'clock in the morning, he heard something running through the grass. Soon after the sighting, he told me, "Out of the corner of my eye I could see these two extremely bright eyes, just like it was standing there watching me." But as he turned toward it, it disappeared.

Hayslip returned to the site about 6 A.M. He found that the heavy steel grommets in a tent that had been intact at 3 A.M. now were ripped out. A quilt lying nearby was torn to shreds. The Farmer City police chief, who had earlier expressed the curious view that the so-called monster was nothing more than a Shetland pony (evidently one of the bipedal variety), now decided to lock the gate that led to the ten-acre area.

The creature apparently moved on. Or at least the witnesses to it could no longer get to the area where it was being seen, and the Farmer City flap ended.

Then during the first week of August, Vicki Otto contacted me to let me know that she had sighted something near Ireland Grove Road three miles southeast of Bloomington. She figured everyone would think her crazy, so she wrote me a letter about it. She said she saw a pair of eyes reflecting her automobile headlights as she approached what she at first thought was a dog. Then, she told me, "I saw this ape running in the ditch. The thing I saw was the size of a baboon."

Next, on August 16, 1970, at around 9:30 P.M., Dan Lindsey and Mike Anderson encountered a similar Bigfoot creature while driving on Route 136 approaching the Kickapoo Creek Bridge north of Waynesville. "My first thought was a tall man or maybe a bear or a gorilla," Anderson said. The thing stood six feet five inches tall, was all brown, and had stooped shoulders. Walking on two legs and illuminated by the car lights, it more or less trotted across to the west side and along the creek's edge. And then it was gone.

Flap of 1972   During the summer of 1972, even though far more dramatic events were going on just across the border in Louisiana, Missouri, where a smelly, red-eyed creature dubbed Momo was being reported (see chapter 9), a "monster" was seen in Illinois.

The *Peoria Journal-Star* for July 26 told of Randy Emert, eighteen, who reported seeing a "monster" two different times over the previous two months. Emert said the thing resembled Momo in most particulars, although its height was between eight and twelve feet and it was "kind of white and moved quick." It also had a rancid odor and seemed to scare the animals living in the woods near Cole Hollow Road. Said Emert, "It lets out a long screech—like an old steam-engine whistle, only more human."

Emert's friends had also seen either the creature or its footprints. "I'm kind of a spokesman for the group," he said. "The only one who has guts, I guess." Ann Kammerer of Peoria corroborated

Emert's story, stating that all of her children, friends of Emert's, had seen the thing. "It sounds kind of weird," she admitted. "At first I didn't believe it, but then my daughter-in-law saw it."

According to Emert, an old, abandoned house in the woods had large footprints all around it and a hole dug under the basement. Emert thought this might be where the creature was staying. Interestingly enough, Edgar Harrison, the chief witness in the Momo affair, believed the creature might temporarily be residing in an abandoned building.

On July 25 a Pekin resident reported seeing "something big" swimming in the Illinois River, which also flows through Peoria. On the night of the twenty-seventh "two reliable citizens" told police they had seen a ten-foot something that "looked like a cross between an ape and a caveman." According to a UPI dispatch, it had "a face with long, gray, U-shaped ears, a red mouth with sharp teeth, [and] thumbs with long second joints." It smelled, said a witness, like a "musky wet-down dog." The East Peoria Police Department said it had received more than two hundred calls about the creature.

Then Leroy Summers of Cairo saw a ten-foot, white, hairy creature standing erect near the Ohio River levee during the evening hours of July 25, 1972. The Cairo police found nothing when they came to investigate, and Police Commissioner James Dale warned that henceforth anyone making a monster report would have his breath tested for alcohol.

Enfield
Horror
The following year, when creatures descended upon White County in southeastern Illinois and I received some national publicity for my search there, Sheriff Roy Poshard Jr. took an even sterner stance: he threatened to arrest the key witness.

Whatever it was that Henry McDaniel of Enfield saw, it was not a classic Bigfoot. Nonetheless, an undoubted apelike creature was observed during the resulting "monster scare."

McDaniel claimed that late in the evening of April 25, 1973, he heard something scratching on his door. Upon opening the door, he did a double take, for the "something" looked as if it had stepped out of a nightmare.

"It had three legs on it," he said, "a short body, two little short arms coming out of its breast area, and two pink eyes as big as flashlights. It stood four and a half to five feet tall and was grayish colored. It was trying to get into the house."

McDaniel, in no mood to entertain the visitor, grabbed a pistol and opened fire.

"When I fired that first shot," he said, "I know I hit it."

The creature hissed like a wildcat and bounded away, covering seventy-five feet in three jumps, and disappeared into the brush along a railroad embankment that runs near the McDaniel home.

I also interviewed ten-year-old Greg Garrett, who lived just behind McDaniel. Garrett had been playing in his backyard half an hour before McDaniel's encounter, when the creature approached him and stepped on his feet, tearing his tennis shoes to shreds. The boy had run inside, crying hysterically.

On May 6 at 3 A.M., the howling of neighborhood dogs awakened McDaniel. Looking out his front door, he saw the creature again.

"I seen something moving out on the railroad track and there it stood," he said. "I didn't shoot at it or anything. It started on down the railroad track. It wasn't in a hurry or anything."

The publicity McDaniel's report received brought hordes of curiosity seekers, newsmen, and serious researchers to Enfield. Among them were two young men whom Deputy Sheriff Jim Clark arrested for hunting violations after they said they had seen and shot at a gray, hairy creature in some underbrush. Two of the men thought they had hit it, but the thing had sped off, running faster than a man. Two of their friends, Roger Tappy and Mike Mogle of Elwood, Indi-

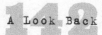

ana, who were not arrested, confirmed the incident of May 8, when I spoke to them.

Another witness I talked with was Rick Rainbow, news director of radio station WWKI, Kokomo, Indiana. On May 6 he and three other people saw a strange creature near an old, abandoned house close to McDaniel's place. They didn't get a good look at it because it had its back to them and was running in the shadows, but they described it as apelike, about five and a half feet tall, grayish, and stooped. Rainbow taped the cry it made, a distinctively apelike, short, screeching sound. Rainbow's companions shot at and missed the creature. Rainbow was shaken by the experience and called me back to discuss the reality of such creatures, as he could hardly believe what he had seen.

Then on May 12 I heard the creature myself. I was on-site with Richard Crowe, a Chicago investigator and writer on the unknown, searching the area around McDaniel's home, when we heard a high-pitched screech. We had spent our time interviewing witnesses, measuring and photographing the sighting locations, and just looking around the area. Suddenly, while examining a plowed field for fresh tracks in the late afternoon, we heard the most ungodly, piercing shriek you can imagine. Though startled, we attempted to locate the source of the sound in a wooded section that abutted the field. We looked around, searched through some sheds, but did not see the creature or any signs of it. We felt we were close, but then we also thought we were the ones being seen.

On June 6, a month after the Enfield events, the police in Edwardsville, Illinois, received and checked three reports of a musty-smelling, red-eyed, human-sized creature said to be lurking in the woods on the eastern edge of town. It was said to be more than five and a half feet tall and broad-shouldered, with eyes that apparently were sensitive to light. It made no sound when it walked. The witnesses said the thing chased them, and one man told police the creature had ripped his shirt and clawed his chest. All told, three sightings occurred, two on June 4 and one on June 8, all in the wooded area near Mooney, Little Mooney, and Sugar Creeks.

The Big Muddy Monster

The rest of the summer months of 1973 were taken up with the events near the Big Muddy River.

The creature—which would quickly be called the Big Muddy Monster after the nearby river—first appeared shortly after midnight on June 25, 1973, and was seen by Randy Needham and Judy Johnson, who were parked on a boat ramp to the Big Muddy River near Murphysboro, a town in southwestern Illinois. The couple was startled by a cry "about three times as loud as a bobcat, only deeper," emanating from the nearby woods. When they looked up, they saw a huge biped lumbering toward them, still shrieking but now in altering tones. It was not a human sound.

Randy and Judy agreed the thing was about seven feet tall, white, its short body hair matted with river mud. They were not interested in examining it at close range, and by the time it had approached within twenty feet of them, they were bound for the Murphysboro police station. Officers Meryl Lindsey and Jimmie Nash checked the area and found "impressions in the mud approximately ten to twelve inches long and approximately three inches wide," according to the report they filed later.

Needham later described the impressions as "something like a man with a shoe on would make—only the thing wasn't wearing shoes." He suggested that toe prints might not have registered in the mud.

At 2 A.M., Nash, Lindsey, Needham, and Deputy Sheriff Bob Scott returned to the scene. This time they discovered fresh tracks, similar in general appearance to those they had seen an hour earlier, but deeper and smaller. The police report noted an especially strange detail: "The prints in the mud were very irratic [sic] in that no two were the same distance apart and some were five to six feet apart. Also prints were found very close together."

Officer Lindsey left to get a camera to take pictures of the prints, and while he was gone, the other three followed the tracks. While they were bending over to examine some of them, there came "the most incredible shriek I've ever heard," Nash recalled. Apparently the creature was hidden in the trees less than a hundred yards away, but the trio didn't stick around to find out. They beat a hasty retreat to the squad car. In the hours that followed, the officers scoured the area in pursuit of an elusive splashing sound, but found nothing. When daylight came, things quieted down, but with darkness the creature returned.

The first to see it this time was four-year-old Christian Baril, who told his parents he had seen "a big white ghost in the yard." They didn't believe him, of course, but ten minutes later, when Randy Creath and Cheryl Ray saw something very much like that in a neighboring yard, parents and police reconsidered the youngster's words.

About 10:30 P.M. Creath and Ray were sitting on the back porch of the Ray home when they heard something moving in the trees just beyond the lawn. They saw the creature standing in an opening in the trees, quietly watching them through glowing pink eyes. Cheryl Ray insisted, during an interview with my associate and friend Jerome Clark, that the eyes were glowing, not reflecting, since there was no nearby light source that could have caused the effect.

The creature was either the same one the other young couple had seen the night before or similar to it. It was white and dirty, weighed close to 350 pounds, and stood seven feet tall. It had a large, round head. Ray thought its arms might be "ape-length," although she wasn't certain because it was standing in waist-high grass.

Creath went down to get a closer look while Ray went inside to turn on the yard light. The light did not reveal much more of the creature than they had already seen.

Finally the thing ambled off through the trees, making considerable noise. Later, investigators found a trail of crushed weeds and broken brush, as well as imprints in the ground too vague and imperfect to be cast in plaster.

Cheryl Ray's mother called the police. While waiting for them to arrive, they suddenly began to smell a "real strong odor, like a sewer," the Ray teen said, but it lasted only a short time.

Soon Officers Nash and Ronald Manwaring pulled up in their car. What happened then is recounted in the official report they shared with me:

> Officers inspected the area where the creature was seen and found weeds broken down and somewhat *[sic]* of a path where something had walked through. Jerry Nellis was notified to bring his dog to the area to see if the dog would track the creature. Upon arrival of Nellis and dog [a German shepherd trained to attack, search buildings, and track] the dog was led to the area where the creature was last seen. The dog began tracking down the hill where the creature was reported to have gone.
>
> As the dog started down the hill, it kept stopping and sniffing at a slime substance on the weeds; the slime appeared periodically as the dog tracked the creature. Nellis put some of the slime between his fingers [and] rubbed it and it left a black coloring on his fingers. Each time the dog found amounts of it, the dog would hesitate.
>
> The creature was tracked down the hill to a pond, around the pond to a wooded area south of the pond where the dog attempted to pull Nellis down a steep embankment. The area where the dog tracked the creature to was too thick and bushy to walk through, so the dog was pulled off the trail and returned to the car. Officers then searched the area with flashlights.

Officer Nash, Nellis, and the dog then proceeded to the area directly south of where the dog was pulled off the tracks. The area was at the end of the first road to the west past Westwood Hills turnoff. The area is approximately one-half mile south of the area of the pond behind 37 Westwood Lane.

Nellis and the dog again began to search the area to see if the dog could again pick up the scent. Nellis and the dog approached the abandoned barn and Nellis called to Officer Nash to come to the area as the dog would not enter the barn. Nellis pushed the dog inside and the dog immediately ran out. Nash and Nellis searched the barn and found nothing inside. Nellis stated that the dog was trained to search buildings and had never backed down from anything. Nellis could find no explanation as to why the dog became scared and would not go inside the barn. Officers continued to search the area and were unable to locate the creature.

The Murphysboro creature was reported twice more in 1973. During an evening July Fourth celebration in a city park near the river, carnival workers said they had seen it watching some Shetland ponies. And on July 7, Mrs. Nedra Green heard a shrill, piercing scream from near the shed on her isolated farm. She did not go out to investigate.

The monster season of 1973 ended on the night of October 16, when four St. Joseph, Illinois, youths—Bill Duncan, Bob Summers, Daryl Mowry, and Craig Flenniken, all high school seniors—encountered a hairy "gorilla-like" creature on a road south of the town. They had stopped their car to investigate what they had thought was a campfire near the bridge on the Salt Fork. One of them lit a match and they all saw the creature, approximately five feet tall, about fifteen feet away. They did not linger to investigate further.

Nevertheless, the Big Muddy Monster again made brief return appearances in July 1974 and July 1975. Officials didn't know what to make of the Big Muddy Monster. "A lot of things in life are unexplained," concluded Police Chief Toby Berger, "and this is another one. We don't know what the creature is. But we do believe what these people saw was real. . . . These are good, honest people. They are seeing something. And who would walk through sewage tanks for a joke?"

I cut my teeth on those hominological investigations, and they form a body of cases that give me insights into the diversity of the Eastern Bigfoot. The variety of Southern "Bigfoot" would prove to be another matter entirely, one that would hark back to one of my earliest discoveries, that apelike track I had found near Stevens Creek. Deep down in Dixie, an entirely different kind of ape appears to live in the palmettos.

right: Native Americans represented the Pacific Northwest Bigfoot through masks and totems. This mask of a Tsonokwa—a wild woman of the woods—was carved by a British Columbia Coast Indian. (© René Dahinden/Fortean Picture Library)

below: This California Giant Lettuce crate label was created about 1930 and is critical evidence for the awareness of hairy giants in northern California before the modern Bigfoot era. (Label supplied by Dwayne Rogers)

Jerry Crew holds the
now very famous first
1958 Bigfoot cast.

Researcher René
Dahinden stands next
to Jim McClarin's
Bigfoot statue at Willow
Creek, California.

Frame 352 from the Roger Patterson–Bob Gimlin Bigfoot film footage, taken at Bluff Creek, California, on October 20, 1967. (© René Dahinden/FPL)

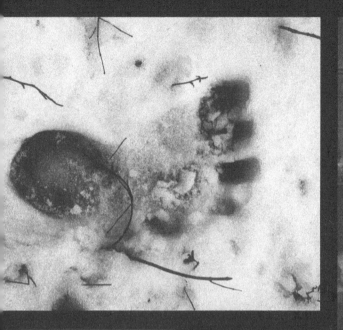

above: The famed
"Cripple Foot" track
found in snow at
Bossburg, Washington,
in 1969. (© René
Dahinden/FPL)

left: One of the
most popular films
ever made on Bigfoot
is *The Legend of Boggy
Creek* (1972), which
appeared on DVD
for the first time in
2002. (© Hen's Tooth
Video 2002)

Anthropologist Grover Krantz holds the 1982
Bigfoot cast on which he first noticed dermal
ridges. (© René Dahinden/FPL)

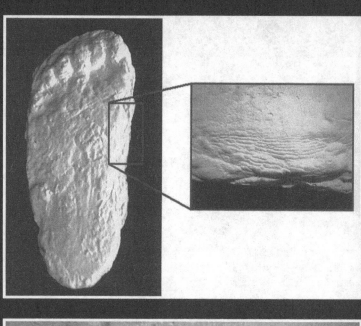

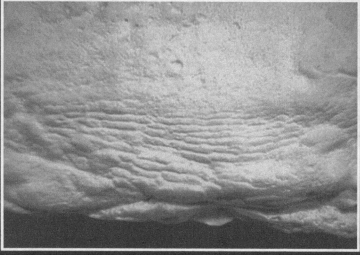

Close-up of dermal ridges visible on the side of a footcast from the right foot of a Bigfoot print found on Blue Creek Mountain, Blue Mountains, Washington State, 1982. (© Zack Clothier 2002)

The Myakka "Ape" allegedly photographed by an elderly woman in Sarasota County, Florida, in the fall of 2000. (© David Barkasy and Loren Coleman 2001)

above: Richard Noll of the Bigfoot Field Researchers Organization points to the thigh area on the cast of the partial Bigfoot body imprint found in mud at Skookum Meadows, Washington, September 2000. (© Dan Bates 2001)

left: An authentic Bigfoot Crossing sign is posted in Pike National Forest, Colorado, at the site of frequent Bigfoot sightings (© Chris Kraska 2002)

BIGFOOT!

Part 3

Reflections

11 Myakka and Other Southern Apes

To accept the existence of a population of giant, hairy, upright man-beasts in the forests of the Pacific Northwest is one thing, but to think that a whole group of more chimpanzee-like or orangutan-like apes are being seen throughout the warm, wet bottomlands of the South is more than some folks can accept. But in reality more than a hundred years of eyewitness reports and footprint finds of this Southern swamp creature are on record. In the South these Bigfoot-like creatures are called booger, swamp monster, or as they call them in Florida, Skunk Ape, due to their appearance and awful smell.

Two remarkable new photographs of what may be a Florida Skunk Ape have recently come to light thanks to Sarasota resident and animal welfare specialist David Barkasy. The story behind the photographs is intriguingly innocent.

In early autumn 2000, an elderly couple living near I-75 in Sarasota County, Florida—an area that includes the Myakka River and Myakka State Park—began to experience routine visits from an apelike animal. The couple did not know what the animal was, but since the husband of the pair said it looked like an orangutan, they called it an orangutan.

During one visit, the wife took two relatively clear photographs of the animal. "For two nights prior," she wrote, "it had been taking apples that my daughter brought down from up north off our back porch. These pictures were taken on the third night it had raided my apples."

She went out into her backyard after hearing deep "woomp" noises. She aimed her camera at the hedgerow at the back of her property and was startled to see what her flash revealed. "I didn't even see it as I took the first picture because it was so dark. As soon as the flash went off for the second time, it stood up and started to move. I then heard the orangutan walk off into the woods." She judged that the animal was "about six and a half to seven feet tall in a kneeling position" and noticed that its "awful smell" lasted long after it had left her yard. Eyewitnesses regularly report larger sizes for animals that are hair-covered and seen in the dark.

Reflecting on what had occurred, she said that the anthropoid "sounded much farther away" than "it turned out to be." She thinks she was about ten feet away from it, and it looked to be crouching, then standing: "As soon as I realized how close it was, I got back to the house."

"It only came back one more night after that," the woman photographer remarked, "and took some apples that my husband left out in order to get a better look at it. We left out four apples. I cut two of them in half. The orangutan only took the whole apples. We didn't see it take them. We waited up but eventually had to go to bed." When they put a dog in their backyard, the apelike animal did not return.

The Anonymous Letter

The woman provided these details in a letter signed, "God Bless. I prefer to remain anonymous," and mailed it to the Sarasota Sheriff's Department on December 22, 2000, according to the evidence provided by the postmark on the envelope. The sheriff's department received the letter on December 29, 2000, although most people in the office were unaware of it until after the holidays. According to the department's official report created later, the filing officer wrote: "I received an unusual letter addressed to the animal services of the sheriff's office. The letter told of an encounter with a monkey or ape and contained two photos. The letter was anonymous."

The letter begins: "Enclosed please find some pictures I took ... My husband thinks it is an orangutan. Is someone missing an orangutan?"

The woman said nothing about a "Skunk Ape" or "Bigfoot" in the letter. She was simply worried about her grandchildren's safety and her own. She wanted to alert the police and requested, "Please look after this situation."

From what I have been able to gather, the people in the sheriff's office did not take the letter and photographs seriously at first and did not create a file or permanent record right away. The photographs were passed around the office and were the butt of jokes.

The case began to be treated differently when a member of the animal control division contacted David Barkasy, owner of the Silver City Serpentarium, Sarasota, Florida. Barkasy, who had an interest in unusual animal reports in the area, was informed that local authorities were matter-of-factly discussing the local "orangutan animal" problem and some interesting photographs had been sent to the department. On January 3, 2001, Barkasy was told of the case and given some black-and-white photocopies of the photographs. Barkasy, who was aware of Florida's history of Skunk Ape reports due to his animal welfare interests, felt that these photographs might be firm evidence for the existence of these mystery anthropoids.

That night, Barkasy contacted me, as well as a local Bigfoot enthusiast. Barkasy wanted assistance and opinions on what he had discovered, to explore the possibility of a hoax, as well as to conduct certain anthropological, zoological, and photographic analyses if the case proved authentic. Over the week that followed, Barkasy worked to gain the trust of the sheriff's department and got closer to finding some answers to the who, what, and where of the photographs.

The sheriff's office finally created a file on the incident on January 18. Unfortunately, the sheriff's department filing and the artifacts of the photocopying process led to staple holes, scratch marks, and other damage to the original photographs. Later, critics of the photographs would claim that many of these marks were evidence of a hoax.

Barkasy's attempts to discover all the particulars of the photographs were frustrated by the unfolding events, although the officers did inform him of rumors of an animal bothering neighborhoods in east Sarasota County. Barkasy felt the trail was still hot. He discovered that no feral apes or lost pets had been reported lost or recovered. Finally, Barkasy asked me to release all the details of the story to the Bigfoot community.

The Myakka Photographs

My overview of the case, entitled "The Myakka Ape Photographs," appeared on my Web site (www.lorencoleman.com) on February 5, 2001. I said that the photographs were perhaps the first good photographs of a so-called Florida Skunk Ape, but I made no claim of authenticity and emphasized that further investigation was needed. For a point of reference, I designated these photographs the "Myakka Ape Photographs" until further analyses discovered a definite identity.

When those involved in cryptozoology and Bigfoot studies began to discuss the photographs, or at least the initial poor-quality scans of the photographs, on-line, people thought the photographs were:

1. a cardboard cutout

2. a dog

3. a man in a mask

4. a Bigfoot-like exhibit at a well-known tourist attraction found in various parts of the United States.

5. a man wearing a furry coat

6. a computer-enhanced or -created image

7. or an authentic Skunk Ape

David Bittner, well-known videographic, photographic, and film analyst, and partner of Pixel Workshop, Inc., noted that some caution must be given to any consideration of computer-posted JPGs from photocopies of prints of photographs. Some critics of the posted images thought the "photographs" appeared as if they were, as one person put it, of a "possible cardboard prop." But Bittner told me, "There's definitely a whole collection of artifacts that color Xeroxing will introduce, including edge enhancement and color field flattening, which contributes to a 'flat' look."

Later, after looking at better-quality scans provided by Barkasy and me, Bittner commented, "I'm pretty impressed with it so far, at least in terms of it being a real photograph, and not a compositing job or a cardboard cutout."

Newspapers in Florida, the Art Bell show, and other radio programs discussed the Myakka photographs in mid-February. The hope was that the woman photographer would be identified. In the meantime, meaningful analyses of the eyeshine, the pupil diameter, the dentition, the tongue, hair color, and exhibited behavior of this apparent primate took place.

Tracking Down the Details By tracking down the photo processing numbers on the prints, David Barkasy discovered that the photographs were developed near an exit off I-75. He found at the Eckerd photo lab at the intersection of Fruitville and Tuttle Roads that the photographs were taken in the fall of 2000 and printed in December of 2000. Finding out by whom and where the photographs were taken remains a goal of the ongoing investigation, but other angles must be explored too.

A few primate, Bigfoot, and cryptozoological students and scholars have sent in other insightful comments. For example, Jay O'Sullivan, Ph.D. candidate, Department of Zoology and Florida Museum of Natural History, University of Florida, points out the eyeshine is useful in determining whether the photographed animal was alive or a mask. The expectation is that the pupils will contract in response to exposure to the first flash. The eyes would be wide open for the first photo, but smaller in the second. The pupils do appear to be smaller in the second shot. Based upon O'Sullivan's and my initial measurements (index of pupil size vs. orbit minus distance of withdrawal), the eyeshine is about 40 percent larger in photograph one than in photograph two.

Another line of investigation involved the possibility that the animal was displaying a "pant-hoot" in its facial expression. An individual interested in primate studies initially suggested this idea as a reason the photographed Myakka animal had its mouth open. But in mid-2001, Wendy Shaw, a primate specialist who has worked for a dozen years, firsthand, with apes (such as Washoe) at the Chimpanzee and Human Communications Institute, wrote to tell me that she felt "that the expression displayed in the photo is not in the least like the facial expression which accompanies a pant-hoot. And indeed, one would not expect an animal startled by a flash to pant-hoot or to display a hoot face. The alleged ape in the photos appears to be displaying the 'full open grin,' an expression of extreme fear or anger in which the teeth (top and bottom) are exposed with the jaws parted. Behaviorally, this expression is also more consistent with the circumstances of an animal startled and frightened by a sudden camera flash than a pant-hoot would be. It's great to see that you folks are really trying to evaluate the photos objectively. Good luck to you!"

Considering the controversy these photographs have stirred up, we'll need it.

Tentative Conclusions

The two photographs have held up to analysis—there is no evidence of computer fakery or apparent hoaxing involved. But could this be a feral or escaped orangutan? The two witnesses used this moniker, and in the better scans of the photographs, its orangutan-like features are clearly visible. Perhaps the Skunk Apes are feral orangutans. Perhaps they are unknown orangutan relatives, or perhaps we will discover an affinity to orangutans previously unimagined.

I find the comparisons of the photographed Myakka apes with orangutans compelling. A young male Sumatran orangutan, *Pongo pygmaeus abelii,* photographed by the American Museum of Natural History and found in two of Ivan T. Sanderson's books, *Abominable Snowmen* and *Monkey Kingdom,* shows the manlike nature of these primates. Concurrent with my thinking, Canadian Wildlife Service biologist Tony Scheuhamme has pointed out that certain facial features present in the Myakka creature compare favorably with those found on a Sumatran orangutan. These include unique wrinkling between the eyes, the flatness of the nose, the specific opening of the nostrils, the curling fringe of hair above the eyes, pale coloring on the upper cheeks, and the exact shape of the lower lip. This is not to say the Myakka photographs are necessarily of an orangutan, though the comparison of the known animal with this unknown one is informative. Or that they aren't a hoax.

In any case, the Myakka photographs have refocused the debate on the "types" of mystery primates in America back to the compelling evidence for Unknown Pongids in Florida. Some current critiques of the Myakka photographs have mentioned that the animal does not look enough like a Bigfoot. Indeed, it doesn't, nor should it.

Long History of Southern Apes

Funny thing is that no one should expect a Bigfoot in Florida. Ramona Clark and other researchers from the Sunshine State gathered reports from the 1950s to the 1970s that described unknown anthropoids, not hominids. Even *Sports Illustrated* magazine in 1971 did an article on the "latest" Skunk Ape reports from Florida. That article quite straightforwardly noted that these animals were more chimplike than Bigfoot-like.

The Myakka Ape Photographs are only the most recent of a long history of Skunk Ape and related mystery anthropoid reports. I have files and letters from people who lived along the east-central coast of Florida who told me of their encounters with apelike animals, especially during the 1963–68 period. These are mostly from the Holopaw-Brooksville area and discuss algae-covered unknown apes seen on the extensive wild areas of the huge Mormon Ranch.

The classic Skunk Ape—as opposed to the apparently hoax south-Florida images of Patterson-film-modeled Bigfoot clones seen on recent "reality television" programs—is a much different animal from the Sasquatch of the United States and Canadian Northwest.

Florida's largely subtropical location is only the most obvious reason why the mystery apes of the South should be radically different from the traditional Bigfoot. They have been seen and tracked throughout the lower Midwestern and Southern, swampy woods and bottomlands of oak, cottonwood, and willow. Whereas the classic Bigfoot is upright, walking on two legs, from six to eight feet tall on average, and leaves a giant footprint that looks like an oversize human footprint, complete with five toes, the Skunk Apes or North American Apes, or Napes as I call them, are more apelike, shorter, often not much more over five or six feet tall, go down on all fours sometimes, and leave behind prints that look like your hand—that is, with their big toe sticking out to the side.

The word *gorilla* has been used to describe the creek-bottom sightings of these animals in the last fifty years. In Boone County, Indiana, in 1949, fishermen Charles Jones and George Coffman were chased from the banks of Sugar Creek by a brown "gorilla." In 1962 farmer Owen Powell of Trimble County, Kentucky, spotted what he called a "gorilla," about six feet tall, black, walking on its hind legs, and having front legs or arms hanging down to its knees. In 1968, a boy was snatched and then released in the backyard of his home in Kinloch, Missouri, by what he called a "gorilla." A screaming aunt and barking dog led the "gorilla" to eventually drop the boy. At Hamburg, Arkansas, also in 1968, the *Arkansas Gazette* noted stories of a prowling "gorilla." In the 1970s, the reports of Knobby, seen in North Carolina, some of the Fouke Monsters of Arkansas, the "manimals" of the Red River, and the Lake Worth Monster of Texas all describe similar gorilla-like creatures. At least one bottomlands resident believes the animal he saw was a "chimpanzee." Over a three-year period, from 1967 to 1970, Howard Dreeson of Calumet, Oklahoma, left out bananas and oranges for the animal, which he had hoped to capture. The reports of these much more anthropoid beasts are often buried in "Bigfoot" files because the term is so widely used today.

Sometimes the sightings leave a lasting impression on the local geography. One such place is Allen County, Kentucky, where, according to folklorist Harold Holland, "the name Monkey Cave Hollow apparently was given to one locality about four miles northeast of [Scottsville, Kentucky] by the earliest settlers for the simple reason a forested valley was inhabited by a tribe of what the pioneers identified as some sort of monkeys. These creatures foraged in the woods and took refuge in small caves."

Holland mentions that he once talked with an old-timer who, when a boy of seven or eight, saw the carcass of the last "monkey." He stated that a hunter came by his father's house and displayed the dead beast. He said that he could not recall exactly what it looked like (after all, it had occurred eighty years or so previously), but the creature had hands and feet "like a person," was about the same size as he, had no tail, and was covered with brown hair.

Other times, the events become part of the local folklore, and as the years move on, the details get cloudy. Take, for example, an incident from Hannibal, Missouri. One day around 1900, mainland residents noticed a mysterious animal moving about on a large wooded island in the Mississippi River near that city. The locals notified the sheriff, who subsequently saw it and thought it might be a hyena, except that it was eating grass. When the sheriff and others captured it, it turned out to be "the man from Borneo," who had allegedly escaped from a circus. Said circus was most happy to get him "back." Fine. But I should point out that the orangutan of Borneo and Sumatra is constitutionally incapable of swimming the Mississippi or any other river, while our primate friends from the bottomlands seem to be able to do so without difficulty.

The known species of great apes do not swim. But from all indications, Napes do. They range up and down the Mississippi waterways as well as the gallery forests bordering the river systems. A high percentage of Nape sightings take place along the creek bottoms of rural America, in such places as Sugar Creek (Indiana), Walnut Creek (Alabama), and the Anclote River (Florida). The popular film *The Legend of Boggy Creek,* really a docudrama (mostly factual in the details but melodramatic in the re-creations) about Fouke, Arkansas's apelike "monster," notes several times that "he always travels the creeks."

The sighting of a swimming ape by Charles Buchanan reinforces the point. On November 7, 1969, Buchanan was camping out on the shore of Lake Worth, Texas, when he awoke at about 2 A.M. to find a hairy creature that looked "like a cross between a human being and a gorilla or an ape" towering above him. Buchanan had been sleeping in the bed of his pickup truck when the thing suddenly jerked him to the ground, sleeping bag and all. Gagging from the stench of the beast, the camper did the only thing he could think of—he grabbed a bag of leftover chicken and shoved it into the long-armed beast's face. The beast took the sack in its mouth, made some guttural sounds, then loped off through the trees, first splashing in the water, then swimming with powerful strokes toward Greer Island.

The Tale of the Toe

The great toe of the Napes, as evidenced in their footprints, sticks out to the side, at anywhere from a fifty-degree to almost a 90-degree angle. All primates are pentadactyl—five-toed. Among the higher primates, hominids (men) and pongids (apes) have a foot that is plantigrade. Both hominids and ursids (bears) leave behind a footprint clearly showing the foot is plantigrade with a big toe that is not opposable. One of the great differences between the foot (and thus the footprints) of humans and pongids is the human great toe, the hallux, which lies alongside and points in the same direction as the other toes. More than anything else, these strange footprints found in the South and border states strongly support the notion that another kind of unknown ape—different from humans or the classic Bigfoot—exists on our continent.

In the spring of 1962, as I mentioned in the last chapter, I came upon apelike footprints in a dry creek bed near Decatur, in south-central Illinois. As Mark A. Hall demonstrated in his discussion of Iowa and related pongid tracks, at the fringes of the Nape range activity is often apparent. The Decatur discoveries are thus no surprise. These Illinois tracks are similar to ones found throughout the bottomlands of the South.

For example, an ape observed near Clanton, Alabama, in 1960, was first seen by the Reverend E. C. Hand of the Refuge Baptist Church and some locals. The creature left a series of tracks near where rural Route 31 crosses 65, south of the town, and also two miles to the west. Large and small tracks were found, as if there were at least two of the animals. Sheriff T. J. Lochart and Deputy James Earl Johnson investigated. Johnson described the tracks as the "strangest things he had ever seen." No one could figure out what kind of animal made the prints. One of the tracks, preserved in a cement cast, was "about the size of a person's foot but looking more like a hand," according to what *Clanton Union-Banner* editor T. E. Wyatt told me in a letter forty years ago. Of course, the pongid foot does resemble a human hand more than a human foot. Editor Wyatt, I learned years later, died in 1974.

In 2002, T. E. Wyatt's grandson Brian contacted me with more information on the Clanton reports. Brian Wyatt, a twelfth-grade social studies teacher in an Alabama high school, recalls how he grew up hearing his mother and father talk about the creature in his hometown of Clanton and how it was nicknamed Elijah Mae's Booger or the Hairy Booger. At one time, the footcast made from the track of this creature was on display at the courthouse in Clanton, he recalled. Brian Wyatt thought the cast was still in existence and volunteered to make a new attempt to find it. I had tried for years to locate the cast. Finally, in August 2002, Brian Wyatt learned through his mother, who stills lives in Clanton, Francis Lynn, the daughter of editor T. E. Wyatt, some horrible news. Apparently, in 2000, when a new administration took over the sheriff's office, the concrete cast from the apelike beast was found in the evidence room, thought to be a worthless curio, and discarded in a general housecleaning. What a shame.

Farther south, in Florida, the forensic ichnological finds are overwhelming. In 1965, following a late-night visit by a stooping figure in Hernando County, investigators discovered rounded tracks with "one big toe stuck out to the side like a thumb on the hand." In 1971, a "Skunk Ape" prowled through the Big Cypress Swamp, producing footprints from which casts were made. These casts show a footprint about nine inches in length, with an opposed great toe.

Arguing most convincingly for the pongid nature of the Skunk Ape, however, is the existence of knuckle prints. Broward County, Florida, rabies control officer Henry Ring, investigating sightings of two apes by the residents of the King's Manor Estates Trailer Court during August 1971, reported that he had "found nothing but a bunch of strange tracks, like someone was walking around on his knuckles." What Ring discovered was hardly "nothing"—to the contrary, it was striking evidence of the presence of anthropoid apes in Florida. Whereas most quadruped mammals, as well as monkeys, "walk" on the flats of the hands, the gorilla, chimpanzee, and orangutan use the backs of their fingers to "knuckle-walk." Officer Ring's finding of knuckle prints is a vital clue in any effort to piece together the Napes puzzle.

Handprints resembling those of a gorilla-like man or manlike gorilla are also part of the puzzle. Near El Reno, Oklahoma, in December 1970, something that moved on all fours raided a chicken coop, leaving a handprint or footprint on the door. The door and the seven-by-five-inch print were taken to Lawrence Curtis, director of the Oklahoma City Zoo, for an opinion. Curtis was frankly baffled. He found the "thumb" of the print quite unusual—it was crooked as if deformed or injured. Curtis thought it was from a primate but was uncertain of what kind. (Howard Dreeson, it will be recalled, said he had fed a "chimpanzee" in the same area from 1967 to 1970.) An examination of the photograph of the "handprint" left on the chicken coop door shows not so much a deformed hand as a typical anthropoid footprint. In a good-quality reprint of the photograph, dermal ridges (those lines we call fingerprints on human fingers, which are also found on the hands, feet, and toes of all primates) are slightly visible.

Similar tracks were reported at the Skunk River near Lockridge, Iowa, in 1975, and in Humboldt County, Iowa, in 1978, as chronicled by Mark A. Hall in *The Minnesota Archaeologist*.

The Waynesboro Wonder

The range of the Napes appears to sometimes intrude into states bordering the South. Several classic Bigfoot researchers have acknowledged for the first time that Napes might really be around in Pennsylvania during warm winters. The reason? Some remarkable anthropoid footprints were found in 2002, in southern Pennsylvania.

Local Waynesboro, Pennsylvania, *Record Herald* reporter Don Aines broke the dramatic story: "As you read this story, there is either a large apelike creature wandering the woods and hills skirting the Waynesboro Reservoir, or some good ol' boy laughing his head off."

It all began on Valentine's Day in February 2002 when Mike Hilton and Steve and Denny Gates went to look at the drought-lowered local lake and discovered a long series of tracks along the creek feeding into the upper end of the reservoir. More than three hundred prints stretched along a thousand feet. Plaster casts, videotape, and lots of looking around convinced them this was for real. Steve's brother-in-law, Paul Scott, went up to the lake to see for himself. Scott told his mother, Darlene Taylor of South Carolina, via e-mail, about the find. Then Taylor typed in *Bigfoot* on a search engine and came up with the Bigfoot Field Researchers Organization (BFRO). Scott was contacted by Ron B., on behalf of BFRO. Actually several people had been contacted, including me, and I was able to interview, by phone, Paul Scott and Steve Gates. The BFRO, and Rick Fisher of the Pennsylvania Bigfoot Society, in separate forays, trekked to the Waynesboro Reservoir to gather more evidence.

While some early reports said the tracks were between sixteen to seventeen inches in length, seven inches wide at the heel, two inches deep, with twenty-six to thirty-two inches of stride between the tracks, later measurements proved otherwise. From a close examination of the photographs (which included a ruler), taken by the researchers and the news staff, the tracks actually seemed to be between twelve and a half and thirteen inches long, with some strides being very short, less than two-foot lengths. In any case, whatever left the prints walked totally upright, with no handprints or knuckle-prints visible anywhere in the extremely muddy conditions. It appeared to maintain its balance well.

The prints showed five toes, with the large toe clearly sticking out to the side. Researchers wondered if this could be evidence of a Nape, different from the classic Bigfoot, in Pennsylvania. No sightings or other reports of an apelike creature had been heard in those parts of the state for a few years, however, so the tracks had to stand alone.

When the first article about the tracks appeared in the Frederick, Maryland, paper, many people with no organized plan, motive, or direction began tracking through the site, destroying evidence.

During the investigation, the researchers shared with me scores of confidential photographs, which have still not been released. Though they show an exciting array of footprints, I found some troublesome details in the configuration of some of the tracks. The sides of the prints were almost always rigid, as if made by a cookie cutter. Even more bothersome was the repeated imprint of a V-shaped object, apparently human-made, in the middle of the arch of several of the tracks.

As I said to a reporter at the time, I can't identify the brand of the sneaker, but part of the logo seems to be there! It is as if someone, perhaps even innocently fooling around in "monster" feet, or a type of glove or fixture made semirigid and placed on the front of worn footwear, had tracked through the muddy area along the lowered reservoir.

I might be wrong, and it would not be the first time. The BFRO is keeping its options open and I look forward to the results of their analysis. No one ever saw or claimed a Nape was in Pennsylvania, but the Waynesboro tracks have raised a few hopes.

While I accept that Napes exist in America, I find the Waynesboro tracks rather dubious. Reality can be a harsh teacher.

If They Exist Once again, I will state the obvious. I know it is difficult enough convincing mainstream scientists that the classic Bigfoot exists out West, and perhaps in the East as a smaller geographic race. Why muddy the waters with an additional unknown in the American Southeast and parts of the Midwest, the Napes?

The simple answer is because authentic tracks and credible eyewitnesses seem to identify an unknown primate quite different from what I call the classic Bigfoot. During the last forty years, I have entertained numerous theories as to the Napes' origins. Did they come over in the 1700s and 1800s with ships carrying slaves and cargo from Africa or Asia? While slave-trading between Africa and the United States began in the early 1600s, it did not become routine until after the invention of the cotton gin in the 1790s. It is possible that some chimpanzees, or a subspecies, might have been brought over then, since slave-ship captains often kept chimps as pets. In fact, the first chimpanzee to reach a zoo in England was brought to Bristol in the autumn of 1834 by a Captain Wood, who had picked it up on the Gambia coast. Some people today do not even think this was a chimp at all, but the very different bonobo.

The first four gorillas to be brought from the wild into captivity arrived in 1855, 1883, and 1897 at Liverpool, and in 1883 at Berlin. The first gorilla in Liverpool was thought, at first, to be a chimpanzee. The first two gorillas in the United States did not arrive until 1897, at Boston, and 1911, at New York. But for many reasons, particularly their swimming behavior, it is unlikely that the source of the American apes were the known chimpanzees or gorillas brought over on slave ships.

Could they have been an unknown form of ape then? Much confusion still exists about just what kinds of apes live in Africa. In 1959 through 1964, the mystery of the unknown Ufiti, an unknown ape monster seen around Lake Nyasa, Africa, turned out to be a gray silver-backed female chimpanzee, a rare comixture of traits more often found in the male gorilla. In his book *The Apes,* primatologist Vernon Reynolds reported on a group of four "chimpanzees" seen swimming in the Benito River, Spanish Guinea, which he thought was "some other species." In 1967, the Basel zoo received an alleged koolokamba, or gorilla-like chimpanzee *(Pan troglodytes koolokamba),* which turned out to be a red-backed, female gorilla. In 2001, National Public Radio brought to the attention of listeners something known in cryptozoological circles for years, the search for the Bili Ape of the Congo. NPR's Alex Chadwick told how Richard Wrangham of Harvard University and the Leakey Foundation, and Christophe Boesch of the Max Planck Institute for Evolutionary Anthropology in Leipzig, finally concluded that they were not searching for a gorilla, as originally thought, but a possible new race of chimpanzee.

My own sense of this is that a wide-ranging, supposedly prehistoric dryopithecine, which paleontologists tell us existed in Africa, China, and Europe, may be the source of the swimming apes of Africa and the bottomlands of the United States. The dryopithecines seem to be the perfect candidate to explain the North American apes. Anthropologist Napier writes that they were "a highly successful family living in both temperate and subtropical woodlands." Theodosius Dobzhansky remarks that it is not surprising that fossil apes have been found in Europe "since that continent,

together with North America, enjoyed warm temperate to tropical climates during the Tertiary period." *Dryopithecus fontani* was found on the continent of Europe and occurred during the middle Miocene. Naturalist M. Fontan discovered the holotype of this species near the village of St. Gaudens, France, in 1856.

Even the name *Dryopithecus* furnishes a clue. It means "oak ape" and was so called, Alfred Sherwood Romer wrote in *Man and the Vertebrates,* "because of the presence of oak leaves in the deposits from which the first remains of this form were obtained." All evidence points to the occurrence of "oak apes" in North American marshy habitats and temperate bottomland hollows.

This idea, I realize, is heretical enough, since the pongids of the Dryopithecinae are supposed to have lived only from the Miocene to Pleistocene times. *Gigantopithecus,* anthropologist Grover Krantz's candidate for the Bigfoot/Sasquatch of the Pacific Northwest, is merely the evolved giant end of the dryopithecines. Dryopithecines appear to be important in the mystery primate picture in North America—from the chimp-sized small Napes of the South to the classic Bigfoot and Sasquatch, the gigantopithecines or paranthropines of the West and occasionally, perhaps, in the East.

12 High Strangeness

Not everything about Bigfoot is, let's say, straightforward. One reason is that people tend to use Bigfoot as the canvas for their own fears, which in some cases is darkness incarnate. If you open this door a bit, the shadows come rushing in.

The Sinister Mirror of Sasquatch

To encounter a Bigfoot is to die. This early belief grew out of one often-told story by John Green, who, in writing about the Ruby Creek Incident (see chapter 5), mentioned that for "an Indian to see a Sasquatch was believed to be bad luck, in fact the observer was in danger of dying."

Then Ivan Sanderson propelled the "if you see a Bigfoot you die" legend into the lore of the field with a short passage in his book *Abominable Snowmen: Legend Come to Life,* in which he refers to the primary witnesses in the Ruby Creek incident, the Chapmans: "It is just as well that we crossed the Fraser River just when we did, and so met the Chapmans, because about a month afterward they were drowned crossing at the same spot late one night. The irony and tragedy of this event upset me greatly. . . . The Chapman family at the time of the incident consisted of George and Jeanne Chapman and three children."

Then in early 2002, rumors spread on the Internet that "Patterson died not long after his encounter." Or those who were involved with the Skookum cast might be star-crossed, after the deaths of Dr. LeRoy Fisher and Dr. Grover Krantz.

Is there any reality to this sense of bad luck and death after seeing a Bigfoot? I don't think so. The Patterson-Gimlin film footage was taken in October 1967; Roger Patterson died in January 1972 — more than four years later. The Skookum cast was found in 2000, and Fisher and Krantz died in 2002. The Chapmans had their sighting in 1941 and died in 1959 — about eighteen years later. Nevertheless, the folklore lives on.

Writing in *Salon* in 2001, former Bigfoot researcher Kyle Mizokami wrote: "In my time investigating the hairy linebacker, I expended most of my efforts researching Native American legends about the creature. Many tribes believed in a Bigfoot-type being, and many agreed that to see Bigfoot was a bad sign. Often, someone who actually witnessed Bigfoot would have a run of bad luck, go insane, grow sick, or even die. I have always believed that these legends, no matter how fantastic they sounded, had some grains of truth to them. However, the belief of bad luck associated with Bigfoot, while consistent across multiple tribes, was a little too out there, a little too metaphysical for my liking. I wanted facts, not superstition. I didn't know what to do with the bad luck aspect of the legend, so I ignored and eventually forgot about it. Bad idea. Ironically, by ignoring the bad luck theme I had ignored perhaps the most personally relevant 'fact' about Bigfoot of all. All that talk of 'seeing' Bigfoot (figuratively or otherwise) as being a bad luck sign turned out to be true. It's the scarlet B in action, viewed through the lenses of another culture. It's dozens of ancient cultures collectively sending the warning: 'Hey, don't get involved with Bigfoot. You will *so* regret it.' The warnings were in plain view—and I completely missed them."

The theme of Mizokami's article is that his association with Bigfoot has ruined his social life and no one will take him seriously anymore. Mizokami, of course, only extends this folklore into the modern world through his magical thinking.

Bigfoot is more than a creature of the wild; it is often what people want to make of it—and it was especially so during one recent period of "high strangeness."

Defining
the Times

Sometime in the 1960s, we all woke up and the world had grown decidedly weirder. Was it the antiwar, peace, and hippie movements? Was it the music revolution and new sexual freedoms? Could it have been the breakout from the Eisenhower doldrums and the shock of the JFK assassination? Historian Edward J. Rielly's *The 1960s* informs us that it was much more than the Beatles and Vietnam that changed us all. This "something" did happen, and it altered the landscape of Bigfoot studies too. From the Patterson-Gimlin film to the Minnesota Iceman, and Bossburg, a hint of this bizarre new age was in the air. The ensuing period became known as one of "high strangeness."

This was an era in which several threads of the inexplicable overlapped, danced about together, and merged. Bigfoot met UFOs, cattle mutilations, electromagnetic effects, and other bizarre imports from the world of the paranormal. It was an unfortunate marriage that still scars the field.

Most unfortunate of all was the mix of UFOs and Bigfoot. Ufologist Jerome Clark in his 1996 encyclopedia, *High Strangeness: UFOs from 1960 through 1979,* noted that this was a period during which people spoke "falsely or sincerely" of sightings of "hairy bipeds," some in conjunction, supposedly, with UFOs. During the

1970s, individuals such as California researcher Peter Guttilla began discussing what he saw as the overlapping nature of Bigfoot and UFO reports. Barbara Ann Slate and Alan Berry would later write about the UFO link to Bigfoot sightings.

In Pennsylvania, UFO researcher Stan Gordon began taking note of the strange hairy-creature reports coming his way. He was especially intrigued by a rash of reports beginning in 1973 that seemed to link sightings of Bigfoot and UFOs. Gordon told of sightings on October 25, 1973, near Uniontown and Greensburg, on November 2, 1974, again near Uniontown, and on February 6, 1974, in rural Fayette County, Pennsylvania, in which Bigfoot would be seen near glowing objects. Alerted by police officers, Gordon and psychiatrist Berthold Eric Schwarz investigated these cases. Linking tracks found at a landing site, reports of Bigfoot seen near a UFO site, and other clues, Gordon became convinced of the interactions. Today, Gordon maintains one of the few remaining active "Bigfoot UFO" hot lines.

Other ufologists were getting into the Bigfoot business at this time too. Carol Lorenzen, Leonard Stringfield, Andrew Collins, Leo Sprinkle, John S. Derr, R. Martin Wolf, and Steven Mayne began looking into hairy-creature sightings during the 1970s, resulting in clear-cut Bigfoot accounts appearing in the UFO literature.

In New York, writer John A. Keel was pondering the material he'd gathered a few years earlier in a place called Point Pleasant, West Virginia, which lumped Bigfoot, dog killings, Mothman, Men-in-Black, and UFOs in the same vortex. The volume he wrote — even before his famous Mothman book was published in 1975 — was *Strange Creatures from Time and Space,* published five years earlier. It was typical of the new wave of paperback books that would capture the mood of the times.

A year before *Strange Creatures,* Keel had introduced Jerome Clark to me and we carried on a lively exchange of stories and ideas. I found myself investigating the reports of glowing-red-eyed creatures, such as those haunting the cornfields of Farmer City, Illinois, in 1970, and the railways of Enfield in 1973. Clark in the meantime was digging into airship reports and exploring fairylore and ufology. By the mid-1970s, Clark and I coauthored articles that merged our two fields of study, full of straight data as well as sociological and psychological assessments, including the now rejected Jungian hypothesis set forth in our *Creatures of the Outer Edge*.

So I must plead guilty to being partially responsible for the amalgamation of Bigfoot and UFOs, which happened in this era of "high strangeness." But today, having reclaimed the firmer zoological and anthropological foundations of hominology, I reject such notions, as does Clark. During the late 1990s, Clark would look back on the "UFO-Bigfoot connection" and state, "These are huge suppositions tied to small evidence. At this stage, given the limitations of human knowledge, there is hardly anything about Hairy Bipeds, or their possible connections with the UFO phenomena, that can be stated with any degree of confidence."

I would agree wholeheartedly. But let's not toss out the bona fide Bigfoot cases with the UFO bathwater.

UFO-Bigfoot Cases   Many alleged UFO-Bigfoot reports exist in the UFO literature. Australian ufologist Marc Moravec even published *The UFO-Anthropoid Catalogue* in 1980, which brings several of these cases together. Here are details of some well-known examples from this literature.

An unusual series of events took place at Presque Isle Peninsula Park, north of Erie, Pennsylvania, on July 31, 1977. Families on a picnic first saw a weird light not far away, near the beach. Betty Jean Klem, sixteen, described the object as mushroom-shaped with three lights. Law enforcement officers, accompanied by one of the family members, Douglas J. Tibbetts, were advancing on the UFO when they all ran back to the car because someone was blasting away on the horn. They found Betty Jean Klem and Anita Haifley, with the two young children, scared to death. Klem reported she had seen a six-foot-tall, apparently neckless, armless, dark, nonhuman animal, moving sluggishly in the underbush. Haifley also saw the creature. Police took them downtown for questioning and returned the next day to find markings where the UFO had supposedly landed. Police Chief Dan Dascanio told psychiatrist and UFO researcher Berthold Schwarz, "I'm convinced that the young people saw something. The girl was a credible person. Of the two individuals involved she was the most specific about what she saw—she made no attempts to fill in her story when she wasn't sure. She was one scared girl when I first saw her. Her hands were shaking, her face was trembling, her speech was more inarticulate, and she had difficulty maintaining her composure. Her eyes were red and she kept shaking her head from side to side."

On a wintry December 4, 1970, Mrs. Wallace Bowers, of Vader, Washington, heard her children calling for her to come outside. Upon doing so, she found mysterious footprints in the inch-deep snow covering her farmyard. She told a reporter for the *Centralia-Chehalis Reporter,* "The footprints were very large, measuring sixteen inches, and five to seven inches wide. The night before, it had snowed, freezing hard afterwards. In comparison of weight, my husband's pickup truck never even went through the snow and ice upon his leaving for work; he leaves around 5:30 A.M. as he is a logger. The morning we discovered the giant tracks, or footprints, alongside his truck in the drive, the prints were like black on white, as whatever made them was so heavy it took the frozen snow with each step, plus leaving one-and-a-half-inch impressions in the frozen gravel beneath."

Bowers recalled that the family dog had acted oddly the night before, as if sensing the presence of an intruder. Vader is in the middle of Bigfoot country, and the tracks in the snow resembled those attributed to the creature.

At 7:15 A.M. three days later, on the seventh, the Bowers children again called their mother, this time to the window, where they observed a "bright star" moving across the sky. The object flew closer to the witnesses and for ten minutes they were able to view it carefully. Its center appeared to be a dome around which a larger circle seemed to be revolving. It was deep orange in the center, with the light diffusing toward the outer edge, but with a definite bright rim.

Bowers said it seemed tipped sideways slightly, rather like an airplane banking, before it hovered briefly over the nearby Bonneville power lines. It changed from orange to a bright, clear light after leaving the power lines, and when it made one last sweep closer, it again turned orange. The children thought they saw a "gray shape" drop away from the UFO just before it vanished in the distance. During the sighting Bowers switched on the intercom in the house, only to hear a peculiar "sharp" sound.

Subsequently, according to Bowers, the family experienced several months of shadowy intruders around their place and heard strange noises in the night and something very heavy thudding across the yard between 2 and 3 A.M., but they never saw anything.

In late January 1972, four teenage boys from Balls Ferry, California, were on their way to Battle Creek to fish on a dark, rainy night when they saw a brilliant-glowing object swoop over their car. Later, as they parked at the Battle Creek Bridge, they heard a noise, then a scream in the bush.

"We heard a bloodcurdling scream," recalled John Yeries, sixteen. "I threw the light over in the brush and there was this weird thing."

The beast was about seven feet tall, dark brown or green, had a large, teardrop-shaped ear, and was hunched over. It appeared to have lumps all over its body, "like pouches in a flight suit."

When it turned and ran, so did the witnesses. "I was wondering what it was," said Darrell Rich, sixteen, "and at the same time I was turning to get out of there." James Yeries and Robbie Cross also hightailed it back to the car. But when they got there, they were horrified to discover that the car wouldn't start (thus, for ufologists, establishing the electromagnetic link to the phenomena). They had to push it before it finally started.

As they sped away, they all had the feeling they were being watched and followed. Soon thereafter, Darrell saw what looked like "firecrackers" going off on the pavement, only without the accompanying sound. John saw them out the rearview mirror, but soon fiery objects, blue and white, orange and red, moving erratically in the open fields on either side of the road, captured their collective attention. At one point two of the "glowing balls" came together in the sky, while another time one shot straight up and disappeared. One of the glowing objects, weirdly enough, took on the appearance of a human figure beside the road. Strangely and suddenly, the lights disappeared at an intersection.

Racing back home, they told Darrell Rich's father, Dean Rich, of the incidents. The elder Rich, though somewhat skeptical, returned with the boys to the Battle Creek Bridge area and walked out into a nearby walnut orchard.

All of a sudden they heard an odd "commotion" in the darkness in front of them. As Dean Rich would later describe it, "It sounded like a real deep growl. It was a real weird type of sensation. It was something I've never experienced before." The boys abruptly fled and the father quickly followed.

The growling, a long, nerve-wrenching *eeeeaaaaaghhhrrr,* continued as Rich ran backward to his car. Once there, he and the boys decided the "thing" wanted them out of its territory. If it was trying to scare them, Rich said, "it succeeded."

The party went to the Anderson, California, police, who returned to the area but found nothing. However, the lawmen said they doubted the story was a hoax. One officer remarked, "They seemed completely sincere. There was no hint of the funnies or something else. They were really scared."

In the midst of a UFO flap in Pennsylvania in September of 1973, researcher Stan Gordon's hot line received an anonymous telephone call about a Bigfoot-UFO report. The unnamed individual reported that three women driving through the forest near Penn had seen a landed, metallic, rectangular UFO. The caller said the witnesses saw a door open, a ramp descended, and then three seven-foot-tall, hairy, apelike creatures ran out and into the woods.

Another Bigfoot emerged from a UFO in a case reported by Linda Moulton Howe in *Glimpses of Other Realities, Volume II: High Strangeness*. During Easter weekend 1977, Steve Bismarck from Snohomish, Washington, said he saw a dark-haired Bigfoot lowered from a large silver disk that was hovering over a forested area near Bismarck's rural house. He sketched the hairy giant and wrote, "This apelike animal walked upright. It had extremely black hair about three inches long, or more. It had a big, cone-shaped head that extended down to a big hump on its back. Its legs were much longer than an ape's. . . . And the arms were shorter than an ape's. They seemed to swing to the extreme as it walked by."

Many Bigfoot-UFO cases can be attributed to coincidence, mistakes, and outright hoaxing. Witnesses of unusual phenomena tend to group all the weird things they experience together, whether related or not. A puzzled witness often just doesn't know how to differentiate one mystery event from another. Adding to the problem was the practice by ufologists in the 1960s and 1970s of asking witnesses to recall everything strange that had happened to them in the days before and after their encounter. This unfortunate situation makes separating the valuable Bigfoot case from its UFO underpinnings problematic at best.

And just in case you are wondering, no, I don't think Bigfoot come from UFOs or the collective unconscious. And I don't think that Bigfoot are to blame for people killing people, either.

Bigfoot and Killer Witnesses

Since Bigfoot is part of the fabric of our culture, it was only a matter of time before the dark side would venture into the Sasquatch realm. Take the case of Charles Starkweather, well-known from the Martin Sheen and Sissy Spacek movie, *Badlands*. The true sad saga of Starkweather and his fourteen-year-old girlfriend Caril Ann Fugate began, in earnest, on January 21, 1958, when Starkweather killed Fugate's mother, stepfather, and her two-year-old sister. Before their Nebraska-to-Wyoming murder spree was over, eleven people were dead.

In the journal Starkweather kept in prison, awaiting death in the electric chair in June 1959, he told of seeing, as a boy, a strange creature outside his Midwestern window in the mornings. He described it as a female whose hairy body "tapered off from a big chest to a small pointed head." The visitations were accompanied by strange whistling sounds. Starkweather thought it was Death visiting him and said of the sounds, "It was close and loud at first, but it got further and further away and the sound became mournful and sad until I couldn't hear it no more." Death did not make him afraid, however: "The world on the other side couldn't be as bad as this one."

Robert Damon Schneck's article "Death Had a Sagittal Crest," which appeared in the February 1999 issue of *Fate* magazine, points out that Starkweather's Bigfoot sighting was, in many ways, classic. "It would be easy to ignore this story, considering the source," Schneck writes, "if it weren't a classic Sasquatch sighting *from before the name 'Bigfoot' was ever applied* [my emphasis]. Starkweather had no idea what

he was seeing. Since he was the kind of person inclined to mass murder, he decided it must be death come to howl at his window."

Could mass murderer Starkweather have actually seen Bigfoot? For Cary Anthony Stayner, the confessed brutal slayer of four
women in Yosemite in 1999, there is no doubt. Stayner stalked the
forests of Yosemite. He told of seeing a Bigfoot in the woods and
being "possessed" by the hunt for these animals, a feeling that obviously reflected a wild rage within himself.

Stayner was obsessed with something else—media attention
and celebrity. His brother, Steven, seven, was kidnapped on December 4, 1972. Search parties and news reports did not lead to Steven,
and he remained missing for seven years. The media storm that
erupted when Steven reappeared was intense for the quiet Mormon
family, especially for the father, Delbert, and his once-missing son,
as is clearly portrayed in the 1989 made-for-TV docudrama *I Know
My First Name Is Steven*. Steven Stayner died on September 15, 1989,
when someone hit-and-run his motorcycle, shortly after the film was
completed. On December 27, 1990, Cary Stayner's uncle Jesse was
found murdered in Merced, in the home he shared with Cary
Stayner. The murder remains unsolved.

Then on Valentine's Day weekend of 1999, Cary Stayner went
on a killing spree. Later that year, he was arrested for murder—
charged with killing three Yosemite National Park tourists and a
ranger. The tourist victims—Carole Sund, forty-two, her daughter,
Juli, fifteen, both of Eureka, and Silvina Pelosso, sixteen, an exchange
student from Argentina—were guests at the Yosemite lodge where
Stayner worked. Stayner is now serving a life sentence in federal
prison for killing the Yosemite park guide, Joie Ruth Armstrong. Late
in 2002, he was found guilty of the three tourists' murders, as well.

Cary Stayner used Bigfoot as his lure to approach and talk with
Armstrong. Soon after his arrest, Stayner freely discussed his Bigfoot ploy in an interview with San Jose television newsman Ted Row-

lands. Stayner was no longer in his dead brother's shadow. And Stayner kept telling anyone he could about Bigfoot. He told of his sighting to the cabdriver on his taxi ride home the February night he says he dumped the bodies of the Yosemite tourists. Stayner talked about Bigfoot with everyone.

Stayner even imitated the call of the Bigfoot for reporter Sean Flynn, who wrote a January 2000 article in *Esquire* on the killings: " 'A horrible shriek,' Cary tells me, animated now, eyes flashing, reveling in the memory. 'Like a woman screaming through a bullhorn right next to the car. And it went on for a long time. And then it faded away to this low growl.' "

During Stayner's 2002 trial for the death of the three tourists, defense witness Dr. Jose Arturo Silva testified that Stayner would often visit Foresta, a town on the southwest edge of Yosemite National Park, where Stayner believes he encountered a large, hairy, humanlike creature and also decapitated nature guide Joie Armstrong. Silva detailed a long history of mental disorders as the forty-year-old motel handyman's attorneys tried to bolster their insanity defense. "He lives in a quasi-magical reality, which involves Bigfoot and premonitions about the end of the world," Silva told Stayner's jury.

Bigfoot links were all over the Yosemite story, even beyond the Stayner angle. Of the early prime suspects in the murders, one was a member of the Modesto Cranksters (local druggies) named Michael Larwick. The Larwick family lived at Long Barn, and a half mile north of Long Barn is where authorities had found Carole Sund's burned-out car and two of the three bodies. Michael Larwick was later cleared of the murder charges due to Stayner's confession, but he remains in jail in 2002, on drug and weapons charges.

Larwick's father, Leroy, had appeared on national television documentaries and in local news reports as a Bigfoot eyewitness. In 1968, he claimed to have seen and filmed a Bigfoot, near Highway 108, not far from Yosemite. Leroy Larwick and Bob James of Tuolumne snapped three Polaroid prints from a plane above the ridge, which is today named Monster Ridge. Later they found two twenty-inch footprints that drew a good deal of media attention. "Larwick and James were famous for a while," neighbor Lance Johnson says. "In fact, I think they even went on some big TV show to talk about it. All the kids at Michael Larwick's school talked about it, of course, giving the son his fifteen minutes of fame."

The Larwick father was a celebrity. "Michael Larwick's claim to fame as a lad was that he was the son of the man who had gotten Bigfoot on film," observed author Carlton Smith. It's been said that Michael Larwick may even have searched for Bigfoot in Yosemite—just like Stayner. Or perhaps more correctly, both may have used Bigfoot to cover their sinister activities in the Yosemite area.

None of this means that these men did not see Bigfoot, however.

The Yosemite "People"

Yosemite, it should be noted, has its own dark side. During the Yosemite Indian War of 1851, mountain man Jim Savage would discover the Yosemite Valley and name it after a word he thought meant "grizzly bear." But as Carlton Smith points out in *Murder in Yosemite,* Savage got confused about the origins of the word *Yosemite.* It had nothing to do with bears, but referred to a shadowy group of "people" that pursued the Indians that lived in the valley. The Miwok word *yohemiti* is really tied to their characterizations of their elusive enemies and means "some among them are killers."

Stories of violent Bigfoot do exist. Giant cannibals in the bush eating women are part of ancient Indian lore, although little discussed today. One of the first stories among nonnatives appears in Theodore Roosevelt's *The Wilderness Hunter,* published in 1890. During the mid-1860s, two hunters, one named Baumann, were camping in the Bitterroot Mountains, on the other side of the Rockies from Yosemite, when they were visited by something that left giant foot-

prints. Then at midnight they saw, in the fire's light, a huge upright form and smelled it too.

The next morning, Baumann went to check traps, while his mate packed up. When Baumann returned, he found his friend's neck broken and four great fang marks in his throat. Roosevelt added, "The footprints of the unknown beast, printed deep in the soft soil, told the whole story . . . his monstrous assailant, which must have been lurking in the woods, waiting for a chance to catch one of the adventurers unprepared, came silently up from behind, walking with long noiseless steps and seemingly still on two legs. . . . It had not eaten the body, but apparently had romped and gamboled around it in uncouth and ferocious glee, occasionally rolling it over and over; and had then fled back into the soundless depths of the woods."

There are also reports of Bigfoot, the Eastern variety, killing dogs. These begin with the hairy giant "wildman" of Gladwin County, Michigan, who killed a dog with one blow of its hand, in October 1891, to such items as the 1970s Louisiana, Missouri, account of Momo seen carrying the bloody carcass of a dog. There is also the Wisconsin encounter in 2000 of a similar beast carrying a dead and bloody animal. John Green too collected cases of Bigfoot killing dogs, but he has only five accounts, other than the Baumann story, of people being killed by alleged Sasquatch. All are secondhand stories. Two from the 1970s came to him from an investigator in Alaska, who told of Bigfoot attacking men living on boats in the Yukon River. Though their dogs drove off the hairy giant, the men later died.

The *Bigfoot Bulletin* of October 31, 1970, published by California researcher George Haas, carried a fantastic letter from an army trainee named Nick E. Campbell at Fort Ord, California. He related that two Texas National Guard privates, one of them a minister, had told him that at Longview where they lived there were reports from about 1965 of a giant, hairy creature roaming the back country between there and Jefferson, Texas. They said that the creature had reportedly killed a couple of people. The Reverend Royal Jacobs had told him that as a teenager he was a member of a posse that hunted the creature and he had seen the body of a person the creature had torn apart.

Reports like this are difficult to confirm. One in my files is a UPI clipping, dated September 20, 1965, from Jefferson, Texas, entitled "Town Fed Up With Monster Hunters." Sheriff Luke Walker is quoted as being upset by the Bigfoot hunters from three states who had overrun his small, northeast-Texas town since a thirteen-year-old boy had come running out of the woods three weeks earlier telling of seeing a big, black, hairy thing. Did something else happen in Jefferson that never made it to the papers? Reports of aggressive Bigfoot still circulate in Texas.

Bigfoot, as a primate, may be no different from his supposedly more "evolved" cousins. There are bad apples in every bunch.

13 Sex and the Single Sasquatch

A conspiracy of silence exists in the Bigfoot world. It is not based on government cover-ups and hidden evidence stored in a military warehouse. It has nothing to do with murders in the Bigfoot community. The deafening quiet that envelops the already controversial area of hominology involves sexual behavior and genitalia. Stated simply, talking about sex and Sasquatch is largely taboo.

Pick up any text on great apes—orangutans, gorillas, chimpanzees, and bonobos—and you will find pages upon pages on the sex lives of these primates. The observers of bonobos have actually created a cottage industry of books and documentaries about their great sexual appetites, their masturbatory habits, and their quite apparent enjoyment of what appears to humans to be "gay sex." But examine any text on Bigfoot, and more often than not you will find no mention of the subject. Even in the books by scientists John Napier, John Bindernagel, and Grover Krantz, no extended discussions on the sexual activity of this unknown primate exist. You'll be

hard-pressed to find more than three pages about sex or genitalia in a 250-page book on Bigfoot.

For whatever reason, the 3 percent difference in DNA between humans and the known apes has made it comfortable for people to deal with the graphic details of such matters when talking about those primates. But within the world of Bigfoot, an upright but hairy primate that mirrors our looks, something else seems to have taken place. That something seems to have more to do with the humans than with the Sasquatch. Simply stated, the attitude of the Bigfoot community has kept the subject away from the general public—and each other too.

If Bigfoot has managed to survive with a population estimated by Grover Krantz to be in the two thousands in the Pacific Northwest, then they had to have bred to continue with their species. Bigfoot must have a sexual drive to reproduce. Juvenile sexual explorations must be occurring. Their genetic design is being passed along.

But where are the reports of Bigfoot sexually conquering and mounting mates? Where are the field observations or the sightings of courtship behavior? Where is Bigfoot's sexual activity hidden in the hominological literature?

"Bigfoot Is Gay" In 2001, I had an intriguing encounter with the stone wall the Bigfoot community has erected around the subject. I was speaking at a well-attended Newcomerstown, Ohio, conference on Bigfoot. Some 225 people had gathered from nearby Ohio, Pennsylvania, and Indiana, as well as from such far-off places as California, Washington, Texas, Maryland, Arkansas, and Florida. The audience included a few families of Bigfoot hunters.

The speakers began their talks in the early evening, and I was given a very late slot to say my piece. Delays, questions to other speakers, and breaks to sell a wide variety of plaster-cast copies of

tracks, tapes, books, and T-shirts put off my slide lecture until after 9 P.M. that cool spring evening. Most of the families had left, and less than a hundred die-hard researchers remained.

I talked for over an hour, showed eighty slides, and discussed a wide range of Bigfoot topics. I quickly touched on the subject of Bigfoot's sexual life and that so little has been written about it. I showed just one slide of an illustration drawn by Harry Trumbore of a Bigfoot seen by a Pennsylvania professor in the early 1970s; artist Trumbore had unconsciously given a slightly effeminate stance to a clearly male Bigfoot.

Drawings of Bigfoot are almost always asexual. Except for the hard-to-ignore large breasts in drawings of the Bigfoot captured on film in the Patterson-Gimlin footage, most sketches of Sasquatch and other unknown hominoids show no sexual or gender guidelines. Bigfoot are most frequently shown without any male genitalia even though a penis might be part of a witness description.

In my Ohio lecture, I noted, quite briefly, how curious it was that this Bigfoot should appear this way, as it is one of the few instances where we had an eyewitness state that he had seen a Bigfoot having sex—here, with a cow. I lightheartedly wondered aloud if 10 percent of the Bigfoot population, matching the figures we have for *Homo sapiens*, might be gay. Then I moved on to the next slide.

At the end of my lecture, the usual questions and answers touched on a variety of topics, but not this one. People asked me about what I had seen, what I "believed" in, what did I think about Bigfoot in Ohio, all the usual questions, but not one person asked me about the sexual activity of Bigfoot. Of the two families that were left in the audience, one mother even came over afterward to say how interested her oldest daughter was in the research.

You can imagine my surprise when I returned home a few days later to find my talk had become the center of a vortex of Internet-driven outrage. People who were not even in attendance at the conference, from the West Coast and the South, were claiming that I was "irresponsible" for having exposed families and their kids to my "disgusting" talk in which I had called "Bigfoot a homosexual" and said that "Bigfoot and cows mate." One person wrote, "Did you really say that Bigfoot is homosexual and likes cows?" And an angry writer wrote, "Talking about anal sex with cattle by an unclassified creature when there are children in the audience who may view Bigfoot as a monster anyway, isn't a subject YOU as the speaker, arbitrarily have the right to inflict upon other families." Another person forwarded this: "The most important point is you have NO credible evidence that Sasquatch have anal intercourse with cattle. What stupid illiterate speculation!!!!!!!!!!!!" Or this: "Come in out of the rain, Loren. You live in fantasy land."

A couple of wags tried to put a different spin on what had happened. One wrote, "Actually, if Bigfoot was gay, he wouldn't be having sex with cows, he'd be having sex with bulls!" Dave Grenier of Olympia, Washington State, clarified the joke by writing that, no, "if Bigfoot was gay, he'd be having sex with another Bigfoot, not a bull."

Now, years later, the only thing that people can remember about my talk in Ohio is the twisted reality that I said "Bigfoot is gay" and "Bigfoot has anal sex with cows"—neither of which were noted exactly that way. Trying to defend yourself on-line is often an uphill battle, especially against misstatements from folks who hear things about you secondhand. I was particularly offended by remarks that I was undermining the youth of all of Middle America as my life has always revolved around education and keeping kids safe. Upon reflection, I see now, what happened to me, post-Ohio, is that whenever sexual data surface in relation to Bigfoot, emotions reign rather than science.

This is far too important an issue to ignore, so I wish to examine those Bigfoot cases in which elements of sexuality have played a part, beginning with the story that got me into so much trouble at this 2001 Ohio Bigfoot conference.

Jan Klement's Creature

It all goes back to a little book, *The Creature: Personal Experiences with Bigfoot* by "Jan Klement," published by Allegheny Press in 1976. When he wrote the booklet, Klement said he was a small-town earth-sciences professor. His book tells of a series of encounters with a large, hairy creature, beginning in August 1972, with some simple sightings near his cabin in the woods of southwestern Pennsylvania and eventually leading to closer contacts with it late in September 1972.

The professor lured the creature close to his shanty by putting out apples. For almost four months, the creature tolerated the professor's close observations. The visiting animal, which Klement affectionately called Kong, was neither apelike nor manlike. It stood seven feet tall and was covered in short brown hair with slightly longer hair on the head, under the arms, and in the pubic area. Its large eyes and expressive mouth sat in a face that was not primitive or too animal-like, but the short hair that grew from the eyes down gave the appearance of a mask. The arms did not reach below the knees. It had a powerful body with strong leg and shoulder muscles, flat buttocks, and thirteen-inch, humanlike feet.

The most notable feature, according to Klement, was its protruding stomach. The professor observed the smelly creature killing a deer and small animals, and eating these and other items in the natural environment. It grew to trust the professor's presence but was always cautious, never left tracks, and invariably made itself scarce when metal objects, cameras, or other people were near.

Finally, in mid-January 1973, Klement found the creature dead and buried it in a wooded area some distance from his cabin. Between 1973 and 1976, he returned to the burial spot but could not find any trace of it. The creature appears to have been dug up.

That's the basic story. But how about the "bits and pieces," as the British euphemistically talk about sex?

At one point, after noting rather matter-of-factly of having seen Kong defecating and then covering his droppings, Klement writes, "The other event is rather humorous now that I reflect upon it but at the time some puritan influence overcame me. Kong had arrived at the cabin with this massive erection. Usually his penis hung limp and after a time it ceased to exist. He never urinated around me so there was no need to dwell upon it. Limp, it seemed to be about an inch in diameter and about six inches long. It looked very human with a red head that occasionally poked out from the foreskin. His testicles were not overly large but they hung to about the same length as the penis."

Uncomfortable at the sight of this erection, Klement went inside his cabin, got some apples to give to the Bigfoot, but "as he stood around I felt uneasy and again embarrassed." Finally, Klement started yelling at Kong to "get the hell out of there," even though he knew the Bigfoot did not understand what Klement meant.

"Kong finally did go away," the professor writes, "and I was relieved. I took up my water jug and walked over the hill toward the stream and the spring from which I obtained water. . . . As I approached the bottom of the hill I could see the cows in the pasture on the other hillside. There was a commotion among the cows and when I put the water jug down and walked over I could see Kong. He was mounted on a large Holstein cow and was shoving away. The cow would start to walk away and Kong would lift his legs and hang on with his hands cupped against the side of the cow until it would stop and then he would begin working his buttocks rapidly again. Again I was stupidly embarrassed."

Klement watched a bit longer, filled his water jug, and returned to his cabin. Later, when Kong, complete with a dripping penis, came back by the Klement's cabin, Klement gave him some more apples and hollered at him to go. Feelings of confusion and morality were stirring in the professor, and he really was at a loss by his own actions.

"I headed for the car and Kong started slowly up the road toward the top of the hill. I hollered after him 'you picked the ugliest one.'"

Is Jan Klement's story a Bigfoot fairy tale, as some critics claim? Or is it one of the best close-up examinations of an unknown hominoid ever chronicled? And who is this mysterious figure? For years, "Jan Klement" was the Bigfoot field's Deep Throat—an unknown college professor who has important data on at least one Sasquatch. Who is or was he? Professor Paul Johnson of Pennsylvania, a well-known local Bigfoot researcher, has been a prime candidate, but he denies being Jan Klement. Rumor now has it that Klement is today dead. According to the book's new description on Amazon.com, he is a deceased biology professor.

Sexual Kidnappings?

From the past are confusing sightings of Sasquatch chasing cows, including one observed on a farm on the southeastern corner of Lulu Island, in British Columbia, during July 1969. Perhaps we should reconsider what these are all about, along with accounts in which eyewitnesses have told of horses and deer being pursued by apparently juvenile male Bigfoot.

As we read between the lines, something more telling, as far as the possible sexual behavior of Sasquatch, may also be revealed in examining accounts of kidnappings. J. W. Burns's 1929–36 articles collected some of these kidnapping accounts (see chapter 3) among the Natives of British Columbia. While the capturing of human females is frequently assumed to be a folkloric motif and appears to have some basis in Indian legend and tradition, the actual twentieth-century firsthand experiences can be quite different. From the recent reports of the unknown upright, Bigfoot-like creatures called the Ucumar or Ucu of northern Argentina to the 1920s accounts of Sasquatch in British Columbia, one hears of men, not women, being the object of kidnapping reports. Why?

A clue appears in perhaps the most famous Sasquatch kidnapping incident of all, the Albert Ostman case, which is said to have happened in 1924, but did not come to light until 1957. When John Green first began publishing Sasquatch sightings in his newspaper, a Canadian lumberjack named Albert Ostman broke his decades of silence, from fear that no one would believe him, and finally told his story.

Albert Ostman, as the story goes, was camping near Toba Inlet, British Columbia, when a huge male Sasquatch abducted him. Plucked from the ground in his sleeping bag, the giant, hairy creature threw Ostman over his shoulder like a sack of potatoes and jogged over hills and valleys to a little canyon unknown to Ostman. Ostman found himself a prisoner of four Sasquatch, an "old man," an "old woman," and two younger, thinner Sasquatch. The older male and young female would stand guard over Ostman while the older female and young male prepared the meals. The Sasquatch group demonstrated they were vegetarian and ate roots, grass, and fir-tree tips. Ostman told of how he was held for a few days, how he observed the exact anatomy of the group, their bedding, and even some simple language, e.g., *sooka sooka,* meaning "get back." In the end, after about a week of captivity, Ostman used the creatures' curiosity and his snuffbox to disorient and distract the Sasquatch so he could escape.

Bigfoot chroniclers such as John Green and Ivan T. Sanderson who actually interviewed Ostman noted Ostman's belief that he had been snatched as a mate for the young female Sasquatch. But here, as in the entire Bigfoot field, the discussion of sexual matters was taboo. It is instructive to note how Sanderson describes this part of his interview with Ostman.

Sanderson found it difficult to obtain primatological details from Ostman about one of the four Sasquatch: "The young female was very shy; she did not approach Ostman closely but kept peeking at him from behind the bushes. He could not estimate her age, but remarks that she was without any visible breast development and was, in fact, quite flat-chested. Like her mother, she had a very pronounced upcurled bang across her brow-ridges. This was continuous from temple to temple. Curiously, no amount of questioning would prompt Mr. Ostman to elaborate any further on this individual, which may in part be psychological since it seems to be his conviction that he had been kidnapped as a potential suitor for her, and I think," writes Sanderson, "he has a sort of subconscious and rather touching modesty about her shyness. Mr. Ostman maintains a delightful old-world delicacy about the proprieties and neatly turned aside some purely biological questions with such noncommittal phrases as 'wouldn't know about that.'"

Ostman did have a bit more to say about the males. Don Hunter, writing for René Dahinden in their coauthored book, *Sasquatch*, noted that in "subsequent talks with René, Ostman made particular reference to the size of the old-male Sasquatch's penis. He indicated that the head was hooded with skin and in this respect resembled that of a stallion—but only in this respect. He seemed puzzled by the fact that the old man's was only about two inches long. Now, if Ostman had been fantasizing about the Sasquatch family, it would seem logical that he would have endowed the male with much more impressive equipment than this, to match the rest of its giant stature. And the instance becomes even more interesting when we consider that the gorilla, the biggest of all known primates, itself has to make do with a penis of about two inches in length."

In e-mail exchanges about this in recent years, John Green recalls that Ostman did describe the penis as "like an inverted funnel, which sounds horselike." Green, writing in *On the Track of the Sasquatch*, does not mention these details but on the reality of the overall story wrote, "It is hard to see how Mr. Ostman, whose story was one of the very earliest, could have known so much without having had an opportunity for close observation of all the individuals he describes, and any sequence of events that could make such observations possible would be certain to sound unbelievable." As Hunter notes in his book with Dahinden, when Ostman was confronted with an individual's reservations with his detailed story, he would reply, "I don't care a damn what you think."

Muchalat Harry Although not as famous as the Ostman story, another one of these early cases, mentioned in some Bigfoot children's books and by retired Bigfoot hunter Peter Byrne, is the kidnapping account of Muchalat Harry, a native Nootka living on Vancouver Island. According to the story, sometime in the autumn of 1928, a Sasquatch kidnapped Muchalat Harry. After being carried a few miles, he was dumped on the ground. When he looked around, he found twenty (yes, twenty!) Sasquatch of different genders, ages, and sizes surrounding him.

The giant, hairy creatures examined Muchalat Harry, pulling at his long underwear (as if it were loose skin, according to one theory). Growing tired of him, they wandered off, as if to gather food. Harry jumped up and ran out of their "camp," out of the hills, to his boat, and rowed back to his village.

It took Muchalat Harry three weeks to recover, his hair turned white, and slowly he began to talk and tell people of the kidnapping incident. He was said to have never traveled into the forest again.

This story is rarely mentioned, hardly ever critiqued by anyone, perhaps because people find the "twenty Sasquatch" detail pushes it into the fantastic realm. Muchalat Harry's account is treated more like a Bigfoot folktale today and perhaps never gained the status of Albert Ostman's account because of its Native origins. Nevertheless, the kidnapping theme is much more pervasive in Sasquatch encounters than many modern Bigfooters would have us believe. The sexual content, once again, seems to prevent these stories from being taken seriously.

Bill Cole A more contemporary incident appears in Roger Patterson's little 1966 book, which reprinted a recollection given in the December 7, 1965, *San Francisco Chronicle*. Retold by Fresno locksmith O. R. Edwards and his Nebraska friend Bill Cole, the strange encounter occurred while they were on a hunting trip in California's southern Siskiyou Mountains during World War II. The two were rounding some bushes, Edwards to the right, and Cole to the left. All of a sudden, while sweeping the area with his eyes, Edwards saw an apelike head sticking out of the woods. By the time he refocused on the spot, the thing was gone. Edwards told what happened next: "I heard the *pad-pad-pad* of running feet and the *whump* and grunt as their bodies came together. Dashing back to the end of the bush I saw a large manlike creature covered with brown hair. It was about seven feet tall and it was carrying in its arms what seemed like a man. I could only see legs and shoes."

The Bigfoot was carrying Bill Cole down the hill, and Edwards, unable to believe what he was seeing, closed his eyes, shook his head, and looked again. The thing was nearly out of sight in the woods about seventy or eighty yards away. Working his way back, Edwards saw two more of the creatures at the bottom of the ravine.

Cole would say later, when he and Edwards got to talk about it two decades later, that the thing had carried him for a time but didn't hurt him. Cole remembered that after he quit rolling, he got up the hill and got his rifle. "I stood there some time and looked and listened. I had a feeling I was being watched and hunted," Cole said.

Edwards observed, "Cole is the only man I know who has had physical contact with a giant." For twenty years, until they talked about it, Edwards said, "I would not believe what I had seen."

Cole replied, "Funny, neither of us has guts to say what happened to us."

Why were Ostman, Harry, and Cole stalked and kidnapped? Could it have been to mate with a female Sasquatch? How has it become a standard unwritten assumption that there are even female Bigfoot?

Big Breasts

You've seen the film footage by now. And so have thousands of people who are interested in Bigfoot. The Patterson-Gimlin footage, as we discussed in chapter 7, is the best visual evidence for the existence of Sasquatch. When the image of that Bigfoot filmed by Roger Patterson on October 20, 1967, was first examined, it quickly became apparent that this upright, hairy creature had something sticking out from the front of its body. Bigfoot authors have described what they saw as "wobbling breasts," "gigantic brown breasts," "droopy breasts," "pendulous breasts," or merely as "heavy breasts." Needless to say, these "breasts" are difficult to ignore and have been used as an obvious sign that the animal filmed was female. While a few nonsensical theories have ventured that the breasts might be vocal sacs on the chest of a male Bigfoot, or babies being carried on the front of this Sasquatch, most students of the film agree they are simply breasts. One researcher, Lloyd Pye, states firmly that they are "indistinguishable from human mammary tissue in motion."

That the breasts of "Patty," as Bigfooters have named the Patterson Bigfoot, are hairy, however, has troubled some researchers such as the late Bernard Heuvelmans. He felt this cast doubt on the entire incident and the film, as he felt such a higher primate would not have hair on her breasts. For others, the hair on the breasts actually fortified their thought, for if this was a hoaxed event, why wouldn't the hoaxer have created a suit that had hairless breasts as supposedly found in human and gorilla females? The counterargument was that, perhaps, the anatomy of the Bigfoot is different and reflective of a colder or subarctic lifestyle. Zoologist Ivan Sanderson pointed out soon after the film was shown to him that human females do, actually, frequently have hair on their breasts.

Patty is not the only female Bigfoot to have been reported from the Pacific Northwest. Carefully but openly, witnesses mention the breasts, giving a good indication of gender. Some of these are from such classic accounts as that of William Roe, who was climbing on Mica Mountain, British Columbia, when he saw a young Sasquatch in 1955. Roe affirmed in a sworn affidavit that when he viewed this upright animal at about 3 P.M. on an October day, his "first impression was of a huge man, about six feet tall, almost three feet wide, and probably weighing somewhere near three hundred pounds. It was covered from head to foot with dark brown, silver-tipped hair." But then as it came closer, the hunter and trapper "saw by its breasts that it was female." A quite famous drawing of Roe's Sasquatch, sketched under his direction by his daughter, shows perky, large, lightly hair-covered breasts (except for the nipples), in many ways foreshadowing those of Patty's.

Mt. Shasta, California's mystical mountain, is today associated with Bigfoot lore, but this only began, according to the Chamber of Commerce there, in 1962, when a woman reported watching a female Bigfoot give birth on the mountain.

The notation that a "female" Bigfoot has been seen, especially during the 1960s, was frequently a clue that breasts were being sighted. In April 1962, on the Bella Coola River bank, British Columbia, a human woman and two children saw a female Sasquatch holding a younger one by the hand. In June 1963, at Lewis River Canal near Yale, Washington, Stan Mattson saw a female Bigfoot with hanging breasts and a young Bigfoot under its left arm drinking water and catching small fish. In the autumn of 1965, near Harrison Mills, British Columbia, a female Bigfoot was seen in the woods near a road. On April 7, 1968, in the Trinity Alps of California, Larry Browning said a female Bigfoot chased him for thirty minutes. And in mid-June 1968, near Clipper, Washington, logger Frank Lawrence Jr. reported a male, female, and child Bigfoot only one hundred yards away.

Sasquatch breasts are usually described as hair-covered, except for one specific place on them, reflective of the Roe report. In the Clearwater River area of Idaho, north of Orofino, in June 1969, investigator Russ Gebhart interviewed the night watchman at a rural sawmill found deep in the forest, who'd seen a six-foot-tall Bigfoot. It was covered in shiny, dark hair except there was no hair on its hands, face, or "nipple area of its very large breasts," according to Gebhart, writing in *The Bigfoot Bulletin*. The skin showing was pink, and the witness thought this Bigfoot might have been nursing a baby, although he apparently never saw a young Bigfoot with this female.

Meanwhile, a month later, on July 12, 1969, near Oroville, California, Charles Jackson and his six-year-old son, Kevin, saw a seven-to-eight-foot-tall Bigfoot that appeared to have three-inch-long, gray hair, and large breasts. René Dahinden interviewed Jackson and noted the witness said the breasts were "huge, pendulous." The Jacksons, who had been burning trash, were frightened and ran inside.

At that same time, in July 1969, a rash of sightings by Grays Harbor County deputy sheriffs and other credible witnesses took place near Hoquiam, Washington. (The casts from this series are some of the best examples of footprint evidence used and exchanged among Bigfoot researchers.) John Green interviewed one deputy, Verlin Herrington, soon after his sighting, which took place at 2:35 A.M., on July 26, 1969. As Herrington was patrolling Deekay Road, by Grass Creek Road, on his way home, he rounded a corner to see what he at first thought was a large bear in the middle of the road. He quickly realized it was a Bigfoot, and, indeed, a female. As Herrington noted, it had breasts located on the body like on a human, but "they were covered with hair except for the nipples."

Later during that active summer of 1969, near Maple Springs, north of Orleans, California, a woman prospector saw an adult male and female Bigfoot several times, and she was able to "interact" with them by leaving out grapes and apples, which they took. In September

1969, along the Kananasis Lake–Ribbon Creek, near Banff, Alberta, three male prospectors saw a female Sasquatch, somewhere between seven and eight feet tall, squatting near their camp in broad daylight.

While the subject of gender differences between male and female Sasquatch is taken for granted historically, such cases are uncommon in today's files, especially in the East. One exceptional example is the account given by two boys, Karl, fourteen, and Steven Traster, ten, who told a *Saginaw News* reporter that on September 5, 1977, near Caro, Michigan, they saw a smelly, eight-foot-tall Bigfoot with long brown hair, large teeth, lengthy fingernails, and, yes, breasts.

Forbidden Valleys Even more exceptional than breasts being seen are eyewitnesses who notice the female genitalia: in all the annals of Bigfoot encounters, only one report seems to exist.

The Glen Thomas encounters of Oregon involve four sightings the witness had between the fall of 1967 and the end of 1968. They all took place in the mountains west of Clackamus Valley, southwest of Estacada. On one occasion, in the spring of 1968, Thomas watched a female Bigfoot eat willow leaves. The creature was about one hundred feet away and he noticed it had breasts like a human woman but a bit lower on the chest. But the incident that concerns us the most happened while Thomas was hunting in the same area in November 1968. Thomas crossed a 3,500-foot ridge and found two sets of tracks in the snow. He followed them for miles and came upon two Bigfoot. John Green records what he learned from Thomas, who was using binoculars to observe them from two hundred yards away: "He found himself looking at two Sasquatch sleeping out in the open, with their backs to the sky and their knees and elbows drawn in under their bodies." After watching them sleep for an hour, Thomas then saw them get up and go down to a creek to eat water plants. "Both were obviously females," Thomas noted, "with more pendulous breasts than the ones he had seen before, and one appeared to have a swelling in the genital area and kept rubbing itself," giving an intermittent loud call "like a scream in an echo chamber." Thomas watched the six-foot-tall Sasquatch slowly work their way from the area, but was "too spooked" to go over to look for evidence.

Did Glen Thomas have a rare glimpse of the swollen genitalia of an unknown primate, mirroring those of chimpanzees so familiar to most of us from the work of Jane Goodall and the documentaries on *National Geographic*? Or were these descriptions merely issuing from an active imagination of a Bigfoot hunter?

The Playmate, er, Redwoods Video

The modesty of modern Bigfootery is again illustrated with perhaps one of the better videotapes of a Bigfoot creature since the Patterson-Gimlin film. Taken a mere thirty miles from the Bluff Creek site of that famed 1967 footage, professional videographer/filmmaker Craig Miller captured something with his personal camcorder on August 28, 1995, while socializing with members of a shoot. The story has drawn outright skepticism from serious hominologists, more because of the individuals involved than due to the actual images.

At the time, Miller was enjoying a relaxing postproduction evening in a thirty-four-foot recreational vehicle on Walker Road, in the Jedediah Smith Redwoods State Park, near Crescent City, California. Earlier in the day Miller had been working on a new cable television series, *Adventures,* by shooting *Playboy* magazine's fortieth anniversary Playmate, Anna-Marie Goddard. Colin Goddard, the model's husband, was at the RV's wheel and first saw the upright, almost eight-foot-tall, hairy creature crossing the road. Miller rushed forth and caught five seconds of the creature on video.

Considering the taboo subject of Bigfoot and sex, the "Playmate Video," as it was called, quickly became a burden for some researchers. Anthropologist Jeff Meldrum thought this troublesome name would immediately exclude serious-minded scientists from examining what he felt was valuable evidence of Sasquatch. Therefore Meldrum proposed to the Bigfoot community that the footage be known as "The Redwoods Video," and the name has stuck.

The video is compelling, and such Bigfooters as Jeff Meldrum, Pixel Workshop director Dave Bittner, and Bigfoot investigator Daniel Perez, who was initially a skeptic, all very much accept the reality of this video today. But two problems with the video have caused others to feel the footage is a hoax or to ignore it.

One troubling item for many is the apparent penis seen on the Bigfoot being videotaped. This is such an underdiscussed detail in sighting reports to be a rarity in the record, except, of course, for the examples in this chapter. Wildlife biologist John Bindernagel used only one sentence in his book to discuss the entire nature of *male* sexuality for Bigfoot: "The genitalia of male Sasquatch are rarely observed."

Jeff Meldrum and Richard Greenwell put it this way in "The Redwoods Video," published in *BBC Wildlife* magazine in September 1998: "The Redwoods film may also reveal an anatomical detail not reported previously in Sasquatch encounters—the male genitalia. As the subject passes in front of the RV, a reflective object can be seen at the front of the body, just below waist level. The object in question has a thick, hair-covered base and a reflective, tapering portion that curves upwards in a sickle shape. One interpretation is that the subject is displaying an erect penis, perhaps as a form of threat—as has been observed in some other apes."

The second difficulty for many people wishing to study this video was the involvement of Anna-Marie Goddard, the Playmate who has appeared nude in *Playboy* on more than one occasion. Her presence in the midst of a Bigfoot sighting was seen as some sort of publicity stunt. The *Adventures* cable program never took off, so this now seems rather a weak argument.

The tape has little or nothing to do with just Goddard, other than that she was the one celebrity witness. But the video has followed her, much more so than Craig Miller, through the years. She has suffered a good deal of ridicule for her Bigfoot experience. She appeared on *The Tonight Show with Jay Leno* in 1995 to recount her experience, while taking the butt of Leno's jokes. In 2002, she was on *The Weakest Link* where only *Playboy* Playmates appeared and got kicked off early by her peers, because, according to Goddard, the other contestants were "jealous" of her Bigfoot encounter.

The Redwoods Video footage is now available on the Internet, but Anna-Marie Goddard and the erect penis remain troublesome topics in the "proof" of Bigfoot.

Why the Silence? Grover Krantz acknowledged and briefly theorized about the underreporting of Sasquatch sexuality. He wrote in 1992, "Sightings often include female breasts and sometimes male genitalia, though most observers are so overwhelmed by the overall phenomenon that they do not notice, or remember, details like these." Also at issue, no doubt, is the modesty of the witnesses and the neglect of researchers who have not asked the right questions. The Bigfoot community has failed to look at the "whole picture." Witnesses are not deeply interviewed about the sexual details of the creature seen, and if they are, those details are not generally recorded. Frankly, the subject of sex and the Sasquatch is avoided. Never mentioned are Bigfoot bestiality, Sasquatch penises, and that more human males than human females have traditionally been kidnapped by Bigfoot.

If Bigfoot, however, is to be treated as a truly unknown animal, the cryptozoological and hominological communities will have to overcome their embarrassment over the evidence that, yes, Bigfoot do have a sex life—and the organs that go along with this very biological activity.

14 The Changing Image of Bigfoot

While thousands of Americans claim to have seen Bigfoot, millions more have only experienced these creatures through the movies. And some of these movies have been the source of many a Bigfoot seeker's passion for the subject. More recently, a spate of television documentaries have brought a newfound respectability to the subject.

Our view of Bigfoot has evolved through time; despite that the real creature behind the images has apparently remained the same. We have seen this happen before with another large primate, the gorilla. Before the gorilla was discovered by "Western" science, white hunters and travelers would tell of native accounts of a fantastic giant ape that would squeeze village women to death. Firsthand experiences of gorillas by Europeans were related as attacks on members of safaris encountering the beasts in the bush. Today, of course, we know these early descriptions were misinterpretations and elaborations on observed roaring, chest beating, bluff charging, and big, bared teeth—normal "threat" vocalizations and displays by male and female gorillas, to protect their family groups. Gorillas are mostly nonviolent, gentle, and mainly vegetarian animals, which do not fit the nineteenth-century image found in travelers' tales. So too it appears to be with Bigfoot.

Images of Sasquatch

Aside from the many Native tales of apelike, hairy giants in the woods, there emerged, more than a hundred years ago, stories of Sasquatch as "another tribe," a lost race of humans out there in the rain forests of the Pacific Northwest. This is the version of Sasquatch portrayed in the early work of Indian agent John W. Burns. He was writing of the Sasquatch as if they were merely another Indian tribe, just hairy. In the 1990s, I was able to discover, on eBay of all places, a relic from these days—an eight-inch-high, furry little female, humanlike figurine. Covered in what would appear to be short brown hair from head to toe, the figure also sports long head hair down to her waist. It was labeled a "Young Sasquatch" on the front of its little stand and "Souvenir of B.C." on the stand's back. It originates from Langley, British Columbia, and represents an image frozen in time of how some tourists viewed Sasquatch, thanks to Burns and other writers like him in the 1920s until the modern era of Bigfoot.

The "Sasquatch as hairy Indian" closely mirrors the view in early newspaper stories of Sasquatch as "wildmen" who were naked and hairy. These representations were an attempt to fit the notion of a supposedly human-looking but hairy creature into the human cosmos.

America's Abominable Snowmen

In the 1950s, the media began carrying reports from parties climbing Mt. Everest of the giant, hairy monster of the snows called the Yeti or the Abominable Snowman. When the *Daily Mail,* a newspaper in London, decided in 1954 to launch a scientific expedition in search of the Yeti, newspapers around the world took note. The Abominable Snowman had arrived.

What followed was a flood of films. Although Canada had an active tradition of real-life encounters with the Sasquatch, Hollywood viewed the Yeti as the monster of the hour. Not coincidentally, 1954 saw the release of a United Artist film from the brothers of the famous Hollywood writer/director Billy Wilder. Produced and directed by W. Lee Wilder, and written by Myles Wilder, *The Snow Creature* is the first major Abominable Snowmen motion picture ever made. The movie's plot followed a formula that would be repeated time and time again. An expedition goes in search of the Yeti, encounters the beast, and the trouble begins. In this movie, the "Snow Creature" is actually captured; the problem surfaces when Customs agents try to figure out if this is a man or an animal, thus foreshadowing the "human versus ape" debate that would arise over Bigfoot years later.

The Snow Creature was followed by *Man Beast* (1955), *Half-Human: The Story of the Abominable Snowman* (1955 in Japan, 1957 in the USA), and Hammer Studios' classic *The Abominable Snowman of the Himalayas* (1957). The greatest fictional film treatment of the Abominable Snowman was probably the original Japanese version of *Half-Human*. Writing about this Japanese version, called *Ju Jin Yuki Otoko,* in July of 2001, Joe Winters stated on the Horror-Wood Web site that it was a pity that the movie had "all but disappeared, the result of a dispute with Ainu tribe lobbyists. That film may well have proved to be the best of the lot."

The lead character in all these films was the Himalayan Yeti, clearly an upright, hairy, humanlike creature with intelligence and, more often than not, a family. In this way, the myth of the lone Abominable Snow*man* was put to rest in the drive-in theaters and television parlors of America.

That image of groups of animals—a population versus a single monster—was easily transferred to Bigfoot when it was so dubbed in

1958. For about a decade afterward, as previously noted, these new American creatures were molded after the Yeti. Ivan T. Sanderson's *True* magazine article in 1959 was entitled "The Strange Story of America's Abominable Snowman." Roger Patterson's little 1966 book was called *Do Abominable Snowmen of America Really Exist?* Eventually, however, the Snowman would make room for Bigfoot.

Making of a Modern Monster

The naming of "Bigfoot," which *Humboldt Times* editor Andrew Genzoli did on October 5, 1958, was a significant cultural event. The widespread use of the term *Bigfoot* has been, in one sense, quite beneficial, making it easier for people outside the Pacific Northwest to "own" the creatures too. Before reports of "Bigfoot" were widely published in the press, the pervasive nature of these shaggy forest giants was inadequately acknowledged. But since the advent of *Bigfoot,* this word has actually made it easier for law enforcement officers, media reporters, and the general public to "accept" and "file" sightings of all kinds of unknown, hairy, upright creatures. Reports of a seven-foot-tall, brown-haired, white-maned creature seen in Ontario or Illinois might have been ignored in 1941, but in 2003, would be duly collected and written up as an "out-of-place" or "neighborhood" example of a Bigfoot. Such has been the positive effect of the name.

On the downside, the enormous popularity and humorous connotation of the term *Bigfoot* has been a tremendous drawback to funding research on these primates. Bigfoot tends to get the tabloid treatment whenever the topic arises in a mainstream publication. While it only took about sixty years of moderately financed hunting and collecting parties in search of mountain gorillas to "discover" and verify those giant African primates, the label *Bigfoot* just does not lend itself to university, zoological-society, or museum funding. The moniker that was rather universally avoided by most main-

stream zoologists and anthropologists is just now starting to loose the chains of its silly origins in describing a certain body part. There's a change in the wind and the trend is one of more open-mindedness, divorced from the jokes about the name.

"Home Movie" For the media and movie producers, it took more than a decade for Bigfoot, the real creature, to push aside the "presence" of the Abominable Snowman. Between 1958 and 1967, there was a drought of films about hairy, bipedal creatures. The Patterson-Gimlin film footage (see Chapter 7) changed all that. Seeing was believing, and this was no hairy human; it was a giant, unknown beast. It was peacefully walking away, but it was big and menacing. The image of creatures in the woods was no longer merely a fantasy, but a real-life incident, caught on film. Here was a real "home movie" of one such beast.

This event changed the picture-making landscape, and in no time, fictionalized versions of the hairy beasts of the Pacific North-west would grace the silver screen as Bigfoot.

The first movie using the "new" name was, not surprisingly, called *Bigfoot*, which appeared in 1970, directed by Robert F. Slatzer, a former newspaper writer. Tag lines for its ad campaign indirectly referred to that seminal 1967 "home movie": "Has a 150 Year Old Legend Come True?" and "America's abominable snowman . . . breeds with anything!"

Producer Anthony Cardoza made all the sounds of the beast and its kids himself and even appeared in *Bigfoot* as an extra, the "fisherman." The film's plot has Bigfoot kidnapping women, and bikers deciding to rescue them. One biker is played by Christopher Mitchum, the famed Robert Mitchum's son. The big star, however, was none other than John Carradine, who also was the American star of *Half-Human*. Carradine (whose sons David and Keith are movie and TV celebrities to the present generation) thus personalized the jump from the Abominable Snowman to Bigfoot. Six Bigfoot are in the film, including a "lead" Bigfoot, an evil, thin Bigfoot, three females, and one child (played by veteran actor Jerry Maren, who was the Munchkins Guild leader in the original *Wizard of Oz*).

The most memorable line from *Bigfoot* is spoken by the female lead, Joi Landis: "They're practically subhuman, except that they still live like animals!" (This sentence, similar to an earlier Yeti movie hint, pinpointed the emerging debate about the affinities of Bigfoot.)

An unrelated Landis, John Landis, shows up the following year in the grade B movie *Schlock*. This film, with director John Landis playing the role of the very thin Bigfoot, had a financially risky sense of humor, which was captured by the ad campaign's tag line: "Due to the horrifying nature of this film, no one will be admitted to the theater." The plot was right out of the Beauty and the Beast, or the old King Kong and Yeti movies. The Bigfoot kidnaps a girl, and the army is called to the rescue. As briefly mentioned in chapter 7, the captain in the National Guard is played by John Chambers, the makeup artist who won an Academy Award for *The Planet of the Apes*, and who some blamed for making the Patterson Bigfoot. The makeup artist for this movie was Chamber's student Rick Baker, who pops up again a little later.

By the 1970s, Bigfoot exploitation movies had come into vogue. Other films, such as the soft-porn movie *The Beast and the Vixens*, also entitled *Beauties and the Beast* (1972 or 1973), about a horny Bigfoot terrorizing horny couples, were not widely seen and had little influence. But one Bigfoot movie from this time would play a bigger part on the B-movies circuit than all the rest.

Journey to Boggy Creek

Something shocking happened in 1972. A drive-in Bigfoot movie became a surprise moneymaker. The movie was *The Legend of Boggy Creek*, released in 1972, and out for the first time on DVD in 2002.

Although people around the Boggy Creek area had been seeing Bigfoot-type creatures since the 1940s, their encounters in the late 1960s and then especially in 1971 received a good deal of press attention. The six-feet-tall, hairy "Fouke Monster" gained notoriety when it harassed two families (the Fords and the Crabtrees) living outside Fouke, Arkansas (pop. 600), in the southwest part of the state. The monster was said to smell awful and apparently made a habit of killing chickens, dispatching livestock, and mauling a number of dogs. Director Charles B. Pierce decided to use real eyewitnesses (mostly the Crabtrees) and the actual locations near Boggy Creek to re-create Fouke's experience with their local monster. The docudrama or semidocumentary thriller became a smash success, a cult classic.

Although it was a scripted movie, the spooky footage of the river bottoms, fog, and vegetation along the Boggy Creek make for a captivating, and for most filmgoers, scary setting. The terrifying encounters were re-created quite realistically, even though the movie budget is reflected in an almost amateur feel to the filmmaking. The "based on true stories" tag line only reinforced the wonder generated by the film.

Between the lonely, piercing cry of the monster and the eerie music, the auditory experience from the film is haunting too. For example, these lingering lyrics (Earl E. Smith, 1972) waft through the theater as the audience's attention drifts over the swampy bottoms:

> Here, the sulfur river flows,
> Rising when the storm cloud blows,
> This is where the creature goes,
> Lurking in the land he knows.
> Perhaps, he dimly wonders why,
> Is there no other such as I?
> To love, to touch before I die,
> To listen to my lonely cry.

The impact of *The Legend of Boggy Creek* was far-reaching. A couple of modern reviews from the Internet give more than a hint of its significance: "Bigfoot was, and still is, a celebrity because of this movie!" and "This may be the movie that made 'Bigfoot' a national star."

A self-published book by Smokey Crabtree entitled *Smokey and the Fouke Monster* (1974) followed the film, giving "another point of view" of the events portrayed in the movie. Crabtree wrote that director Pierce didn't "invest anything and had millions to gain." Smokey and I lectured from the same podiums in Ohio and Texas in recent years, and he's still talking as if it all happened yesterday. Crabtree, whom I sincerely like, may not admit it, but the movie more than the monster changed his life. He never saw the Fouke Monster, but he's made a career out of lecturing about the movie.

The movie also created a whole new generation of dedicated Bigfoot hunters. Young people between the ages of ten and thirteen who were first attracted to Bigfoot research in the 1970s speak of *The Legend of Boggy Creek* as the source of their passion in the subject. In his 1988 book, *Big Footnotes,* Daniel Perez wrote, "My personal interest in monsters was first ignited at about the tender age of ten, by the movie *The Legend of Boggy Creek*. This was the trigger which led to casual to casually serious to serious full-fledged involvement in this subject matter." *Maryland Bigfoot Reference Guide* author Mark Opsasnick notes this movie inspired his interest in Bigfoot at the age of eleven. Ditto for cryptozoology artist Bill Rebsamen, who told me, "I was about ten years old when I saw it. I went immediately to the library the next day and checked out all the books I could find on Bigfoot after seeing the movie." And Chester Moore Jr., Texan outdoors journalist and author of *Bigfoot South* (2002), writes, "Seeing *The Legend of Boggy Creek* lit my interest in the Bigfoot phenomenon into a full-blown passion. While the Pacific Northwest seemed a world away to me, Arkansas did not. . . . The impact it had on me as a youngster was immense."

Many people in the current organization the Texas Bigfoot Research Center (TBRC), including Monica Rawlins, Robert Dominguez, Tim Clay, Rick Hayes, and Jerry Hestand, told me that they had seen the movie in their youth, and it had been the one thing that brought them into the field. TBRC director Craig Woolheater said, "It sealed the deal for me." *The Legend of Boggy Creek* was also the entry point for cryptofiction author Lee Murphy and for Chad Austin, president of Interactive Pilot, Inc.

A smash hit, *The Legend of Boggy Creek* spawned two sequels, *Return to Boggy Creek* (Tom Moore, 1977) and *Boggy Creek 2: The Legend Continues* (Charles B. Pierce, 1985, and thus the latter is actually the third movie, although the second from Pierce). Following in the footprints of Pierce's movie, *Creature from Black Lake* (Joy N. Houck Jr., 1976) was filmed at Caddo Lake, as was *The Legend of Boggy Creek*. *Creature from Black Lake* was about a group of men searching for Bigfoot in nearby Louisiana. *Sasquatch: The Legend of Bigfoot* (1978), with great footage from the Three Sisters Wilderness in Oregon, was patterned after *The Legend of Boggy Creek*, mixing allegedly real-life incidents with scary scenes of Bigfoot attacking people.

This era of Bigfoot movies was capped with *The Capture of Bigfoot* (Bill Rebane, 1979), where we find a town that has exploited Bigfoot for tourist dollars is upset by a local businessman who hopes to trap Bigfoot once and for all, so that he can make the big bucks all at once. The film was a box-office disaster.

The image of Bigfoot in these motion pictures harks back to women-kidnapping, upright, hairy beasts in the Yeti movies, but with a twist—these Bigfoot are even more violent. From *Bigfoot* (1970) through all the Boggy Creek movies and clones, one finds a decidedly vicious, aggressive Bigfoot. This cinematic Sasquatch only slightly reflects what was actually happening across the country with real Bigfoot reports during this time of high strangeness. Bigfoot, especially in the Pacific Northwest, continued to be mostly reported in nonviolent encounters and through footprint finds. Bigfoot may scare people at the movies, but not really in the woods or near their country homes. Nor, it should be noted, did the Hollywood Bigfoot movies lead to a rash of real Boggy Creek–type creature sightings in most places in North America.

Era of the Bigfoot Documentaries

The B-movie Bigfoot did not rule the day. On a parallel plane during the 1970s, thanks in large part to the existence of the Patterson-Gimlin footage, Bigfoot began to stalk the world of nonfiction films on the drive-in circuit and on television screens.

While John Carradine confronted a fictional hairy giant in *Bigfoot* in 1970, the documentary *Legend of Bigfoot,* by executive producer Ivan Marx, was released. It was a Sunn Classics film of a man pursuing Bigfoot from Alaska to the Pacific Northwest. Sunn Classics, a Utah-based film company owned by members of the Church of Latter-day Saints (Mormons), would become a driving force behind Bigfoot documentaries.

Sunn Classics also produced *The Mysterious Monsters*, also known as *Bigfoot the Mysterious Monster* (Robert Guenette, 1975), with Peter Graves as the narrator. This movie, shown commercially in theaters, would have a long-term impact, though not as widespread as *The Legend of Boggy Creek*. Nevertheless, I've been told by Eric Altman, director of the Pennsylvania Bigfoot Society, Mike George, director of the Western New York Bigfoot Investigation Center, and Forrest Halford, head of the Colorado Bigfoot e-mail group, to name a few, that *The Mysterious Monsters* was the film that motivated them to study Bigfoot.

Meanwhile, on television, documentaries about Bigfoot began to crop up. The most prominent and significant of these was the *In Search Of (ISO)* series, the most memorable episode of which was

"In Search Of Bigfoot" (Alan Landsburg, 1976), narrated by Leonard Nimoy (of *Star Trek* fame). Other *In Search Of* programs, for example on the Bay Area Group and the Honey Island Swamp Monster, also touched on Bigfoot. These programs would also spark a growing interest in Bigfoot. Gregg Hale of Haxan Pictures in Florida, the man behind *The Blair Witch Project,* has often been quoted in the press and discussed with me how the *ISO* programs on Bigfoot from the 1970s got him interested in the strange and the unknown. In 2000, when the new series of *ISO* programs was commissioned, Gregg Hale got the call. Hale asked me to be the senior series consultant, and we worked closely together on, you guessed it, programs about Bigfoot and other cryptozoological topics, before the series was moved to other producers in California.

Documentary films and television programs on Bigfoot made Bigfoot more credible to the general public. These Bigfoot documentaries were nature films that because of their elusive subject needed to work outside the parameters of formal biological-science-class films. These films lead the way in our questioning of the authority of science to expand or limit inquiry about this apparent primate. Almost every one of these documentaries was produced with the Patterson-Gimlin footage as its centerpiece. The Bigfoot television programs and drive-in fillers mixed the flavor of old safari, romance zoology, biography, and adventure films with new graphics, special effects, and a growing ecological advocacy. This early trend would be revisited and highlighted years later, but only after a very hairy Hollywood detour.

Hello to Harry

Twenty years after the filming of the Patterson-Gimlin film, Hollywood released the most popular Bigfoot film of all time, *Harry and the Hendersons.* The prerelease tag line gave a hint of what the movie held for its mostly youthful audience (and their parents): "According to science, Harry doesn't exist. When you can't believe your eyes, trust your heart."

The plot merely reinforced the journey of compassion portrayed in this movie. Returning from a trip into the wilderness, the Henderson family's car hits a large animal on a backwoods road. Banishing a gun to kill it, the Hendersons discover they don't have to shoot it, as it appears to be quite dead, and they secure it to the top of their station wagon for the trip back to their Seattle home. But of course, in this lighthearted comedy, "Harry" is not dead. He revives and the Hendersons adopt him with the predictable resulting laughs. They have to hide him from the authorities, the press, and a Bigfoot hunter. And that's where all the movie's edgy moments dwell, on the "to kill it to prove it" versus "no kill" tension.

The movie represented the debate taking place using characters based on real people in the Bigfoot field. The heavily accented French-Canadian, obsessed "pro-kill" hunter "Jacques LaFleur," played by David Suchet (famous for his role as Hercule Poirot), was clearly but loosely modeled on Swiss-born Canadian Sasquatch hunter René Dahinden. The "no kill" Bigfoot expert, "Dr. Wallace Wrightwood," a tall, thin, intelligent character played by Don Ameche, seems to be a combination of three real Bigfoot personalities, the tall, lean, bright Canadian chronicler John Green, anthropologist Grover Krantz, and Bigfoot Central Museum owner Cliff Crook. Crook says he was an official "consultant" on the movie, and many of the Bigfoot castings and artifacts shown in the film are from his museum. He feels the Wrightwood character is modeled on him, but it appears Hollywood blended several people into the role. Dr. Wrightwood's looks and publications mirror Green's, his academic status mirrors Krantz's, and of course, the museum reflects Crook's.

Director William Dear, who worked on the 1985 television series *Amazing Stories* created and produced by Steven Spielberg, was asked by Spielberg's Amblin Entertainment to steer *Harry and the Hendersons* onto the screen. What they got met their wildest expectations. Released the last weekend in June 1987, the movie ranked ninth in the USA, received $2.3 million for that opening, and grossed over $21 million in total during its summer run.

And of course, Harry lives on. A television series spin-off was mildly successful, airing seventy-two episodes from January 1991 through June 1993. The movie is still popular on DVD, and Bigfoot memorabilia collectors actively accumulate videos of the television series and *objets d'art* tied to the movie.

The likeness of Harry in the film, on television, and for years on the tours at Universal Studios was created through the makeup magic of Rick Baker, who won an Academy Award for his work on the movie. For a few years Harry was what people had in mind when the word *Bigfoot* was mentioned, replacing the Patterson-Gimlin footage's zaftig Bigfoot shown crossing the Bluff Creek sandbar. The Harry of the movies is a very, very tall, smiling, gentle giant, a male without a penis but with a pronounced hairless forehead, stark white beard, and white mustache in the midst of a body of brown hair. Field observations of Bigfoot do not reinforce the reality of Baker's Harry, but the forehead and white facial hair have become a prominent reflection of how the "modern" Bigfoot should appear, at least, to the generation that was ten to sixteen in 1987.

Harry and the Hendersons was followed by more family-entertainment fare, such as *Bigfoot: The Unforgettable Encounter* (Corey Michael Eubanks, 1995), *Little Bigfoot* (Art Camacho, 1997), and *Little Bigfoot II: The Journey Home* (Art Camacho, 1997). All three were about children who befriend a young Bigfoot. The few real-life encounters between children and Bigfoot that Ivan Sanderson had written about in 1961 had finally made it into Sasquatch cinema. It was a time for a friendlier Bigfoot. The period of the comedic, gentle, giant, nonsexual Bigfoot had arrived. But not for long. After all, something very real was still happening out in the woods. Or as the character Malcolm says in the *Jurassic Park* movies, "Nature has always found its way."

Reality Sasquatch TV

On April 27, 1986, Geraldo Rivera stood in front of Al Capone's tomb, for two hours. When he opened the tomb and discovered it was empty, it seemed as if "The Mystery of Al Capone's Tomb" would be declared a failure. Instead, it was the highest-rated syndicated television program of all time. The appearance made Rivera a star. It also got television producers all over America talking the morning after about how reality television programs, especially ones about mysteries, were so cheap to make, and so very successful.

With a major mystery, a television-magazine format, a famous host, glamorous reporters, the heavy use of economically available archival footage, and re-creations and reenactments—bingo, the reality-television-show formula came into being in the late 1980s. The high-quality prototype for the times was *Unsolved Mysteries*, which began broadcasting weekly on September 14, 1988, on NBC-TV, and continues today on the Lifetime cable network. In *The Complete Directory to Prime Time Network and Cable TV Shows*, authors Tim Brooks and Earle Marsh state, "This unassuming documentary series was one of the most popular reality programs of the late 1980s and the inspiration for dozens of network and syndicated imitators."

In the 1990s, *Unsolved Mysteries* ran reports, for example, on the expeditions of Tom Slick, the Minnesota Iceman, and Peter Byrne's search for Bigfoot. Other series, from *Sightings* to *Evening Magazine*, carried regular reports on Bigfoot. As the twentieth century was coming to a close, the "real" Bigfoot, at least a version of it, was making a comeback, and the Hendersons' Harry was fading into the background.

Back to Nature

Another trend in television and documentary filmmaking, the explosion of interest in nature-oriented topics, would also have an impact on

the Bigfoot field. With animals being a perennially interesting topic and outdoor recreation being rediscovered as a family-friendly activity, discovery-adventure-nature programs on Bigfoot began to appear rather regularly in the 1990s.

Ancient Mysteries, History Mysteries, Animal X, and other seemingly documentary contributions to solving the Bigfoot mystery blossomed during this decade. Most of these shows took a straightforward zoological approach to the subject. Viewers have come to view Bigfoot as part of the outdoor landscape, an animal to be discussed, and a mystery to be pondered. The production companies for these programs also began to serve as a source of funding for some mini-expeditions, taking the place once filled by zoological institutions in the nineteenth century.

No other current documentary captures the modern view of Bigfoot, the enjoyment experienced by seekers, and the outdoors nature of this subject like *Sasquatch Odyssey: The Hunt for Bigfoot* (Peter von Puttkamer, 1999). This film profiles the pursuit of Bigfoot mostly through the eyes of Grover Krantz, René Dahinden, John Green, and Peter Byrne, who formed the "Four Horsemen of Sasquatchery"—they laid the foundation work on these mysterious creatures of the Pacific Northwest from the 1960s onward. It is more than a biopic about the seekers, however, as it gives a great overview of the country, various pieces of the evidence (including the Patterson-Gimlin footage), and the ongoing debates about how to "hunt" for Bigfoot. The viewer is given a good, nature-oriented, factual overview that is compelling in its support of the Sasquatch.

Tracking these creatures from the ancient oral traditions to their modern celluloid images, it's clear that our picture of the creature has changed, as has the purpose of our quest. Today, Bigfoot has become a gateway through which people are realizing their passion for the outdoors, mysteries, and wildlife.

15 The Bigfooters

No one told me about this part. I had been in California's Mendocino wilderness area for nearly two weeks, alone, camping in a tent, going out at night and during the days, and looking for signs of Bigfoot. Near the end of my time there, I went to move my tent because the ground seemed to have settled onto some lumps that weren't there when I'd originally pitched it. And there it was. That bulge was a damn scorpion under the tent!

In my early Midwestern Bigfoot hunting days, I got used to all kinds of ticks and other critters that had decided to use my body as their feeding ground. Swooshing around the rivers, creeks, and swampy bottoms of southern Illinois, each trek into Bigfoot country held its own tortures. I still remember the time I was poking around the Big Muddy, on the fringes of some active Bigfoot area, when I walked waist-deep into near freezing water.

I've been all over North America, camping out, trekking through, and searching for Bigfoot. My various "research" vehicles (from that old Datsun truck in California to my beat-up station wagon out East) have taken me deep into some mighty wild places in the country. Mostly, I have used my head, eyes, nose, and ears to try to discover what's out there. Like most Bigfooters, I have had little actual success. Like I said earlier, I have found prints, heard noises, but never seen a Bigfoot. But that has never stopped me from going back again.

Adventures in Bigfooting

Take my days of searching in the Shasta-Trinity National Forest of California, in 1974. Back then there wasn't much high-tech equipment available, and besides, I couldn't have afforded it if there were. I gathered together a camera, a tent, a sleeping bag, some plaster of paris, and headed for the hills. I took five days off from my work as head of a group home for troubled children and journeyed with a female friend into a secret location of recent Bigfoot activity. In August of a previous year, during a fishing trip and other visits, several Bay Area–based Bigfooters, including Sharon Gorden, Richard Foster, Ben E. Foster Jr., and Archie Buckley, had multiple Bigfoot sightings there including seeing a Bigfoot throw a rock, one prowling around a campfire, another flipping a car aerial, some communicating by gesture, and another being attracted nearby. Tracks, a dead fawn, and feces had been found. It was an active area, and I thought I would take a look.

Bigfooting means different things to different individuals, of course, but for me, when not interviewing eyewitnesses and arriving at the site of a late-breaking sighting or track find, it simply means waiting. Waiting for Bigfoot to come to you. Waiting to discover some tracks on a hike. Waiting for the night, for its sounds and smells. And sometimes you have to wait for other people to go away. Luckily, on this trip into the Trinity-Shasta area, no humans were around except for my companion and me, so it was mostly a time of walking and waiting.

And not leaving. Bigfooters refuse to exit their quiet, despite all kinds of problems thrown at us by Mother Nature. On this

Trinity-Shasta trek, first there was the cold. It's really cold at night in the mountains of California in August. Next, there was the rain. It rained one whole day and night. But I wasn't going to leave. I would wait out the storm. Wait for Bigfoot.

In between the rain and the cold, of course, I found I was literally in God's country. I discovered myself surrounded by deep, dense, rich green forests that hugged the hillsides. Here is quiet so pure that you can hear a bubbling brook miles away. Birds. Small mammals. You could hear everything.

I did all the things you are supposed to do, like baiting with peanut butter, staying awake until ungodly late hours, getting up early, trekking about silently, and waiting.

But no Bigfoot. Perhaps it was the smell of my truck, parked too close down the hill? Or the smell of the female I had with me? Or maybe the Bigfoot just were over in another valley right during the time I was in this one? Whatever the reason, it just wasn't my time. And so, typical of many of my trips into the field over forty years, I came out of the woods and never wrote about it until now. But that's what most searches are like. Lots of looking, waiting, and you come up empty. Except for the experience, which I would not trade in for anything.

I am not the only one to feel this way obviously.

They come to the field with a sparkle in their eye and a quickness in their step. Something has stimulated their interest—a book, a movie, a footprint find, an encounter, whatever—it has struck a chord. A few stay for a while and make memorable contributions. For others, it becomes a lifelong passion. Or is it an obsession? It is a special federation without membership cards or a secret handshake, but it is a club nevertheless. They are the Bigfooters.

In the beginning, they were few, and now they are many. I am one of them and have meet and grown to know hundreds during my over forty years in the Bigfoot field. Here are a few of them.

The Tracker

John Green believes that Robert Titmus, born in 1919, really deserves the title of the "First Horseman of Sasquatchery."

An animal tracker and a taxidermist in Redding, California, Titmus was an old friend of Jerry Crew's, the down-to-earth construction worker who was one of the first to come upon huge, unknown tracks at Bluff Creek, California, in August 1958. It was Titmus who taught Crew how to work plaster of paris and how to make the first impression of the Bluff Creek track that was cast on October 1, 1958, and led to the name *Bigfoot*.

Titmus could find prints, recognize individual Bigfoot by their tracks, and openly showed his cast collection to all those interested in Bigfoot. René Dahinden, Tom Slick, Ivan Sanderson, and many others visited Titmus over the years.

Beginning in 1962, Titmus tracked the elusive Bigfoot from Alaska to northern California, although the casts he made during this period were all lost when his houseboat was destroyed by a fire. Nine days after Roger Patterson and Bob Gimlin took their film of an alleged Bigfoot in 1967, Titmus was there, tracking and examining the distance the creature had reportedly covered during the encounter. He told of having seen Sasquatch two times and of having tracked Sasquatch dozens of times during those years. Titmus's last forays to Bluff Creek were in 1994 and 1996. Titmus, long ill, died of a heart attack on July 1, 1997, at Chilliwack, British Columbia. He was seventy-eight years old.

Titmus never wrote about his work, instead sharing his discoveries with others, including Green, Dahinden, Slick, Grover Krantz, Jeff Meldrum, and me.

The Hunter

One of the first men that Titmus met on his search for Bigfoot was René Dahinden. If Titmus was the first tracker of Bigfoot, then Dahinden was probably Bigfoot's first hunter. Dahinden was born in Switzerland and

moved to Canada in 1953. Two months after he arrived, he heard about the Sasquatch and was within three years conducting serious research on the hairy primates, sometimes with British Columbian researcher and chronicler John Green, whom Dahinden met in 1956.

Dahinden was involved with the early investigations in California in 1959, but after a month and a half he left, disgusted with what he saw in these early attempts to find the creature. Dahinden had little tolerance for silly ideas, such as traps, baiting, or teams of men. When the effort in the Pacific Northwest wasn't going his way, Dahinden would seek his own counsel and go off to search alone again. Dahinden was never afraid to speak what was on his mind and often walked away in loathing.

Dahinden conducted numerous field investigations throughout the Pacific Northwest, interviewed many witnesses, and examined the physical evidence for the creature.

Dahinden was the first to show the Patterson-Gimlin film in the former Soviet Union, and he worked hard to see to it that the film got the scientific attention he felt it deserved. His only book, *Sasquatch*, was written with Don Hunter. In the 1980s and 1990s, Dahinden's time became more and more occupied in technical legal and copyright affairs, as he owned the photographic images of the Patterson-Gimlin film. He died on April 18, 2001, in British Columbia.

The Chroniclers John Green, a newspaper publisher, started collecting and publishing British Columbia's hairy-giant stories in 1955, mostly for their entertainment value. He first came to regard Sasquatch as a real animal in 1957, when he interviewed William Roe about his 1955 encounter and Albert Ostman, who stepped forward with his 1924 kidnapping episode after the Roe incident was published. John Green was at Bluff Creek just days after the news broke of the huge footprints found in Bluff Creek.

Green was what people called one lucky Sasquatch investigator. He arrived at the Bluff Creek area in 1958 soon after all the publicity broke. On Green's way up to the site, he was told that, unfortunately, the day before he got there the whole site had to be plowed over due to the progress of the construction. Green thought skeptically to himself, "Oh, ya, how convenient, that is one way to make sure no one debunks this thing." The construction fellows said, go on up and just look around. John Green drove up and parked his car. His wife opened her door, and to their mutual surprise, she found a footprint right there, in freshly graded dirt.

Green began publishing a series of monographs on Sasquatch in the early years, which became standard references for Bigfoot investigators. These were followed by his classic work on the subject, *Sasquatch: The Apes Among Us* in 1978.

Other investigators who detailed the 1958–60 activities and are today called chroniclers included zoologist Ivan T. Sanderson, California newspaperwoman Betty Allen, and writer Marian T. Place. All three visited and interviewed the principals of the Bluff Creek incident and wrote about it. Sanderson was first to tell the world about these "new" hairy beasts of the rain forests of California through his popular articles in *True* magazine, his book *Abominable Snowmen: Legend Come to Life,* and later in the pages of such publications as *Argosy* and *Pursuit.*

Big Money, Big Game There was mounting excitement over the quest in California. An active population of Bigfoot appeared to be within the grasp of an expeditionary effort, and funding was seen as a key. The prize seemed within reach. The Bigfooters were getting close.

All hopes for an American Bigfoot expedition turned to Texas millionaire Tom Slick, who was an early backer of Abominable Snowmen hunts during the 1950s. Slick was thrilled to learn of a mystery

hominoid in America he could pursue. After expeditions to the Himalaya in search of the Yeti, he felt the timing was right to refocus his effort closer to home. Ivan T. Sanderson was a consultant to those Asian expeditions and had been throughout western North America in August 1959, gathering Sasquatch and Bigfoot accounts, talking it over with his fellow Slick consultant, anthropologist George Agogino. Through contacts between Agogino, Sanderson, and Bob Titmus, Slick received a Bigfoot track cast from a series Titmus had found on November 1, 1959, at Bluff Creek. A couple weeks later, negotiations between Slick and Green, Titmus, Sanderson, Dahinden, and others lead to the creation of what Slick called the Pacific Northwest Expedition. Tom Slick's California effort hired Titmus as its original field leader for several months in the late 1950s.

The significance of Texas millionaire Tom Slick's expeditions cannot be understated. His efforts set the stage for the way in which Bigfooters would work together—and not work together—from the 1950s up through and into the twenty-first century.

To Slick's backers, the search for Bigfoot was rather like a big-game hunt for an African trophy. Slick flew into the hunt in December 1959 via helicopter. Texan F. Kirk Johnson Jr., Slick's financial partner on the Yeti expeditions, and Slick's secretary, Jeri Walsh, would later visit the Expedition's campsite themselves. In late December 1959, Titmus and Slick hooked up with parties of a dozen heavily armed men. The quest was in full swing, and the quarry, to Slick, at least, seemed only days away. Then the hunt started to unravel.

Slick had several groups of people hunting for Bigfoot in the bush at the same time. Despite his millions, Slick spread the funding around so that no one team had enough to make their life easy. They used their own vehicles, did not have high-tech equipment, and were mostly being supported to look around and find prints. The cast of characters hired by the expedition grew to include Ivan Marx, Ray Wallace, George Gatto, and John La Pe. Mismanagement

of Slick's money and equipment by some of these minor characters led to hard times for the dedicated Bigfooters. Slick's financial management may have added to the problem of interpersonal tensions because he placed so many teams in the field at one time. The conflicts of those days left a legacy on Bigfoot research that lives on to this day.

Slick liked to be in control of everything. While he was the "leader" and Titmus was the "field leader" or "deputy leader," the pull of Slick's other obligations distracted him from the hunt. Slick needed someone he knew to be in charge, and that someone was Peter Byrne, who had been his point man in the Yeti hunt.

Byrne, Irish-born, refined, a dashing and successful big-game hunter of tiger and elephant in India and Nepal, had found his first Yeti print in 1948 in Sikkim. He had first met Tom Slick in a valley in the Himalayas in 1956 and had grown to know Slick through their shared love of adventure, women, and a similar lifestyle. He had headed Slick's rather successful searches for Yeti in 1957, 1958, and 1959, which had discovered tracks in snow and mud, and the mysterious Pangboche Yeti hand.

So Slick flew his friend Peter Byrne and Peter's brother, Bryan, over from Nepal, and early in 1960, Byrne had become the new leader of the Pacific Northwest Expedition.

The Byrnes did their best to organize the effort, but money, equipment, and men had been lost. Before they returned to Canada, Titmus, Green, and Dahinden shared duties in the Pacific Northwest Expedition with the Byrnes. Everyone has his own view of those days, and it is obvious that no one got along with one another—or Peter Byrne. Dahinden called the expedition a "total screwup," but Dahinden was not an easy person to be around either. "René had a nasty habit of pacing in front of the campfire and spitting into it," John Green recalled for *Vancouver Courier* reporter Robin Brunet in 2001. "And while René tended to sleep in, another fellow was prone to rising early and firing his rifle. René would lose his temper, go stamping off into the bush, and make so much noise that no creature would come within a mile of them."

John Green made an interesting observation about these times in the documentary *Sasquatch Odyssey:* "People who are prepared to stand up against the entire continent and go looking for something that everyone else says doesn't exist have a tendency to be pigheaded. And when you put several of them together and try to organize something, they all have their own ideas of what they should be doing."

The Byrnes never saw a Bigfoot, but they claimed to have found twelve sets of footprints. Titmus, along with Canadians Green and Dahinden, soon moved lock, stock, and barrel to British Columbia. Once there, in 1960, Slick sponsored an effort he called the British Columbia Expedition—with Titmus as its head. Slick even sent Titmus to the University of Washington Hospital to study embalming techniques, on the belief that the 1961 British Columbia Sasquatch hunt would capture or kill a specimen quickly.

Green would somewhat humorously observe that the British Columbia expedition never consisted of more than a leader, deputy leader, co-deputy leader, and a cook. However, this small party very much reflected the method of hunting Bigfoot Slick thought would succeed. The BC group did find tracks in July 1961, on an island off the coast, and in October of the same year, on a little island near the larger one of the earlier find.

The California and BC expeditions ended abruptly in 1962, when Tom Slick died in a midair explosion of his Cessna over Montana.

Byrne returned to the Bigfoot hunt in 1971, apparently with funding by Ohio millionaire Tom Page. In 1975, Byrne wrote *The Search for Bigfoot: Monster, Myth, or Man?* but left the hunt again in 1979. A dozen years later he came back, promoting a no-kill position, when he got new funding from New Hampshire millionaire Robert Rines. Byrne directed the Bigfoot Research Project from 1992 until

1997. In between, Byrne, wearing a trademark ascot, would make a career out of appearing regularly in television documentaries about Bigfoot. In the documentary *Sasquatch Odyssey,* Peter Byrne tells of having used "three million dollars of other people's money" during his life to search for Yeti and Bigfoot.

Green and Dahinden would remain active continuously, funding their efforts from their own pockets, but they had a falling out over the questions of sharing data and killing Bigfoot. Green thought it important to share info and get a Bigfoot body; Dahinden did not wish to share his work and over time moved from the kill to the no-kill position.

Many strong-willed people were involved in Tom Slick's North American expeditions, but then it takes a special kind of person to look for Bigfoot and deal with the ridicule of the public, the press, family, friends, and academia.

One such person inhabited the halls of ivy.

The Doctor Another pro-kill advocate was the celebrated fourth horseman of Sasquatchery, Grover S. Krantz, an outspoken academic who came into the field after reading Ivan T. Sanderson's book of 1961. For two decades beginning in the 1970s, Krantz was the embodiment of the "scientific Bigfooter." As the modern era's first academically affiliated physical anthropologist to openly involve himself in Bigfoot research, Krantz was the most quoted authority on the Bigfoot controversy.

Grover S. Krantz, born a Mormon in 1931 in Salt Lake City, grew up in Rockford, Illinois, and moved with his family to Utah when he was ten. Krantz went on to study at the Universities of Utah, California (BA, 1955; MA, 1958), and Minnesota (Ph.D., 1971), with a concentration in human evolution.

Krantz began his Bigfoot research in 1963 and fully accepted the reality of the 1967 Patterson film. He found the Bigfoot's loping gait "consistent with a five-hundred-pound biped." He said, "I've attempted to imitate it, and I really can't do it worth a damn."

He began teaching at Washington State University in 1968 and remained there until his retirement, as a full professor, in the 1990s. Getting tenure was not easy for Krantz. He once said that studying Bigfoot was "something of a problem in the academic world. My university supports my Sasquatch research. They don't fire me."

He wrote and edited several scholarly papers on the Sasquatch published in *Northwest Anthropological Research Notes* and *Cryptozoology,* and four books, the best known of which is *Big Footprints*.

Krantz believed that the survival of the giant ape *Gigantopithecus* could explain the source of modern Sasquatch reports. He was also the primary North American spokesperson for the view that a Bigfoot should be killed to prove they exist.

Krantz died from pancreatic cancer on Valentine's Day, February 14, 2002, in his Port Angeles, Washington, home. Krantz was never afraid to take the professionally risky position that the primates called Bigfoot actually exist.

Bay Area Group After the "founding" phase of "Bigfootery," a new generation of baby boomer Bigfooters arose. One such group organized themselves into the Bay Area Group (BAG), so named because of their location in the San Francisco Bay area. In 1974, I first met their spokesman, the gentlemanly George Haas, at his Oakland, California, home and returned often, into 1975, to visit with him. Haas lived in a little apartment chock-full of hundreds of books and artifacts from his years of interest in Bigfoot. During one visit, I met Archie Buckley, the group's founder and leader. The group's fame derived from Haas's widely distributed newsletter, *The Bigfoot Bulletin,* which was first issued on January 2, 1969.

Haas's files included over three thousand news items and specialized collectibles on Sasquatch, such as rocks used by the creatures in stacked piles. Haas and his colleagues were opponents of killing Bigfoot, reflective, in a fashion, of the peace movement ongoing throughout the Berkeley-Oakland area at the time. Members of the BAG had several close encounters with Bigfoot at an undisclosed location in the Shasta-Trinity area during the late 1960s and early 1970s.

The Guy That Carved That Statue

A famous life-size statue of Bigfoot created in the late 1960s is on display in Willow Creek, California, which is often called the Capital of Bigfoot Country. In the 1970s, this Bigfoot sculpture was "the" obligatory shoot for every documentary on the Bigfoot subject. Although he has been out of the search since 1974, the sculptor, Jim McClarin, keeps popping up in Bigfoot books. Besides being remembered for having carved that famous wooden icon of Bigfoot, he also appeared in John Green's analytic re-creation of the Patterson-Gimlin film, published ever so briefly the most scientific newsletter on the creatures up to that time, the *Manimals Newsletter,* and compiled one of the first databases on Bigfoot.

McClarin was born in 1946, in Buffalo, New York, and moved with his family around the country, ending up in California when he was a freshman in high school. McClarin and I grew to be friends during my days in California. I've kept in touch with him, off and on, throughout the last quarter century. When I last spoke to him in 2002, I asked him about 1966 and that famous statue of his.

In the summer of 1966 I drove up to Arcata, California, site of the Humboldt State College campus, to find housing and have a look at the campus. I then drove up to Willow Creek, the Hoopa Indian Reservation, and into the

Bluff Creek area. I remember getting out to look around near the ridge dividing the Blue Creek and Bluff Creek basins and feeling rather spooked, imagining that a giant, hairy hominid was staring hard, sending psychic daggers to strike fear into me. To try getting into a Bigfoot frame of mind I ate salal berries there, wild onions at nearby Onion Lake, and several raw bites of a rattlesnake I killed on a steep trail on the Hoopa Indian Reservation.

During the ensuing school year I organized a search expedition on campus, and the following summer, three other students and I spent ten days trekking down the still-wild Blue Creek basin dressed in camouflage coveralls and moccasins to soften our footsteps. My companions were Bob Betts, Bill Henderson, and Don Orsburn. We carried prepared food packets with us but ate off the land as much as possible and built no fires the first several nights.

When we did build a fire, some large body was heard moving noisily in the undergrowth up the hillside from our camp. We thought it sounded like a biped. Betts and Henderson rush up there with flashlights, though not until the twig and branch snapping had subsided. Whatever it was had retreated and no discernible prints could be found in the hard, dry soil.

After we emerged from the woods we learned that a great many footprints in several sizes had been found in the dust along logging roads near Onion Lake, and that Dr. Lauk, who was the Humboldt zoology department chair and my adviser at the college, had traveled to inspect them. (As I recall, he was not impressed. To him they looked too flat to be real.)

I also arranged another Bigfoot activity in Willow Creek that summer—carving an eleven-foot-tall represen-tation of Bigfoot from a local redwood that, because it was planted some one hundred years earlier outside its natural range, was suffering a beetle infestation that was judged to be lethal. Under the auspices of the town's Chamber of Commerce, the tree was felled and the base section trucked to a rest area alongside the highway in Willow Creek, where it was erected on a concrete pad—a canvas awaiting the artist.

I had meantime carved a small version of the statue. It was my first attempt at carving a statue. My only prior wood-carving experience had been a tiki god face in the end of a fruit lug. I was full of confidence, though, and wanted to produce something that resembled what people were reporting seeing. I had previously driven over to Eureka to view the collection of a full-time redwood sculptor whose talented work included a superbly crafted but far-off-base rendition of Bigfoot as a giant Indian in a loincloth. I learned a few tricks of the trade from him, but after seeing his stupid Bigfoot impression was more eager than ever to produce a giant, hairy hominid in public view.

I used Sanderson's drawing of Ostman's young male Sasquatch as my model for the head, although that is the only report I ever encountered describing bangs looping up in a backward curl over the forehead. In years since, I have often wished I had not included that feature. It was commonly interpreted as an extremely heavy brow ridge, giving a false impression to viewers.

I got way too involved in Bigfoot pursuits. . . .

Today McClarin lives in New Hampshire and describes himself as a "multidisciplined public relations tactician with proven talent for getting major news coverage." He's still a Bigfooter at heart; it's not something that ever really leaves you.

American Yeti Investigators Just about everyone who becomes involved in Bigfootery has a strong personality; it just comes with the territory. The 1970s saw the emerging presence of Robert W. Morgan. He was born in 1935 and grew up in Ohio. With his friend attorney William "Ted" Ernst, Morgan began their Bigfoot research, first in Ohio, then in Florida, through their American Yeti Expeditions, where they sponsored numerous searches for the Skunk Ape of the Florida everglades. They then moved their efforts to the Pacific Northwest. In 1969, Morgan was responsible for having the county commissioners of Skamania County, Washington, create, and then pass, the first ordinance in the United States for the protection of Bigfoot. Violators of this ordinance would be fined $10,000 for shooting a Bigfoot.

From 1974 through 1996, Morgan, Ernst, and the American Anthropological Research Foundation, which they founded in 1974, sponsored four formal expeditions and more than two hundred field studies in North America. Their efforts in the western United States resulted in a commercially successful documentary film, *The Search for Bigfoot,* and they were featured on the Smithsonian series *Monsters: Myth or Mystery,* both broadcast in 1975.

The two vanished from the Bigfoot scene in the late 1970s but resurfaced in 1996 with a new twist to their pursuit, as portrayed in Morgan's tape *Bigfoot: The Ultimate Adventure.* The audiotape claimed that it could "teach you how to come face-to-face with" Bigfoot. The how-to includes meditative techniques Morgan learned from native peoples. Two years later, Morgan's close associate Ernst died mysteriously in a Florida swimming pool, but Morgan has remained active to this day.

Morgan's no-kill, nonviolent stance had growing support among many Bigfooters in the 1970s. The pursuit of Bigfoot was not so much a hunt for a creature any longer, but a quest for under-

standing, an attempt at contact, and a belief in the peaceful coexistence of humans and Bigfoot.

Scientific Hominologists

The end of the 1970s and the 1980s saw an increasing emphasis on science in Bigfoot studies. Cryptozoologists Richard Greenwell, Roy Mackal, and Bernard Heuvelmans founded, along with Grover Krantz, the International Society of Cryptozoology, and California anthropologist Constance Cameron began publishing *Bigfoot Co-op Newsletter*. Krantz, along with other academics—Vladmir Markotic, Marjorie Halpin, and Michael M. Ames—began publishing books that viewed Bigfoot through a scientific lens, but there was hardly any activity, either groups or individual, actively searching for Bigfoot. Among non-Ph.D.s, Mark A. Hall wrote Bigfoot articles that were published in *The Minnesota Archaeologist* in 1978 and 1979. Daniel Perez founded his Center for the Bigfoot Studies in 1979 and began his *Bigfoot Times* newsletter. Cliff Crook opened his Bigfoot Central Museum in 1982.

In 1982, anthropologist Grover Krantz became involved with a group of Bigfooters at Walla Walla, Washington, and found more scientific evidence for the local reports of Bigfoot. Wes Sumerlin, Paul Freeman, and Vance Orchard showed Krantz prints in which Krantz found unique markings, dermal ridges, he compared to fingerprints.

The 1982 Walla Walla findings would eventually lead to the involvement in 1995 of Jeffrey Meldrum, an associate professor of anatomy and anthropology at Idaho State University. Because he'd grown up in the Pacific Northwest, Meldrum, raised a Mormon like Krantz, had heard about Bigfoot at an early age and had long been interested in the controversy surrounding the legendary creature. After graduating with a Ph.D. in physical anthropology in 1989 from

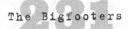

the State University of New York at Stony Brook, Meldrum specialized, through his initial fieldwork with African monkeys, in foot mechanics. He studied the implications for bipedal adaptation and locomotion in early hominids. Meldrum also participated in paleontological field projects to South America, collecting new fossil primate specimens from the Miocene of Columbia and Argentina.

One thing led to another, and Meldrum found himself getting deeper and deeper into the Bigfoot mystery, beginning with Freeman's Walla Walla footcasts and eventually on to the Redwoods Video and the Skookum cast. Meldrum became one of the new breed of young anthropologists who have an open-minded approach to Bigfoot studies.

Groups, Groups, and More Groups

The 1990s saw a more nature-oriented rather than scientific approach to Bigfoot, however. This is reflected in John A. Bindernagel's 1997 book, *North America's Great Ape: The Sasquatch,* for example, and in other activity around that time.

In 1991, Ray Crowe, who was born and raised in Oregon, founded a Portland-based organization called the Western Bigfoot Society. A few years later, it moved to Hillsboro and changed its name to the International Bigfoot Society. Crowe runs the organization by holding monthly meetings, talking to school groups, conducting annual gatherings, and publishing a monthly newsletter, *The Track Record.* Acknowledging the educational and entertainment value of Bigfoot, Crowe's club is typical of the new wave of groups that not only conduct fieldwork but also bring Bigfoot people together for social and recreational networking.

By the mid-1990s the era of the "CyperSasquatcher" had arrived. Henry Franzoni, who would find twenty-three thousand locations in North America that have been named after a Native

word for Bigfoot, saw that the Internet could be a valuable tool in Bigfoot research. Franzoni decided to create an Internet group, calling it the Internet Virtual Bigfoot Conference (IVBC), a format for the open exchange and debate of ideas, cases, and insights. When Franzoni got out of the field, he turned the list over to Bobbie Short and Michael Krein, and when they quit, I took over as moderator and continue to run it today. Bigfoot groups have blossomed on the Internet with some thirty to forty groups in existence today.

The dominant Bigfoot organization on the Internet today is the Bigfoot Field Researchers Organization (BFRO). Here is how the BFRO was profiled in the August 2000 issue of *Outside* magazine: "Founded in 1995 by Matt Moneymaker, a thirty-six-year-old Orange County, California, information technology consultant and lifelong Sasquatch enthusiast, the Bigfoot Field Researchers Organization claims thirty top 'curators' (experienced Bigfooters who interview witnesses, examine fresh evidence, and debate the finer points of Sasquatch theory) and more than three hundred 'investigators' (junior associates who help with the fieldwork)."

The BFRO sponsored the field search that uncovered the Skookum cast. Their geographical database of sightings serves as a welcome resource to anyone seeking Bigfoot. With sightings listed by state, and counties, with matching maps, there is no doubt the BFRO.net Web site is the leader in the field.

Bigfooters Everywhere In May 2000, the Bigfoot Museum opened. Not in Seattle or Vancouver. Not in Washington, D.C., or New York City. But in Willow Creek–China Flats, California, a one-hour drive over rough roads from Eureka, on the coast.

In the sphere of commercial ventures, Sasquatch awareness is popping up all over, keyed to the new brand of Bigfooters out there. Take BigFoot Safari, for example, which is "an innovative and thrilling

4x4 Travel Adventure. Designed to introduce corporate and private parties to the vast Eco-system of Vancouver Island, original home of the legendary Sasquatch," according to their promotional material. "Challenge yourself to tackle the off-road trails in this rugged, pristine wilderness. You will be at the wheel of one of our Toyota Land Cruisers, Land Rovers, and Mercedes Unimogs. In the company of other adventure travelers and with expert instruction, each participant will attend our 4x4 School. After some theory and practical application, you'll learn the arts of winching, vehicle recovery, safety, and trail etiquette. From sea to sky!! Fantastic scenery!! Mountain lakes and meadows!! Wildlife viewing!!! Adventure travel where the ancient people of the forest have lived for millennia. On the edges of civilization, experience this wonderland where few have ventured. All in our backyard!!! . . . On this Safari, we are offering a three-day package if you can't make the entire six days. . . . We also offer custom-designed treks including a 'Women Only Challenge.' "

Then there is Idaho's Bigfoot Outfitters, Inc. promotion: "Horseback or mule ride in Windy Saddle, the gateway to Hell's Canyon, the deepest gorge in North America. Spend 3–7 days riding through the majestic Seven Devils Mountains in Idaho." Or you can go camping at Sasquatch Provincial Park in British Columbia, or take the Bigfoot Trail, a twelve-mile moderate hike in the Joshua Tree National Park. Even a British tourist company has gotten into the act, calling itself Bigfoot Travel Ltd.

The *Denver Post*'s Theo Stein recently acknowledged this trend in outdoor recreation when he asked: "Looking for a new thrill to put the fun back into your backpacking trips? Try searching for Bigfoot on your next outing." The paper noted that a discussion forum on the Colorado Bowhunters Association Web site had become a busy electronic chatting place about Bigfoot's existence in Colorado.

Finally, in July 2000, the Audubon Society of Portland, Oregon, developed and held a five-day-long Bigfoot tracking camp for fifth- through eighth-graders. "We don't want to give people the wrong idea, that the Audubon Society believes there's a Sasquatch," said Steve Robertson, the Audubon Society's education director, to the Associated Press. "The idea is to use the Bigfoot as a vehicle to increase children's wilderness awareness skills, to get them to carefully interpret the animal signs they encounter." The environmental organization, which usually deals with bird-watching and guided hikes in the forest, decided to use Bigfoot as a way to interest adolescents in the outdoors. The camp was set up in the foothills around Mt. Hood and Mt. St. Helens, where there is a history and concentration of sightings. Video cameras were available, if the campers actually ran into a Sasquatch.

But then, the most important lesson that the Audubon Society has to teach these teens is not how to pour the plaster of paris or to make certain the lens cap is off the videocam when the Bigfoot comes into view. The most significant lesson that comes out of Bigfoot hunting is learning how to wait. Being patient.

One Bigfooter, Kyle Mizokami, who was in the field from 1995 to 1998, then left frustrated with the lack of immediate results, reflected in 2001 on his time in the Bigfoot community: "Bigfooters are an army of Egyptian stonemasons building the pyramid at Giza," he wrote in *Salon*. "They'll get the job done, though it might take them several hundred years. Too late for me to care, really, what the eventual outcome is."

I care. I'll wait.

16 Three Big Questions

Several major questions arise when considering the reality of Bigfoot, but one stands out above all the rest. People ask me this question all the time. It's the same question that all Bigfoot researchers face at one time or another.

First Question

If Bigfoot is real, why hasn't anyone found a dead Bigfoot?

Anthropologist Grover Krantz had a great rejoinder to that troubling question: "Well, if bears are real, then why don't we find their bones? I've talked to hunters, many game guides, conservation people, ecology students, and asked them how many remains of dead bears have you found that died a natural death? Over twenty years of inquiry my grand total of naturally dead bear bones found is zero! Now the best population estimate guess we can make is there are at least one hundred bears out there for every one Bigfoot, and we haven't found the first bear yet. We would very much like to find the remains of a naturally dead Sasquatch, but the chance is just simply so remote it's not even serious to even think about it."

Though we have no dead Bigfoot to study, we do have a good deal of physical evidence that points directly to the reality of this animal, beginning with its footprints. The number and reasonable variety of Bigfoot tracks are quite compelling. Just think of it: over hundreds of years we have found hundreds of miles of Bigfoot tracks in mud, snow, and sand—all looking very human with five toes straight ahead and showing individual differences. They have been discovered in long series, in small sets, and individually, exactly as we would expect from a large, intelligent primate. To top it off, these tracks have been found in the most out-of-place locations, not where they would immediately be noticed or be available for the six-o'clock news.

Since they were first described for the Canadian Sasquatch, the Bigfoot footprints have been remarkably consistent over the years. Obviously there can be no truth to the news stories that appear every dozen years or so about one individual being responsible for *all* Bigfoot tracks ever found. To think, for example, that retired Washington State logger Rant Mullens's "confession" in 1982, in which he claimed to be responsible for the legend of Ape Canyon by carving wooden feet to leave large footprints and was somehow involved with the Bluff Creek 1958 incidents, has any merit, is, well, more unbelievable than Bigfoot.

Bigfoot footprints actually support the case for population and individual animal diversity. People taking casts often go for the best-looking print, but researchers today now collect series that illustrate the animal's movement and individuality. Furthermore, the footprint, along with the Bigfoot behavior, indicates regional differences. The argument for a distinct geographic subspecies in the East is strong and growing stronger, based upon its routinely more curved footprints and more aggressive behavior. This Eastern Bigfoot, which I have called Marked Hominids and Mark A. Hall has dubbed Taller Hominids, are probably the *Windigo* of old. (The Napes from the American South and lower Midwest have quite different tracks, with footprints that look like human hands. These are so dissimilar that these cannot be grouped with the classic Bigfoot. Since these Napes are so rare and pose such a distraction to most Bigfoot hunters, I will not concentrate on them here.)

Probably the most significant aspect of Bigfoot footprints, however, has to do with the dermal ridges—or "fingerprints"—that have been discovered on many cast footprints. The late Grover Krantz initially discovered dermals in tracks cast in Washington State in 1982 and published the first paper on Sasquatch dermatoglyphics in 1983, in the journal *Cryptozoology*. Since 1995, however, Jeff Meldrum, associate professor of anatomy at Idaho State University, and a specialist in primate feet, has taken the lead on this significant issue. When Krantz and Meldrum began noticing dermal ridges, something others had never really looked for in footprints or casts, they both felt that they had found a sure proof that the prints being left were from a real, albeit, unknown, primate. Furthermore, when Meldrum began a massive project to collect and examine old prints, he found, to his astonishment, dermals on them too. When I and others showed Meldrum cast prints from the 1960s, he quickly spotted the telltale dermals, those distinctive loops and skin folds on these casts. How could hoaxers have known to include dermal ridges on their fake feet so long before the experts thought about looking for them?

Then in 1999, a Texas police fingerprint expert, Jimmy Chilcutt, heard Meldrum talking about dermal ridges in a television documentary and called him soon afterward. Before long Chilcutt was on his way to Idaho to look over Meldrum's casts. With his knowledge Chilcutt was convinced he could debunk Bigfoot, once and for all. "If there is a Sasquatch," he told a reporter for the *Houston Chronicle* in February 2000, "only a handful of people in the world know the difference between a primate and a human print."

When the skeptical Chilcutt began studying the Meldrum col-

lection, he examined a cast Meldrum had shown on TV and quickly determined it to be a fake (although the prints may have been contaminated by the routine practice of "fixing up" tracks for casting). On this cast, Chilcutt determined that the toe prints were actually human fingerprints. Meldrum then allowed Chilcutt the freedom to authenticate or dispute the rest of his collection of about one hundred castings of alleged Bigfoot footprints.

"What I actually found surprised even me," Chilcutt told the *Chronicle*. He had discovered the print ridges on the bottoms of five castings—which were taken at different times and locations—flowed lengthwise along the foot, unlike human prints, which exist from side to side.

"No way do human footprints do that—never, ever. The skeptic in me had to believe that [all of the prints were from] the same species of animal," Chilcutt said. "I believe that this is an animal in the Pacific Northwest that we have never documented."

Besides footprints, other types of physical data have come our way. Hair and fecal samples have been collected since the Pacific Northwest Expedition at the very beginning of the modern Bigfoot era. But the analysis of hair samples has surprised and frustrated scientists trying to figure out what animals these come from. George Agogino, an anthropologist at the University of New Mexico, was given the task by millionaire Tom Slick, of either analyzing or finding other experts to analyze the hair and fecal samples from those early excursions in California and British Columbia. John Green has written that some hair and fecal matter from those early 1960s efforts have "never been positively identified." In 1991, when I interviewed Agogino, he confirmed that some of the stool samples were found to contain "parasites we could not identify." This is significant, as parasites are keyed to their hosts, and if you have parasites that are unknown, then the animal from which it came is likely to be unknown as well. The problem with the results and findings from the Slick years, of course, is that the material has disappeared, most probably destroyed or archived in a Slick institute warehouse. As in the scene from the end of *The Raiders of the Lost Ark,* Slick's wish to stay out of the limelight caused most of his expedition's findings to be lost forever.

The situation in the ensuing years has not improved. During the late 1990s, thanks to Court TV, the O. J. Simpson trial, and other forms of criminal publicity, DNA analysis has been regarded as the dramatic final answer needed to settle the question of Bigfoot. Find a hair sample with a root attached, and shazzam, a DNA analysis can be done. But applying the technique to Bigfoot identification is not enough. A "reference sample" must be available for a matching analysis, and needless to say, there is no "type Bigfoot" available, by which to compare samples. It's a kind of catch-22. You can't identify it as belonging to Bigfoot unless you have identified it as belonging to a Bigfoot in the first place.

Late in 1995, Paul Fuerst, a molecular geneticist at Ohio State University, and a graduate student, Jamie Austin, attempted to analyze some hairs said to be from a Bigfoot. They employed a DNA testing procedure being developed by the FBI for analysis of hair strands that lack the roots normally needed for identification. Walla Walla, Washington, resident Wes Sumerlin, former game warden Bill Laughery, and veteran Bigfoot hunter Paul Freeman had found the hairs in two clumps in the Blue Mountains of southeastern Washington State in August 1995. In November of that year, the Ohio scientists told the Associated Press that they would compare the hairs to those of humans and chimpanzees and expected to announce their results by the end of the month.

Instead, in March of 1998, the third member of the analytical team, W. Henner Fahrenbach of the Primate Center in Oregon, announced to researchers through e-mail messages sent worldwide (and published as an "Interim Statement" on the BFRO Web site), that the Ohio-Oregon group had decided to withhold submission of their analyses. They found that the hair without roots was not an acceptable enough sample for them to obtain the results they needed to determine the phylogenetic affiliation of the creature. Fahrenbach was not deterred by the setback and called for tissue samples to be obtained. Of course, Fahrenbach's statements on the inability to obtain firm DNA evidence was hailed by skeptics as yet more "proof" that Bigfoot does not exist. But such a brush-off is narrow-minded. It completely disregards the difficulties in working with material from an unknown species, even if some misidentifications and pranks do not get into the mix.

Second Question For years, a debate has been raging among amateur and professional Bigfooters, academic hominologists, and cryptozoologists over the question: Is Bigfoot a human or an ape?

When people speak of "apes," what are they talking about? Of course, the image most people have is of a tailless, hairy creature that reminds them of something between a monkey and a man. More formally, of course, apes are any of the various large, tailless Old World primates, including the bonobo, chimpanzee, gorilla, gibbon, siamang, and orangutan. The "highest" forms of mammals, by human definition obviously, are the primates. Within the order of Primates, the "very highest" primates are the species of animals we call great apes and humans.

Sorting through how one group of "great apes" is organized (by humans, please note again) might give us some insights into where Sasquatch and humans fit into the picture. Let us examine, as an example, the great apes in Africa, the bonobos, chimpanzees, and gorillas. Even among these apes, there is more diversity than is often acknowledged. First we have the bonobo or pygmy chimpanzee *(Pan paniscus)*, which inhabits the dense rain forests south of the Zaire (or

Congo) River as opposed to the populations of common chimpanzees who live north of the river, suggesting that breeding isolation encouraged by that geographical boundary led to the different species.

There are various subspecies or types of common chimpanzee, including these three: the Western African chimp *(Pan troglodytes verus)*, the Central African chimp *(Pan troglodytes troglodytes)*, and the Eastern African chimp *(Pan troglodytes schweinfurthii)*. These are the routinely classified three subspecies of common chimps, which are recognized based on their genetic similarity and their location in Africa. Additionally, primatologists now recognize a new fourth subspecies, *Pan troglodytes vellerosus,* from Nigeria, according to the June 2000 *Bulletin of the American Society of Primatologists.*

That year the society also divided the gorillas, previously considered a single species, into two species and five subspecies. The eastern gorilla *(Gorilla beringei)* includes the mountain gorilla *(Gorilla beringei beringei)* of the Virunga volcanoes area of Rwanda, Uganda, and the Democratic Republic of Congo, the yet unnamed, but distinct, population of Uganda's Bwindi Forest, and the eastern lowland gorilla *(Gorilla beringei graueri)*. Western Africa is home to at least two additional subspecies, the western lowland gorilla *(Gorilla gorilla gorilla)* and the Cross River gorilla *(Gorilla gorilla diehli)*. However, some recent attempts at further classification have considered the mountain and eastern gorillas as separate species.

Obviously, the changes in primatology are impacting the way people look at apes, Bigfoot, and humans. When the great primatologist John Napier wrote his book *Bigfoot: The Yeti and Sasquatch in Myth and Reality,* in 1972, his view of where the great apes and humans grouped, in relationship to Bigfoot, reflected the analyses of his times. In 1985, Napier and his colleague wife would author *The Natural History of the Primates,* which was used in graduate primatology and anthropology courses for years. In that book, John and Prue Napier had an extremely simple view of where humans and the great

apes were to be located: apes and men were not really closely related.

DNA findings and other new studies have caused a shift in anthropology. A remarkable realization has occurred within primatology since Napier's day, to wit that humans are closer to some forms of great apes than those apes are to each other. Among primatologists, this was expressed by noting that the family Hominidae contained the subfamily Ponginae and subfamily Homininae, according to Colin Groves in 1997. The evolving classification system finally led to a radical reorganization of the lesser and greater apes by Wayne State University zoologist Dr. Morris Goodman in 1999. This reorganization acknowledges the extremely close relationship between humans and apes—essentially that humans are nothing more than hairless chimpanzees. This idea has been popularized in such books as *The Naked Ape* and *The Third Chimpanzee*.

The amorphous "ape versus human" distinction was brought into sharp focus with a highly ballyhooed, recent fossil find. In July 2002, French scientist Michel Brunet proclaimed that his team had found man's oldest ancestor, a 7-million-year-old fossil skull he christened *Sahelanthropus tchadensis*. But the media storm that began with the July publication in *Nature* of this fossil's formal description was still in full force when Brigitte Senut of the Natural History Museum in Paris (one of the discoverers of *Orrorin tugenensis*, "Millennium Man") stepped forward. She declared, in no uncertain terms, to the *Observer*'s Paris correspondent, "This is the skull of a female gorilla." Her colleague Michael Pickford described the creature's distinctive canines as being typical "of a large female monkey."

An angry Brunet quickly held a news conference at his University of Poitiers. Waving a copy of *Nature*, with the skull of *Sahelanthropus* on its cover, he exclaimed, "Here you see the baptismal certificate of this hominid. If one or two people somewhere disagree with me, that is their problem. But one cannot confuse this with a gorilla."

If knowledgeable scientists cannot even agree on a fossil they hold in their hands, how could we possibly expect a consensus on a creature such as Bigfoot?

Yet an answer lies close at hand. The explorer Roy Chapman Andrews once wrote, "Man is an ape with possibilities." Zoologist Morris Goodman more recently noted, "Genetically, humans are only slighted remodeled apes." We are apes, in other words. It is a simple statement that carries with it all the baggage of soul, intelligence, and religion. But, of course, there is nothing to say that we are not apes who have merely created a world of differences between the chimpanzees and ourselves. After all, we have.

So how does Bigfoot fit into the mix? The discovery may be taken in more calmly than we think.

"If it turns out to be an ape," Jeff Meldrum told *Outside* in 2002, "it's not going to overturn our ideas about human evolution or even primate evolution. In fact, it'll confirm what some of us suspect, which is that descendants of Miocene-period apes populate every northern continent."

They are apes, as surely as we are. Whether Bigfoot ultimately turns out to be more of a hominid (humanlike) than a hominoid (apemanlike) being remains to be seen, based upon a closer physical examination of the animal.

Third Question   And therein lies the dilemma that forms the third most important question regarding Bigfoot: Should we shoot one if given the opportunity?

Shooting an ape is easier to think about than plugging a human with a .22. Should the Bigfoot hunters kill one to provide the physical evidence to prove it exists? That question is the source of much controversy within the ranks of Bigfooters. While the gun-toting Grover Krantz and John Green have argued yes, the peaceful Russian Dmitri Bayanov and George Haas have said absolutely not. To kill or not to kill?

If the prey is determined to be an "ape"—which most read as "nonhuman animal"—then it would not be murder, so the argument goes, to kill it and throw it at the feet of science. Or to make a million dollars off it.

But things are no longer as simple as they were in the 1800s, or even the 1950s. Hunting for the mountain gorilla, the giant panda, and many other animals that had yet to be discovered meant going out and shooting them. Today's technology makes such arguments a thing of the past, however. In the twenty-first century, Bigfoot will hopefully be captured, studied, given some rights, and released. Biological sampling, videotaping, and electronic tracking will accomplish what killing and mounting the animals once did.

We all live a life of contradictions. I am firmly convinced that Bigfoot is an ape, but I also believe there is absolutely no justification in hunting it to kill it, as there would have been one hundred years ago, to prove it exists. Bigfoot is a cousin ape, more familiar to us than the chimps perhaps, but the hairy ape to our naked ape. What it means is that through convergence evolution, another ape has changed, like us, into an upright being, but one that has retained its hairy origins.

Seeking Bigfoot is extremely important, and finding them will change us all forever, for we shall never look at humans in the same way again. What Bigfoot "is" probably does not matter for its future. In the end, how we understand Bigfoot and what it has become to us will determine much about how we think of ourselves. We stand at the edge of the forest together. What we discover about each other may surprise us both.

APPENDIX A
Twenty Best Places
to See Bigfoot

You'll have a better chance of seeing a Bigfoot or finding a footprint in one of the following "hot spots" than anywhere else in North America. The sightings are so routine near some communities that many recognize their good fortune through road signs, memorials, statues, museums, and gift shops.

1. **Bluff Creek, California** Bluff Creek is the mecca of the Bigfoot field, the birthplace of the first "Bigfoot" track finds and the site of the filming of the Patterson-Gimlin footage, made famous by the familiar Frame 352 of a female Bigfoot. Visit the nearby Bigfoot wing of the Willow Creek–China Flats Museum in Willow Creek (take 299 east from 101 at Arcata). It houses Bob Titmus's entire Bigfoot cast collection and other great Bigfoot exhibits. A twenty-three-foot-tall Bigfoot statue by Gordon Burns stands outside the museum, the eight-foot-tall, life-size Bigfoot sculpture by Jim McClarin is nearby, with yet another statue at The Legends of Bigfoot Museum at Garberville, also in Humboldt County. Willow Creek's annual Bigfoot Daze celebration occurs on the Labor Day weekend and features speakers and family activities.

2. **Fouke, Arkansas** The real-life encounters with the Fouke Monster and the filming of the famed Boggy Creek movies occurred near this village. Shop for Bigfoot souvenirs at the local

Monster Mart. An annual Boggy Creek Festival is held every April, complete with books to buy, casts to view, and Bigfooters to meet.

3. Ape Canyon–Ape Caves–Mt. St. Helens– Skamania County, Washington Here is where the "apes" attacked in 1924 and where their relatives continue to be seen today. Signage memorializes the event in the Ape Caves area. The county serves as a gateway into the Gifford Pinchot National Forest, site of the Skookum cast find. Due to a high level of activity, Skamania is the only county in the nation where it is against the law to kill a Bigfoot. The annual Carson Bigfoot Daze is usually held in August with Bigfoot lectures, statues, exhibits, and family fun. To the east, along the Spirit Lake Highway, in Kid Valley, there's a Bigfoot statue near a tourist shop. Drive farther north, and find a Bigfoot Crossing sign on the Mt. Baker Highway.

4. Oregon Caves National Monument, Grants Pass, Oregon Grants Pass has a rich history of Bigfoot encounters. A local service group, the Oregon Cavemen, was established in 1922 and then erected a giant figure of a prehistoric "caveman" at the Interstate 5 exit to Grants Pass. Since the Bigfoot sighting in 2000 at Oregon Caves, local shops have been selling Bigfoot memorabilia. Hillsboro, Oregon, holds an annual International Bigfoot Society conference.

5. Mt. Shasta–Trinity Alps, California The Trinity Alps are also steeped in Native and modern Bigfoot lore. The Sisson Museum, southwest of Mount Shasta city, has Bigfoot exhibits and souvenirs.

6. Harrison River Area, Plus Klemetu and the Nearby Islands off British Columbia Sasquatch habitats exist throughout British Columbia. You can also attend the annual International Sasquatch Sympo-

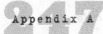

sium in Vancouver or go visit the Sasquatch (Dzunukwa) totem poles at the University of British Columbia's Museum of Anthropology. Campgrounds named Bigfoot and Sasquatch often have statues of the hairy primates at their entrance, especially in the Harrison Hot Springs area.

7. **Pike National Forest, Colorado** The sightings in the Pike National Forest are a local secret. One authentic road sign in the park warns motorists of frequent Bigfoot crossings.

8. **Mt. Hood National Forest, Oregon** Mt. Hood has been an active Bigfoot area since the 1800s. The shops in nearby The Dalles, Oregon, usually have Bigfoot souvenirs because this town was formerly the location of Peter Byrne's now defunct Bigfoot Research Center.

9. **Payette National Forest, Idaho** Payette National Forest is one of the hidden secrets of the Bigfoot world; much more is going on in Idaho than most people realize. *Serious* researchers only are allowed access to Jeff Meldrum's collection of over one hundred Bigfoot casts at Idaho State University.

10. **Jackson County, Murphysboro, Illinois** The home of the Big Muddy Monster is a quiet town. Low-key local acknowledgments like T-shirts are hard to find but surface occasionally.

11. **Tuscarawas-Coshocton Counties, Ohio** On the edge of Appalachia, this is the territory of the Ohio Grassman. An annual Bigfoot conference takes place in Newcomerstown, where casts, books, T-shirts, and more are available.

12. **St. Tammany Parish, Louisiana** This is the stomping ground of the Honey Island Swamp Monster. Boat tour guides are aware of the monster's history. An exhibit at the

Audubon Zoo in New Orleans has a life-size representation of the monster.

13. Everglades-Big Cypress Swamp, Florida Active pockets of Skunk Ape encounters abound throughout the swampy environments. Shops along Alligator Alley carry artifacts from fake ape heads to T-shirts acknowledging the creatures.

14. Marion County, Texas Here lies Caddo Lake, a spooky spot linked to the Boggy Creek activities. An annual Bigfoot conference at Jefferson focuses on the Texas Bigfoot.

15. Pike County, Missouri This is the home of Momo, so active in the 1970s and still seen around today. Talks at the local Louisiana, Missouri, library occasionally discuss Momo's place in Bigfoot history.

16. Allegheny-Fayette Counties, Pennsylvania Still haunted by the hairy relatives of Jan Clement's Kong, this region is abuzz with Bigfoot stories. An annual East Coast Bigfoot Researchers Conference takes place in Jeannette.

17. Lake Louise-Jasper, Alberta Reports of the hairy giant of the woods date back to the 1800s in Lake Louise–Jasper. New reports come in yearly. The Natural History Museum, Clock Tower Village, in Banff, has a life-size exhibit of a Sasquatch.

18. Antelope Valley, California Antelope Valley sees a lot of unusual Bigfoot activity but does not get much publicity, even though it is so close to Los Angeles. South of the city, in Orange County, there is a little Bigfoot museum (with *Gigantopithecus* skull replica, Bigfoot casts, Bigfoot books) at Knott's Berry Farm, near their Bigfoot Rapids water-rafting ride.

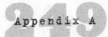

249

19. St. Clair-Sanilac-Huron-Tuscola-Saginaw Counties of Michigan The "thumb" of Michigan has seen decades of Bigfoot encounters, with possible migrations into the Sister Lakes and Monroe areas. Recent activity hints that this could be a good location for searches. The Michigan Magazine Museum on M33 between Fairview and Comins has an exhibit of a Bigfoot track cast taken near there.

20. Northern Maine Ninety-five percent of the state is covered in trees, and indications are that the down east side of the Appalachian Mountains, from Aroostook to Kennebec Counties, still serves as a route of activity for what the Micmacs called the Gugwes. In Sidney, look up Richard Brown to see his Bigfoot track casts. Jay Carr's Outdoor Museum, all the way at the very end of Interstate 95, in Houlton, Maine, has a Bigfoot statue outdoors.

APPENDIX B
Scientific-Quality Replica Bigfoot Track Casts

For those interested in studying Bigfoot further, obtaining well-duplicated footprint casts is an important research and educational step. As early as 1959, Bob Titmus shared copies of his casts. In the 1960s, Roger Patterson sent a copy of a Bigfoot cast as part of the membership to his field research organization. In the 1990s, the International Society of Cryptozoology, a now-defunct scientific body, sold copies of the 1982 Grays Harbor casts to support their mission.

During the 1980s and 1990s, Grover Krantz began molding and recasting, with the assistance of anthropology graduate students, several certified Sasquatch footcasts in the same fashion he had employed to reproduce high-quality skulls of fossil hominids. Krantz wished to share with other Bigfooters and anthropologists this evidence of a unique new primate in America. Krantz passed away in 2002, but various companies and individuals are carrying on his legacy by distributing these artifacts.

Contact the following sources for more information on their products:

GLEN EVANS (private collector)
ADDRESS: 1612 Via Linda
Fullerton, California 92833-1574
E-MAIL: glenevans@earthlink.net

Bossburg, Washington, "Cripple Foot" Footprint Casts with Painted Bone Structure (both feet—right (deformed): 16.5 inches; left: 18 inches), 1969. Full-color, illustrated, foam-core-mounted informational poster included.

Bluff Creek, California, Footprint Cast (17 inches), 1964. Full-color, illustrated, foam-core-mounted informational poster included.

Blue Creek Mountain, Washington, Juvenile "Dermal Ridges" Footprint Cast (14.5 inches), 1967. Full-color, illustrated, foam-core-mounted informational poster included.

Blue Creek Mountain, Washington, Knuckles/Thumb/Thumbnail Cast (10 inches across), late 1980s.

Blue Creek Mountain, Washington, Full Hand Cast (11 inches from third digit to heel of hand, whitewashed by Bob Titmus), late 1980s.

BONE CLONES/KRONEN OSTEO
ADDRESS: 21416 Chase Street #1
Canoga Park, California 91304
E-MAIL: kronen@boneclones.com

Bossburg, Washington, "Cripple Foot" Footprint Casts, 1969, licensed by Dr. Grover Krantz's estate.

Gigantopithecus and *Meganthropus* skulls, reconstructed by Dr. Krantz, and also licensed for reproduction by Bone Clones by his estate.

SKULLS UNLIMITED INTERNATIONAL
ADDRESS: 10313 South Sunnylane
Oklahoma City, Oklahoma 73160
E-MAIL: info@skullsunlimited.com

Grays Harbor, Washington, Footprint Casts (38 x 18 cm; WFP-16 Replica Single; WFP-17 Replica Pair), 1982.

Contact expert tracker Zack Clothier (fox@cryptozoology.com) regarding the availability of his copies of various Bigfoot casts from around the country. He can also assist with instructions on the best techniques for locating and obtaining Bigfoot track casts, refined to the specifics of your locale's fieldwork site.

Copies of or questions about field-obtained Bigfoot casts or other evidence would be appreciated by the author of this book. Contact me at: Loren Coleman, Post Office Box 360, Portland, Maine 04112. **E-MAIL:** bigfoot@lorencoleman.com

On the Matter of Style

The style of this book and the use of capitalization for the undiscovered primates under discussion (e.g., Bigfoot, Yeti, Sasquatch, Abominable Snowman) follows the "manual of style" that has been adopted by the International Society of Cryptozoology's editor, Richard Greenwell, and the ISC scientific, peer-reviewed journal, *Cryptozoology*. Greenwell details the proper capitalization of cryptozoological names, before and after discovery, in a footnote in *Cryptozoology,* volume 5 (1986), page 101. His formalization of this matter is furthermore based on what occurs in systematic zoology, firm ground indeed.

Greenwell is clear in his example:

Native name: *okapi.*

Western name for presumed, undiscovered animal: Okapi.

Common name after discovery and acceptance: okapi.

For our extended use, this translates into:

Native name: *yet-teh* or *yeti.*

Western name for presumed, covered animal: Yeti.

Common name after discovery and acceptance: yeti.

and

Native name: *oh-mah.*

Western name for presumed, undiscovered animal: Bigfoot.

Common name after discovery and acceptance: bigfoot.

Therefore, as Bigfoot has not technically been "accepted" by systematic zoology as of this date, the capitalized form will be employed in this book.

Bibliography

Alexander, Hartley Burr. "North American." In *Mythology of All Races*, ed. L. H. Gray. Vol. 10. New York: Cooper Square, 1964.

Alford, Glenn. "ISU Researcher Coordinates Analysis of Body Imprint That May Belong to Sasquatch." Press Release, Idaho State University, Office of University and Government Relations, October 23, 2000.

"American Yeti Expedition Reports Most Recent Bigfoot Track Find." *Skamania County (Wash.) Pioneer,* October 18, 1974.

Anderson, William, and Clive Hicks. *Green Man: The Archetype of Our Oneness With the Earth*. San Francisco: Harper San Francisco, 1991.

Andresen, Kristen. "Following in Bigfoot's Footsteps." *Bangor Daily News,* August 3, 2000.

Arment, Chad. "Introduction to the Folklore of Henry W. Shoemaker. *North American BioFortean Review* 2, no. 1 (2000).

Barbeau, C. M. "Supernatural Beings of the Huron and Wyandot." *American Anthropologist* 16 (1914): 288–313.

Barcott, Bruce. " 'Sasquatch *Is* Real!' Forest Love Slave Tells All!" *Outside,* August 2002.

Bartholomew, Paul, Robert Bartholomew, William Brann, and

Bruce Hallenbeck. *Monsters of the Northwoods*. Utica, N.Y.: North Country Books, 1992.

Bayanov, Dmitri. *America's Bigfoot: Fact, Not Fiction—U.S. Evidence Verified in Russia*. Moscow: Crypto-Logos Books, 1997.

———. *Bigfoot: To Kill or to Film?* Moscow: Crypto-Logos, 2000.

———. "Why It Is Not Right to Kill a Gentle Giant." *Pursuit,* fall, 1980, 140–41.

Bayanov, Dmitri, and Igor Bourtsev. "On Neanderthal vs. *Paranthropus*." *Current Anthropology* 17, no. 2 (1976): 312–18.

Beck, Fred, and R. A. Beck. *I Fought the Apemen of Mt. St. Helens*. Beck, 1967.

Bernheimer, Richard. *Wild Men in the Middle Ages*. Cambridge, Mass.: Harvard University Press, 1952.

Berry, Rick. *Bigfoot on the East Coast*. Stuarts Draft, Va.: Campbell Center, 1993.

Berton, Pierre. *The Mysterious North*. New York: Alfred A. Knopf, 1956.

BFRO.net Web site.

"Bigfoot Film Sets Enthusiasts at Odds." *USA Today,* January 10, 1999.

Bindernagel, John A. *North America's Great Ape: The Sasquatch*. Courtenay, B.C.: Beachcomber Books, 1998.

Bord, Janet, and Colin Bord. *The Bigfoot Casebook*. Harrisburg, Pa.: Stackpole Books, 1982.

———. *The Evidence for Bigfoot and Other Man-Beasts*. New York: Sterling Publications, 1984.

Boyer, Mike. "He's Tracing the Swamp Monster's Trail." *Elmira (N.Y.) Star-Gazette,* August 24, 1979.

Brandon, Hembree. "Seen Any Beasties Around Your Place?" *Winona (Miss.) Times,* September 5, 1968.

Brewster, David. "Our Last Monster." *Seattle Magazine,* August 1970.

Brunet, Michel, et al. "A New Hominid from the Upper Miocene of Chad, Central Africa." *Nature* 418 (2002): 145–51.

Burgess, Steve. "Loren Coleman, Loch Ness Snowman of Cryptozoology." Salon.com, August 16, 1999.

Burns, J. W. "Introducing B.C.'s Hairy Giants. *Maclean's,* April 1929.

Burns, J. W., and C. V. Tench. "The Hairy Giants of British Columbia." *Wide World Magazine,* January 1940.

Busse, Phil. "Tracking the Bigfoot Trackers." Salon.com, June 8, 2001.

Byrne, Peter. *The Search for Bigfoot: Monster, Myth, or Man?* Washington: Acropolis Books Ltd., 1975.

Chorvinsky, Mark. "The Makeup Man and the Monster: John Chambers and the Patterson Bigfoot Suit." *Strange Magazine,* summer 1996, 6–10, 51.

Ciochon, Russell, John Olson, and Jamie James. *Other Origins: The Search for the Giant Ape in Human Prehistory.* New York: Bantam Books, 1990.

Clark, Jerome. *High Strangeness: UFOs from 1960 through 1979.* Detroit: Omnigraphics, 1992.

Clark, Jerome, and Loren Coleman. *Creatures of the Outer Edge.* New York: Warner Books, 1978.

Clarke, Sallie A. *The Lake Worth Monster.* Fort Worth, Tex.: Clarke, 1969.

Coleman, Sister Bernard. "The Religion of the Ojibwa of Northern Minnesota." *Primitive Man* 10 (1937): 41.

Coleman, Loren. "Abominable Snowmen." *Outdoor Illinois,* April 1970.

———. "Abominable Snowmen Activity in the Southwest." *Bigfoot Bulletin,* April 1970.

———. "Footage Furor Flares." *Fortean Times,* October 1996.

———. *Mysterious America.* Boston: Faber & Faber, 1983.

———. *Mysterious America: The Revised Edition.* New York: Paraview Books, 2001.

———. "Mysterious World: Patterson-Gimlin Film Debunkers Debunked." *Fate,* March and May 1999.

———. "Mystery Animals of Illinois." *Fate* 24, (March 1971).

———. "The Occurrence of Wild Apes in North America." In *The Sasquatch and Other Unknown Hominoids,* ed. Vladimir Markotic and Grover Krantz, 149–73. Calgary: Western Publishers, 1984.

———. "Suits You, Sir!" *Fortean Times,* January 1998.

———. *Tom Slick and the Search for the Yeti.* Boston London: Faber & Faber: London, 1989.

———. *Tom Slick: True Life Encounters in Cryptozoology.* Fresno: Linden, 2002.

———. "Was the First 'Bigfoot' a Hoax? Cryptozoology's Original Sin." *The Anomalist* 2 (spring 1995).

Coleman, Loren, and Jerome Clark. *Cryptozoology A to Z: The Encyclopedia of Loch Monsters, Sasquatch, Chupacabras, and Other Authentic Mysteries of Nature.* New York: Simon and Schuster, 1999.

——. "Swamp Slobs Invade Illinois." *Fate* 27, (July 1974).

Coleman, Loren, and Mark A. Hall. "From 'Atshen' to Giants in North America." In *The Sasquatch and Other Unknown Hominoids,* ed. Vladimir Markotic and Grover Krantz, 31–45. Calgary: Western Publishers, 1984.

——. "Some Bigfoot Traditions of the North American Indians." *The INFO Journal* (Washington, D.C.: International Fortean Organization) 3 (fall 1970): 2–10.

——. "Some Bigfoot Traditions of the North American Tribes." In J. Bergier, *Le livre de l'inexplicable.* Paris: Éditions Albine Michel, 1972.

Coleman, Loren, and Patrick Huyghe. *The Field Guide to Bigfoot, Yeti, and Other Mystery Primates Worldwide.* New York: HarperCollins, 1999.

Colombo, John Robert. *Windigo: An Anthology of Fact and Fantastic Fiction.* Saskatoon, Saskatchewan: Western Producer Prairie Books, 1982.

Coon, Carleton. "Why There Has to Be a Sasquatch." In *The Sasquatch and Other Unknown Hominoids,* ed. Vladimir Markotic and Grover Krantz. Calgary: Western Publishers, 1984.

Cooper, John M. "The Cree Witiko Psychosis." *Primitive Man* 6 (1933): 20–24

Crook, Cliff. "Spoofem Cast." Personal communication, 2001.

Daegling, David J., and Daniel O. Schmitt. "Bigfoot's Screen Test." *Skeptical Inquirer,* May/June 1999.

Dahinden, René, and Don Hunter. *Sasquatch/Bigfoot: The Search for North America's Incredible Creature.* Buffalo: Firefly Books, 1993.

Davidson, D. S. "Folktales from Grand Lake Victoria, Quebec." *Journal of American Folklore* 41(1928a): 275.

——. "Some Tête-de-Boule Tales." *Journal of American Folklore* 41 (1928b): 267.

Dearinger, L. A. "Strange Creatures." *Outdoor Illinois,* March 1970.

DeMillo, Andrew. "Bumper Year for Bigfoot Sightings." *Seattle Times,* July 13, 2000.

Denson, Bryan. "Teacher on Bigfoot's Trail Sees Science Issue in Mystery." *Portland Oregonian,* May 10, 2002.

Dunn, Lori. "20th Boggy Creek Festival Raises Funds for EMS." *Texarkana Gazette,* May 11, 2001.

Eberhart, George M. *Monsters: A Guide to Information on Unaccounted-for Creatures, Including Bigfoot, Many Water Monsters, and Other Irregular Animals.* New York: Garland, 1983.

——. *Mysterious Creatures: A Guide to Cryptozoology.* Santa Barbara: ABC-CLIO, 2002.

Edwards, Keith. "Wisconsin a New Home for Bigfoot?" *Milwaukee Journal Sentinel,* April 5, 2000.

Ellison, Bob. "Don't Shoot That Bigfoot." *Focus on Agriculture, American Farm Bureau,* July 28, 2000.

Fahrenbach, W. Henner. "DNA Updates." Personal communications, 1998–2002

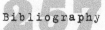

———. "Sasquatch: Size, Scaling, and Statistics." *Cryptozoology* 13 (1997–98): 47–75.

"Fingerprint Expert Tries to Debunk Bigfoot—Reaches Opposite Conclusion." *Houston Chronicle,* February 21, 2000.

Fisher, David. " 'Sasquatch Cast' Makes a Big Impression on Anatomists, TV." *Seattle Post Intelligencer,* June 17, 2002.

Flannery, Regina. "The Culture of Northeastern Indians." In *Man in Northeastern North America,* ed. Frederick Johnson. Papers of the Robert S. Peabody Foundation for Archaeology 3. Andover, Mass., 1946.

Flynn, Sean. "A Voice in the Night." *Esquire,* January 2000.

"Former City Man Believes in Monsters." *Decatur (Ill.) Herald,* May 15, 1973.

Franzoni, Henry. "Skookum." Personal communication, 1998.

Frayer, David W. *"Gigantopithecus* and Its Relationship to *Australopithecus." American Journal of Physical Anthropology* 39 (1972): 413–26.

Freeman, Joel. "Chinook Jargon." Personal communication, 2002.

Gallagher, Dan. "Producer Subjects Tales about Sasquatch to Scientific Method." Associated Press, June 20, 2002.

Gordon, David George. *Field Guide to the Sasquatch.* Seattle: Sasquatch Books, 1992.

Grafton, Carol Beglanger. *Old-Time Fruit Crate Labels in Full Color.* Mineola, N.Y.: Dover, 1998.

Green, John. In reply to Loren Coleman's "California Dreamin' " e-mail. Bigfoot list, March 15, 2001.

———. *On the Track of the Sasquatch.* Agassiz, B.C.: Cheam Publishing Ltd., 1968.

———. *On the Track of the Sasquatch: Encounters with Bigfoot from California to Canada.* 2 vols. Harrison Hot Springs, B.C.: Cheam, 1980.

———. *Sasquatch: The Apes Among Us.* Seattle: Hanover House, 1978.

———. *The Sasquatch File.* Agassiz, B.C.: Cheam Publishing Ltd., 1970.

———. *Year of the Sasquatch.* Agassiz, B.C.: Cheam Publishing Ltd., 1970.

Greenwell, Richard. "Proposed Sasquatch Hunt Stirs New Controversies." *The ISC Newsletter,* summer 1984.

Groves, Colin P. "Order Primates." In *Mammal Species of the World: A Taxonomic and Geographic Reference,* ed. D. E. Wilson and D. M. Reeder. Washington, D.C.: Smithsonian Institution Press, 1993.

Guenette, Robert, and Fances Guenette. *Bigfoot: The Mysterious Monster.* Los Angeles: Sunn Classic, 1975.

Guinard, Reverend Joseph E. "Witiko Among the Tête-de-Boule." *Primitive Man* 3 (1930): 69–71.

Haas, George. *Bigfoot Bulletin,* 1969–76.

Hall, Lawrence. "Bigfoot Believers Shouldn't Be Treated Abominably," *Newark (N.J.) Star-Ledger,* May 24, 2002.

Hall, Mark A. "Contemporary Stories of 'Taku He' or 'Bigfoot' in South Dakota as Drawn from Newspaper Accounts." *The Minnesota Archaeologist* 37, no. 2 (May 1978): 63–78.

———. "Encounters with True Giants, 1829–1994." *Wonders* 4 (1995): 63–79.

———. "The Gardar Skull and the Taller-Hominid." *Wonders* 4 (1995): 3–10.

———. "The Great Swamps." In *Natural Mysteries*. Minneapolis: MAHP, 1989.

———. *Living Fossils: The Survival of Homo gardarensis, Neanderthal Man, and Homo erectus*. Bloomington, Minn.: MAHP, 1999.

———. "On Giant Apes Reported in Africa." Unpublished manuscript, June 12, 1972.

———. "Stories of 'Bigfoot' in Iowa During 1978 as Drawn from Newspaper Sources." *The Minnesota Archaeologist* 38, no. 1: (December 1979): 2–17.

———. *The Yeti, Bigfoot & True Giants*. 2nd ed. Minneapolis: MAHP, 1997.

Halpin, Marjorie, and Michael Ames, eds. *Manlike Monsters on Trial: Early Records and Modern Evidence*. Vancouver: University of British Columbia Press, 1980.

Harter, Kevin. "Search Is On for Bigfoot." *St. Paul (Minn.) Pioneer Press,* August 7, 2002.

Hartlaub, Peter. "On the Trail with Bigfoot Believers." *San Francisco Examiner,* August 6, 2000.

———. "Sasquatch: Kitsch of Death." *San Francisco Examiner,* August 7, 2000.

Heinselman, Craig. "The Media and Bigfoot." *Crypto*. Francestown, N.H., April 1999.

———, ed. *Crypto: Hominology Special I*. Francestown, N.H.: Heinselman, 2001.

———, ed. *Crypto: Hominology Special II*. Francestown, N.H.: Heinselman, 2002.

Heuvelmans, Bernard. "Annotated Checklist of Apparently Unknown Animals with Which Cryptozoology Is Concerned." *Cryptozoology* 5 (1986): 1–16.

———. *On the Track of Unknown Animals*. London: Kegan Paul International, 1995.

Heuvelmans, Bernard, and Boris F. Porchnev, *L'Homme de Néanderthal est toujours vivant*. Plon: Paris, 1974.

Howe, Linda Moulton. *Glimpses of Other Realities, Volume II: High Strangeness*. Reno: Paper Chase Press 1998.

Hume, Mark. "Bigfoot, Big . . . Well, Maybe Not." *National Post,* March 3, 2001.

Hunter, Don, and René Dahinden. *Sasquatch*. Toronto: McClelland & Stewart, 1973.

Husband, Timothy. *The Wild Man: Medieval Myth and Symbolism*. New York: Metropolitan Museum of Art, 1972

Huyghe, Patrick. "Sasquatch!" In *Glowing Birds: Stories from the Edge of Science*. Boston: Faber and Faber, 1985.

Jacobsen, Pat. "California Giant." Personal communication, October 26, 2000.

Johnson, Paul G., and Joan L. Jeffers. *The Pennsylvania Bigfoot*. Pittsburgh: Johnson & Jeffers, 1986.

Jones, Norris. "Abominable Snowmen in Southern Illinois?" *Carbondale (Ill.) Daily Egyptian,* December 11, 1969.

Keating, Don. *The Eastern Ohio Sasquatch*. Newcomerstown: Keating, 1989.

———. *The Sasquatch Triangle*. Newcomerstown: Keating, 1987.

Keeran, James. "Hairy 'Human' Sighted at Kickapoo Creek." *Bloomington (Ill.) Pantagraph*, August 11, 1970.

Kirk, John. "Patterson Film Survives Assault on Its Authenticity." *British Columbia Scientific Cryptozoology Club Quarterly*, March 1999.

Kirkpatrick, Dick. "The Search for Bigfoot . . . Has a 150-Year-Old Legend Come to Life on This Film?" *National Wildlife*, April-May 1968.

Kleiner, Kurt. "Bigfoot''s Buttocks," *New Scientist*, December 23, 2000.

"Klement, Jan." *The Creature: Personal Experiences with Bigfoot*. Pittsburgh: Allegheny Press, 1976.

Klosterman, Chuck. "Believing in Bigfoot." *Akron (Ohio) Beacon Journal*, March 24, 1999.

Knerr, Michael E. *Sasquatch: Monster of the Northwest Woods*. New York: Belmont Tower, 1977.

Krantz, Grover S. *Big Footprints: A Scientific Inquiry into the Reality of Sasquatch*. Boulder: Johnson Books, 1992.

———. *Bigfoot Sasquatch Evidence*. Blaine, Wash.: Hancock House, 1999.

Kraska, Chris. "The Patterson, Gimlin Film: Enmity, Evidence, and Evolution." *Crypto,* (N.H.), April 7, 2001.

Kroeber, Alfred. *Handbook of the Indians of California*. Washington, D.C.: Bureau of American Ethnology, 1925.

LaBarge, Tim. "Believer: Dr. Matthew Johnson." *Salem, (Oreg.) Statesman Journal,* July 9, 2000.

Lambert, R. S. *Exploring the Supernatural: The Weird in Canadian Folklore*. London: Barker, 1955.

Lewis, Mike, and Tim Reid. "Hollywood Admits to Bigfoot Hoax." *London Telegraph*, October 9, 1997.

Lexicographical Centre for Canadian English. *A Dictionary of Canadianisms on Historical Principles*. Scarborough, Ontario: Gage Publishing, 1967.

Mangiacopra, Gary S., and Dwight Smith. "Bigfoot Encounters in Connecticut: Wildmen in the State from 1870–1989." In *Crypto: Hominology Special I.* Francestown, N.H.: Heinselman, 2001.

———. "Wildmen and Gorillas." In *Crypto: Hominology Special II.* Francestown, N.H.: Heinselman, 2002.

Markotic, Vladimir, and Grover S. Krantz, eds. *The Sasquatch and Other Unknown Hominoids.* Calgary: Western Publishers, 1984.

McClarin, Jim. "1960–74." Personal communications, 2002.

Meachum, Lynette. "Tracking Sasquatch." *Bremerton (Wash.) Sun,* July 10, 2000.

Meldrum, Jeffrey, and Richard Greenwell. "Redwoods Video." *BBC Wildlife* magazine, September 1998.

Michel, John, and Robert R. M. Rickard. "In Search of Ape-Men." *In Living Wonders.* London: Thames and Hudson, 1992.

Minor, Les. "Monster Sighting Solidifies Fouke's Spot in Annals of Lore." *Texarkana Gazette,* June 24, 2001.

Mizokami, Kyle. "The Scarlet B: Bigfoot Changed My Sex Life." Salon.com, June 8, 2001.

Moore, Chester, Jr. *Bigfoot South: Examining Cryptozoology's Greatest Mystery in the Southern United States.* Orange, Tex.: Thirteen Promotions, 2002.

Morgan, Robert W. *Bigfoot: The Ultimate Adventure.* Knoxville: Talisman Media Group Inc., 1996.

Moriarty, Leslie. "Bigfoot Lurks in Granite Falls?" *Everett (Wash.) Herald,* September 26, 2000.

———. "Bigfoot's Backside Yields a Clue, Enthusiasts Say." *Everett (Wash.) Herald,* January 13, 2001.

———. "Bigfoot's Fans Keep Close Tabs on His Annual Northwest Tour." *Everett (Wash.) Herald,* September 28, 2000.

Morris, Tom. *California's Bigfoot/Sasquatch.* Pleasant Hills, Calif.: Bigfoot Investigations, 1994.

Moye, David. "Maine Professor Chosen 'Bigfooter of the Year.' " Wireless News Flash, December 23, 1999.

Murphy, Christopher, Joedy Cook, and George Clappison. *Bigfoot in Ohio: Encounters with the Grassman.* New Westminster, B.C.: Pyramid Publications, 1997.

Murphy, Daniel. *Bigfoot in the News.* New Westminster, B.C.: Progressive Research, 1995.

Murphy, Kim. "Science Is Hot on the Heels of Bigfoot Legend." *Los Angeles Times,* January 21, 1996.

Murray, Stephen O., and Regna Darnell. "Margaret Mead and Paradigm Shifts Within Anthropology During the 1920s." *Journal of Youth and Adolescence* 29 (2000): 5.

Napier, John. *Bigfoot: The Yeti and Sasquatch in Myth and Reality.* London: Jonathan Cape, 1972.

Newton, Michael. *Monsters, Mysteries and Man.* Reading, Mass.: Addison-Wesley, 1979.

Norman, Eric. *The Abominable Snowmen.* New York: Award, 1969.

Odor, Ruth Shannon. *Great Mysteries Bigfoot.* Mankato, Minn.: The Child's World, 1989.

"Olympic Peninsula Man Reports Bigfoot Sighting." Seattle, NW Cable News, June 16, 2002.

Opsasnick, Mark. *The Bigfoot Digest: A Survey of Maryland Sightings.* Riverdale, Md., 1993.

———. *Maryland Bigfoot Reference Guide.* Greenbelt, Md.: Opsasnick, 1987.

Orchard, Vance. *Bigfoot of the Blues.* Walla Walla, Wash.: Orchard, 1993.

———. *The Walla Walla Bigfoot.* Walla Walla, Wash.: Earthlight, 2001.

"Oregon Man Says He Spotted Bigfoot." KOIN, Channel 6 News, Portland, Oregon, July 4, 2000.

Otto, Steve. "Absolute Kinda Irrefutable Proof of Skunk Ape." *Tampa Tribune,* February 13, 2001.

Oxley, Jennifer. "Expert on Primate Locomotion Takes Long, Serious Look at Bigfoot." *Idaho Statesman,* March 28, 2001.

Parsons, Elsie Clews. "Micmac Folklore." *Journal of American Folklore* 38 (1925): 56.

Patterson, Roger. *Do Abominable Snowmen of America Really Exist?* Yakima, Wash.: Franklin Press, 1966.

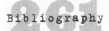

Perez, Daniel. *Bigfoot at Bluff Creek*. Santa Cruz, Calif.: Danny Perez Pub, 1994.

———. *Big Footnotes: A Comprehensive Bibliography Concerning Bigfoot, the Abominable Snowman and Related Beings*. Norwalk, Calif.: Danny Perez Pub, 1988.

Pilichis, Dennis. *Bigfoot: Tales of Unexplained Creatures*. Rome, Ohio: Page Research Library, 1978.

Place, Marian T. *Bigfoot: All Over the Country*. New York: Dodd Mead, 1978.

———. *The Boy Who Saw Bigfoot*. New York: Dodd Mead, 1979.

———. *On the Track of Bigfoot*. New York: Dodd Mead, 1974.

Pope, John. "In Pursuit of Monsters: An Interview with Cryptozoologist Loren Coleman." Sygne.com, May 1999.

Prater, Bill. "Here's a 'Now-I've-Heard-Everything' Story." *Decatur, (Ill.) Daily Review,* September 26, 1970.

Quast, Mike. *Big Footage: A History of Claims for the Sasquatch on Film*. Moorhead, Minn.: Quast Publications, 2001.

———. *The Sasquatch in Minnesota*. Fargo, N.D.: Quast Publications, 1990.

Radford, Benjamin. "Bigfoot at 50: Evaluating a Half-Century of Bigfoot Evidence." *Skeptical Inquirer,* March/April 2002.

"Researchers Disagree on Bigfoot Reports." *Seattle Post-Intelligencer,* July 6, 2000.

"Researchers Using DNA Testing to Verify Bigfoot." Associated Press, November 6, 1995.

Rielly, Edward J. *The 1960s*. Westport, Conn.: Greenwood, 2002.

Robertson, Tatsha. "New Ifs, Butts about Bigfoot." *Boston Globe,* July 14, 2001.

Rogers, Dwayne. "California Giant." Personal communications, 2000–2001.

Rogo, D. Scott. "Ghostly Bigfoot." *Human Behavior,* November 1978.

Roth, John E. *American Elves: An Encyclopedia of Little People from the Lore of 380 Ethnic Groups of the Western Hemisphere*. Jefferson, N.C.: McFarland & Company, 1997.

Sampson, Bob. "Creatures of the Night Are Coleman's Study." *Decatur, (Ill.) Review,* August 20, 1979.

Sanderson, Ivan T. *Abominable Snowmen: Legend Come to Life*. Philadelphia: Chilton, 1961.

———. "First Photos of 'Bigfoot,' California's Legendary 'Abominable Snowman.'" *Argosy,* February 1968.

———. "Missing Link?" *Argosy,* May 1969.

———. *The Monkey Kingdom*. Garden City, N.Y.: Hanover House, 1957.

———. "The Patterson Affair." *Pursuit,* June 1968.

———. "Things," New York: Pyramid, 1969.

———. "The Wudewsa or Hairy Primitives of Ancient Europe." *Genus* 23 (1967): 1–2.

"Sasquatch: Legend Meets Science." Discovery Channel, 2003.

Schmeltzer, Michael. "Bigfoot Lives." *Washington Magazine,* September-October, 1988.

Schneck, Robert Damon. "Death Had a Sagittal Crest." *Fate,* February 1999.

"Search for Bigfoot." Web site, heraldnet.com bigfoot, *Everett (Wash.) Herald,* 2002.

Shackley, Myra. *Still Living? Yeti, Sasquatch and the Neanderthal Enigma.* New York: Thames and Hudson, 1983.

Sharp, Henry S. *The Transformation of Bigfoot: Maleness, Power, and Belief Among the Chipewyan.* New York: Smithsonian Institution Press, 1988.

"Skull Find Sparks Controversy." *BBC News,* July 12, 2002.

Slate, Barbara A., and Alan Berry. *Bigfoot.* New York: Bantam, 1976.

Smith, Carlton. *Murder in Yosemite.* New York: St. Martin's Press, 1999.

Smith, Warren, *The Secret Origins of Bigfoot.* New York: Zebra/Kensington, 1977.

———. *Strange Abominable Snowmen.* New York: Popular Library, 1970.

Soule, Gardner. *Trail of the Abominable Snowman.* New York: G. P. Putnam's Sons, 1966.

Speck, Frank A. "Myths and Folklore of the Timiskaming Algonquin and Timagami Ojibwa." *Anthropological Series,* Canada Department of Mines, Geological Survey 9, 1915.

———. *Naskapi.* Norman: University of Oklahoma Press, 1935a.

———. "Tales of the Penobscot." *Journal of American Folklore* 48 (1935b): 81.

Sprague, Roderick, and Grover Krantz, eds. *The Scientist Looks at the Sasquatch.* Moscow: University Press of Idaho, 1977; rev., 1979.

Steenburg, Thomas N. *Sasquatch: Bigfoot—the Continuing Mystery.* Seattle: Hancock House Pub Ltd., 1993.

———. *The Sasquatch in Alberta.* Calgary: Western Publishers, 1990.

Stein, Theo. "Bigfoot Body Imprint Reportedly Uncovered." *Denver Post,* October 24, 2000.

———. "Colorado Sightings, Tracks Hard to Ignore," *Denver Post,* January 14, 2001.

———. "Legend of Bigfoot Put to Test." *Denver Post,* January 14, 2001.

St. Hilaire, Roger. "Bossburg." Personal communications, 2002.

Stienstra, Tom. "Latest Bigfoot Sighting Might Be True—or Not." *San Francisco Examiner,* July 19, 2000.

Strasenburgh, Gordon R., Jr. "*Australopithecus robustus* and the Patterson-Gimlin Film." In *The Sasquatch and Other Unknown Hominoids,* ed. Vladimir Markotic and Grover Krantz. Calgary: Western Publishers, 1984.

———. "More on Neanderthal vs. *Paranthropus.*" *Current Anthropology* 20, no. 3: 624–27, 1979.

———. *Paranthropus: Once and Future Brother.* Arlington, Va.: The Print Shop, 1971.

Taylor, Troy. "The Wendigo: The North Woods of Minnesota," Alton, Ill.: PrairieGhosts.com Web site, 1998.

Tchernine, Odette. *In Pursuit of the Abominable Snowman.* New York: Taplinger, 1970.

———. *The Snowman and Company.* London: Robert Hale, 1961.

"Tells of Early Days on Sound, F. W. Brown Records Thrilling Experiences in the Northwest." *Tacoma Daily Ledger,* October 15, 1911.

Terry, James. *Sculptured Anthropoid Ape Heads Down In or Near the Valley of the John Day River, a Tributary of the Columbia.* New York: J. J. Little, 1891.

Thibodeau, Sunni. "The Fouke Monster 30 Years Later." *Texarkana Gazette,* June 24, 2001.

United Press International. "Student to Study Ape-Like Creature." *Champaign-Urbana (Ill.) News-Gazette,* May 13, 1973.

Unsolved Mysteries, "Tom Slick." NBC-TV, Hollywood, February 12, 1992.

Vieira, Mischa. "Tracking Myakka's Wily Skunk Ape." *Sarasota, (Fla.) East County Observer,* July 12, 2001.

Von Koenigswald, G. H. R. *"Giganto-pithecus blacki:* A Giant Fossil Hominoid from the Pleistocene of Southern China." *Anthropological Papers of the American Museum of Natural History* 43 (1952): 295–325.

Wallas, James. "Big figure." In *Kwakiutl Legends.* Blaine, Wash.: Hancock, 1981.

Wallis, Wilson D., and Ruth Sawtell Wallis. *The Micmac Indians of Eastern Canada.* Minneapolis: University of Minnesota Press, 1955.

Warren, Sidney. "Sasquatch—Sort Of." In *Farthest Frontier: The Pacific Northwest.* New York: Macmillan Company, 1949.

Wasson, Barbara. *Sasquatch Apparitions: A Critique on the Pacific Northwest Hominoids.* Bend, Oreg.: Wasson, 1979.

Wasson, David. "Bigfoot Unzipped—Man Claims It Was Him in a Suit." *Yakima (Wash.) Herald-Republic,* January 30, 1999.

Webster, Jack. "Roger Patterson Interview." John Green Archives, November 1967.

Weidenreich, Franz. *Apes, Giants and Man.* Chicago: University of Chicago Press, 1946.

"Wildman Craze of 1895 Made Things a Little Hairy." *Waterbury (Conn.) Republican American,* July 13, 2002.

Wilkinson, Eric. "First-of-a-Kind Bigfoot Discovery Has Skeptics Taking Notice." Seattle, *King5 News,* October 2, 2000.

Willoughby, David P. *All About Gorillas.* New York: A. S. Barnes and Company, 1978.

Witthoft, John, and Wendell S. Hadlock. "Cherokee-Iroquois Little People." *Journal of American Folklore* 59 (1946): 413–22.

"Wood Bison *(Bison bison athabascae)."* In *Endangered Wildlife of the World.* New York: Marshall Cavendish, 1993.

Wyatt, Brian. "Clanton Ape Print." Personal communication, 2002.

Wylie, Kenneth. *Bigfoot: A Personal Inquiry into a Phenomenon.* New York: Viking, 1980.

Yorke, Malcolm. *Beastly Tales: Yeti, Bigfoot, and the Loch Ness Monster.* New York: DK Publishing, Incorporated, 1998.

"Youth Enjoys Unusual Hobby." *Decatur (Ill.) Herald,* June 29, 1964.

Index